PAUL YANDELL

SECOND TO THE BEST

A Sideman's Chronicle

NORM VAN MAASTRICHT

Schiffer Publishing Ltd®

4880 Lower Valley Road • Atglen, PA 19310

Library of Congress Control Number: 2016937040

Cover design by John Cheek
Type set in Minion Pro/Times New Roman
ISBN: 978-0-7643-5048-1
Printed in China

Published by Schiffer Publishing, Ltd.
4880 Lower Valley Road
Atglen, PA 19310
Phone: (610) 593-1777; Fax: (610) 593-2002
E-mail: Info@schifferbooks.com
Web: www.schifferbooks.com

Other Schiffer Books on Related Subjects:
Nashville Steeler by Don Davis
Gretsch 6120 by Edward Ball
Blues Hands by Joseph A. Rosen

For our complete selection of fine books on this and related subjects, please visit our website at:
www.schifferbooks.com.
You may also write for a free catalog.

Schiffer Publishing's titles are available at special discounts for bulk purchases for sales promotions or premiums. Special editions, including personalized covers, corporate imprints, and excerpts, can be created in large quantities for special needs. For more information, contact the publisher.

We are always looking for people to write books on new and related subjects. If you have an idea for a book, please contact us at proposals@schifferbooks.com.

Dedicated to uncredited musicians, singers, and dancers who give their talent to enhance a star performer's presentation. They are willing to work in the background and see the glory go to someone else. All too often they get little or no credit for a job well done and always at far less pay than the supported person receives. It is this way in every business, every profession, every walk of life. And to Marie Yandell; couldn't have done it without her.

CONTENTS

Foreword by Steve Wariner *6*
Foreword by Pat Kirtley *8*
Preface *9*
Acknowledgments *11*

Prologue: Stardom … an Illusion 14

Chapter 1: Down On the Farm... 16
Chapter 2: Tuning Up.. 25

       Interlude 1: Mose Rager *30*
       Interlude 2: Instrumental Evolution....................................... *33*

Chapter 3: The Louvin Brothers 38
Chapter 4: Professional Musicianship 53

       Interlude 3: The Grand Ole Opry Tent Show.......................... *68*

Chapter 5: Kitty, the Bus, and the Road... 70
Chapter 6: Jerry Reed.. 77
Chapter 7: The Business of Recording 88

       Interlude 4: Product Endorsement: On and Off the Record *97*

Chapter 8: The Genius of Paul Bigsby.. 100

       Interlude 5: A Word about Sustain *107*

Chapter 9: The D'Angelico.. 109
Chapter 10: A Split Pickup and a Solid Top..................................... 118
Chapter 11: The Legendary '59 124
Chapter 12: Three Iconic Amplifiers.. 136

       Interlude 6: The Echo Effect *138*
       Interlude 7: Another Kind of Sideman *144*

Chapter 13: Then Came Chet: Seconding to Mister Guitar 147
Chapter 14: Recording with Chet 157
Chapter 15: On the Road with Chet 176
Chapter 16: Showtime! 185

Interlude 8: "It's in the Hands" 189

Chapter 17: The CGP Award 191

Interlude 9: Lenny Breau 195

Chapter 18: Research and Development 198
Chapter 19: Pssst … Want Some Action? 225
Chapter 20: Paul's Workshop 231
Chapter 21: Oddnotes and Advice 247

Interlude 10: A Little Style History 247

Chapter 22: Some Grumbles, Some Fun, Some Love 257
Chapter 23: Presidents and Pundits 261
Chapter 24: The Best of Times … The Worst of Times 281

The Legacy 286

FOREWORD

BY STEVE WARINER

It's 1958 or 1959. As a wide-eyed kid I'm sitting on the floor real close to the right side speaker of our "stereo console," the kind that today brings real good bucks in the retro and antique stores. The LP of choice this evening was the Louvin Brothers and I couldn't get enough.

My father is giving me a lesson this night. I would later realize just how lucky I was to have a father who:

- loved country music so … and passed it on.
- was very, very knowledgeable about country and bluegrass.
- was incredibly talented musically himself and was a great teacher … but I digress …

"Hear that guitar right there? That's Chet Atkins, son!," he'd say. The next song would begin with an awesome guitar intro. I'd say, "Is that Chet too Daddy?"

He'd say, "No, that's Paul Yandell on that one!" (Dad proudly told me that like himself, Paul was a Kentuckian). He would then point out which were Paul's tracks, and which were Chet's.

At that early age I had already picked up on Chet and Paul's unique style and technique. It was easy to tell they were very special and, well, just on another planet from other guitarists! Simpatico! Those two always seemed to be joined at the Gretsch! How could I know that just a few short years later, all three of us would be musically entwined?!

Paul's musical journey blasted off from Mayfield, Kentucky and took him to Nashville, straight to the very heart of Country music … WSM and the Grand Ole Opry. The Opry was hillbilly headquarters (I use the term "hillbilly" affectionately), and Paul was there in the thick of it! The Louvin Brothers were white hot and Paul found himself touring and recording with them on so many of their important records. (By the way … what was in the water over in that part of Kentucky? Not far from Paul's hometown were the hometowns of other great thumbpickers; Mose Rager, Ike Everly, and Merle Travis!)

Paul also would go on to tour with such country greats as George Hamilton IV, Kitty Wells and Johnny Wright, and Jerry Reed. All along though, he was becoming so sought after in the studio that the touring was put on hold. He soon became part of the famous studio force, the A-Team. Paul played on the hit recordings for so many artists that I would list a few if only I had the space!

The studio became Paul's sanctuary, his haven. Then he quit the road altogether and cut back on his studio work. He later would tour again with Jerry Reed and ultimately with his mentor and friend, Chet Atkins. That is when my time and rest-of-life friendship with Paul began. I am so thankful that it did. He would stay by Chet's side till Chet's passing in 2001.

I loved how you never were unsure of what Paul thought. He let you know with brutal honesty … that was just Paul! He continued to work and hone his craft on a personal level. His appetite for learning was insatiable. He was also very unselfish.

He loved sharing any new licks or tunes he came upon. If he knew it, he wanted you to know it too.

There are a lot of brilliant guitarists. But they are usually proficient in one style. Paul's versatility and breadth of knowledge was and still is amazing. How could one person know so much? There will never be another Paul!

In these pages you will learn more about this intense, humble, funny, kind-hearted, wonderful guitarist. There is no question he was a master … no question he was like a big brother to me. He most definitely made me a better player and person. Welcome to the world of Paul Yandell, CGP.

Steve Wariner
August 2012

FOREWORD

BY PAT KIRTLEY

Paul Yandell was always a sideman, with the Louvins, with Jerry, and with Chet. But with Chet, he virtually redefined the concept. On stage he was Chet's perfect backup and duet partner, filling the role as no other player could. Offstage, he was Chet's "Man Friday," coming up with ideas and carrying out missions that enhanced Chet's endeavors in many ways. As people say, "there's only one Chet," speaking to his uniqueness, you can say in the same way "there's only one Paul." And there's really no one else with whom you'd compare him that I can think of.

Chet actively avoided being cast in the role of sideman. He wanted to be the out-front star, and he wanted it from an early age. After his beginning radio days in Knoxville, the only sideman gig he accepted of any consequence was with the Carter Sisters. And even then, they featured him as a member of the act, in photos, on stage, and with equal billing. Paul, by contrast, wanted only to be a sideman. He seriously avoided the spotlight even after Chet's death, even when he had produced a couple of videos and five albums under his own name. He wanted no part of fame. It is time that someone told Paul's side of the story.

Pat Kirtley
March 2012

Kentucky born Pat Kirtley is well known in finger style guitar circles as a musician and author.

PREFACE

"Daddy never thought he was a good guitar player, and has always remained humble throughout his life."
— Micah Yandell

This is the story of Paul Yandell, a Kentucky-born guitarist who was the sideman, the accompanying guitarist, to two of the finest guitarists this country ever produced. He called it "playing second" and by that definition he was "second to the best."

When Chet Atkins retired and could no longer play due to health issues (around 1999–2000), Paul cut his own playing to occasional small venues chosen for pleasure rather than need. The computer caught his interest and he signed on to a Chet Atkins oriented online chat board at misterguitar.com. The site is the official website of Chet Atkins. The forum itself is called "The Chetboard" and is owned by the Atkins Estate.

There he kept Chet's fans advised as to how Chet was doing and eventually had the heartbreaking task of announcing Chet's passing. Paul continued to post on the Chetboard. Over the years Paul answered thousands of questions put to him by people interested in Chet Atkins, Jerry Reed, Lenny Breau, and the life of the performing musician. He answered detailed questions about the equipment used by these men over the space of roughly ten years. From time to time, people would urge him to write a book and he refused.

People ask me about writing a book about my experiences with Chet over those years. The problem there is even though a lot of things happened over the twenty-two years I was with Chet I don't think it would be enough for a book.

I had a great experience playing with so many great acts and the best was playing with Chet. I don't know how it all happened. First Jerry Reed, then Chet, but I think something has been guiding me through life. I've had a most wonderful life, more than I ever dreamed of.

There are many stories to tell about different entertainers, some funny, some strange, but if I told some on living artists I might get in trouble.

In spite of Paul's reluctance to write a book, the priceless information he posted on the Chetboard was gathered and saved. After Paul passed on, all of those questions he answered and stories he told were carefully spliced together much in the same way a film buff with a Movieola and a box of film clips might do; put all that information into a continuous form for people to enjoy.

It is the story of a man. It is a story about true musical legends. It describes how guitars are designed and reveals details on some one-of-a-kind instruments that produced iconic tone, tone still sought by guitarists today.

It is a story about the Golden Age of American country music as seen from the stage right view of a sideman ... a shy, humble man, who once said:

You can put it in the archive but don't post it on the forums. After I'm gone people can read it in the archives.
Thanks, Paul
(November 2010)

ACKNOWLEDGMENTS

Jan Hite

Jan gets first call. One day Marie Yandell sent me an email that said, in part: "Jan Hite was really good friends to Paul and I, sent this to me. Read thru it and see if there's anything you can use or want to use."

Marie had sent me a long piece by Jan that had a couple of nice anecdotes. I wrote her and questioned her for clarity on what she had related. That was our beginning.

Jan is a retired principal in the Los Angeles Unified School District and, poor dear, volunteered to be my chief "reader"—the person who takes on the onerous task of combing a manuscript for typos and grammatical errors. Over the next year she would corner me on word usage, punctuation and, most valuably, she would balk and stop me when I wrote something she didn't understand. Something I wrote would be too vague or not make any sense to a non-guitarist. She was stubborn, almost as stubborn as I was and some of our beefs went on for days before they got resolved. But the changes she caused made the book more readable and for that I am grateful. She slogged through the entire manuscript over and over in an effort to make a writer out of me. It must be said that this book would not be what it is without her.

Kevin Jarvis

A personal friend I've known for nearly forty years. He's the former proprietor of Gelb Music in Redwood City, CA, and a well-known, fine guitarist in his own right. I especially valued his input because he is a musician and Kevin was never one to hold back if he thought something seemed off. He was a "reader" too and his recommendations caused a lot of text to get moved around. He preceded Jan in the spelling/punctuation snipe hunt. He is the only contributor in this entire project that I ever communicated with face to face.

Craig Dobbins

Not sure where to start in thanking Craig Dobbins. He not only gave me support but he also gave me laughs and for graciously allowing me to use portions of his book *The Paul Yandell Collection*, published by Craig Dobbins' *Acoustic Guitar Workshop*. He offered me lots of valuable tips and connections. He also provided me with some of Paul's posted quotes I had missed.

Thanks to Gayle Moseley

An inductee into the Thumbpicker's Hall of Fame, he describes himself thusly: "I used to do some "scab sessions" in Nashville and played in groups that backed some fairly big stars at times, but mainly I stuck to being a partner in an insurance agency here in Hopkinsville, KY and made my living that way ... that and investments. I got to be as close to the inside on the music business as I wanted to be."

Gayle gave me a lot of support and shared some great stories, some I included here, some I promised to never divulge. Paul once mused to me that he wished he, Gayle, and I could have had a breakfast or two together.

Thanks to Pat Kirtley

Writer, contributor to *Mister Guitar* magazine (among others) for no-nonsense advice and providing me with hard to find photos. I hadn't planned on including an introduction for the book. I found what became the introduction in a spontaneous email Pat had sent me.

Special thanks to Ed Ball

Author of *Gretsch 6120: The History of a Legendary Guitar.* He helped me navigate the swamp of book stuff. I mean he helped me big time. And of course, none of this would have been possible without the gentle prodding and support of Marie and Micah Yandell, who wanted their Paul to get some of the recognition he deserved. Their husband and father passed away during the creation of this work yet they both were there through the pain of all that with support and reminisces. Marie scanned some long out of print articles about Paul that had invaluable information.

Along with "The Chetboard," I used Paul's words from the following articles with permission (Paul's words are displayed in **boldface** throughout the text):

> "Chet's Right Thumb Man," by Bill Piburn, in *Fingerstyle Guitar*
> "From Mayfield to Music City," by Jim Oldschmidt, in *Fingerstyle Guitar*
> "The Secret's in the Thumb," by John Scroeter, in *Fingerstyle Guitar*
> "Chet Atkins Right (and left) Hand Man," by Jim Oldschmidt, *Frets Magazine*
> "At Top Of The Nashville Studio Scene," by Dennis Hendsley, in *Guitar Player*
> "Here's Paul Yandell," by Bob Guest in, *CAAS Newsletter*

Contributors

These are the folks who sent me brief reminisces and photos. Being on this list it means I have sent a copy of the edited version of their contribution to the contributor and he/she approved it for inclusion in this project. Their contributions are indented throughout the text, and include appropriate credit.

Lists are dangerous things because, invariably, people get left off a list that surely should have been included. To the neglected ones, I can only extend my apologies:

Barry Oliver
Chuck Schwickerath
Craig Dobbins
Denny (Sage) McKinney
Don Birchett
Ed Ball
Eddie Estes
Forrest Yandell
Hendrik Sibca
Jan Hite
John Knowles
Marie Yandell
Micah Yandell
Murray White
Randy Goodrun
Ray Bohlken
Richard Hudson
Vidar Lund
Gary Cochran
John Lewis
Tom Redmond
Ed Preman
Eddie Pennington
Gregg Galbraith
Morgan Scoggins
Sid Hudson

PROLOGUE: STARDOM ...
AN ILLUSION

The illusion ... coming to a park or arena near you ...
"Illusion" is a word usually applied to magicians or strange, shape-changing pictures. Something that is designed to fool or mislead people.

They're here! They're here!

The converted-to-order big bus is arriving and, sure enough, there's the name of the star in that little window over the windshield and painted in big letters on the side! Everybody knows it is bad manners to approach the bus because the star is on the bus. On the other hand, the star would not be a star were it not for the power of the money spent by the fans so the star'd best be stepping off that bus and greeting the fans in pretty short order. Maybe give up an autograph or three.

The fan is there to be entertained. They will attend the show, buy the records, the songbooks, and the tee shirts. The fan will watch the star adoringly, mouthing or even outright singing the words along with the star. Many (if not all of them) will imagine *they* are the ones up on the stage, under the lights, making all that music and making all that money. Vicarious living is a large part of what stardom is all about from the fan's point of view.

But stardom is not a real thing. It is an illusion! A beautiful, shining, diaphanous curtain. A mocking witch of an illusion that neither the performer nor the audience can actually touch. It is a treacherous unreality, this stardom stuff.

The star had better deliver or the fan will hang on to their money to wait for something else. For the fan giveth and the fan taketh away. The fan can turn on the star causing the star to fade into bankruptcy or worse if care is not taken. This is not done with malice. It just happens. The fan loses interest and moves on. There is always something new coming soon ... coming soon.

There is an anomaly in physics called the "Doppler Effect." Everyone is familiar with it. The common descriptive illustration is to be standing at a railroad crossing as a fast train goes by, the engineer sounding the horn as he passes. The sound grows louder, peaks, then drops off again as it fades into the distance.

Stardom is like that. First just a distant glimmer, then a mad, rushing, peak of noise and excitement all too often followed by a fade to oblivion.

This is the greatest fear of the star. The fear of how quickly they might fade into oblivion. Some of them feel they are only one song away from that very thing happening. The star is therefore always hungrily looking for the hit song that will cause their Doppler Effect to maintain the noise and excitement for a while longer.

In the meantime, the fan would like to be treated to something new from the star. But, more importantly, they want to hear the star's "string of hits." They want the reassurance that the star is unchanged from what they were when the fan first discovered them. They want those songs played just like they are on the records they have at home.

To accomplish this trick the bus disgorges these other guys. Some of them are known by the fan because some stars keep and maintain a band. Most stars cannot afford to maintain a full-time band. They cannot afford to keep a band unless they are on the road over 200 days a year. So what some of them do is to hire freelance musicians to work the shows. Musicians willing to get paid by the day or by the show. Playing the same "string of hits" again and again at each stop.

Their musical ability is usually far, far, above the relatively simple fare of country music hits. But it is the star who is, after all on the playbill. The musicians are, to a large degree, faceless.

They are paid to play it like it is on the record.

They are the sidemen. The professional musicians.

CHAPTER 1

DOWN ON THE FARM

Some Local Back Story

A long time ago, it is not recorded when, stone age humans found that a certain tasty animal they had been hunting could be trained to be a beast of burden. Eventually they found that this marvelous creature could be ridden. If they could ride it they could race it. If they could race it, they could bet on it and lo, the horse race gambler was born!

Betting on horse races became deeply ingrained in human civilization. Ancient Rome, as it spread its influence over the known world always included an arena in their settlements and the arena was, first and foremost, designed as a racetrack. Once Europeans discovered and colonized the New World they brought the racetrack with them. With the westward movement, pioneers became settlers who then became townsmen. The townsmen built racetracks; temples, in a way, to the gods of chance, offering enticement for the gambling instinct in the human psyche.

It came to pass in 1817, that a gambler from Mississippi, surnamed Mayfield, was on his way to a place called Mills Point, Kentucky. He was waylaid and kidnapped, for an unspecified reason, by some of his fellow gamblers. These brigands took the intrepid Mr. Mayfield to their camp that was near an unnamed creek. There he was held by his captors while they plotted what to do with him. Oddly, they allowed him to keep a knife, most likely an inoffensive pocketknife, on his person.

Perhaps as a distraction, he took the time to carve his name in a tree that was near the nameless creek. At first opportunity Mayfield bolted the scene, making for the creek. His captors, seeing their prize escaping, fired upon his person with the unfortunate result being a lethal combination of powder, ball, and drowning. The misadventure cost gambler Mayfield his life.

For some reason, perhaps due to the woodworking skill exhibited in his carving, or the more mundane, that he was the first person known to have expired in those waters, the creek was named after the fallen gambler. Eventually a town was built near that very creek. The town took the name of Mayfield.

With the arrival of the railroad in 1858, Mayfield became the county seat of Graves County. Over time, it built up to a sizable town with all the stores and services a citizen could want.

Even as the arrival of the railroad in the 1800s marked Mayfield as a modern town for that day, its timeliness is now marked with that icon of the twenty-first century, the website! The Mayfield website lists some of the notable highlights of the town.

Graves County was considered neutral territory during the Civil War, but most of the citizens of Graves considered themselves Confederates. However, many men from Mayfield fought at the Battle of Shiloh as soldiers in the federal army.

The first female sheriff in the United States was Mayfield's Lois Roach in 1922, who took over for her husband after he was murdered on duty.

Jerry Seinfeld stopped in Mayfield for a barbecue sandwich. He did so at the recommendation of Bruce Willis. (No one turns down a recommendation by Mr. Willis apparently.)

The Mayfield Woolen Mills and the Merit Manufacturing Co., that produced pants and suits, once could boast to be two of the largest factories of their kind in the nation.

Graves County was mostly a dry county. Mostly meaning alcohol could be sold by the drink in restaurants that served one hundred or more patrons and alcohol could be sold at the Mayfield Golf & Country Club. There were no sales of alcohol allowed on Sunday except at the Mayfield Golf & Country Club. This would imply that less moneyed people in Mayfield, those who could not afford the game of golf, or membership in the Mayfield Golf and Country Club would have been hard pressed to buy a cocktail on a Sunday, but such is life.

Tobacco was, for some areas of the South, a cash crop, a side crop, raised for the extra money tobacco could bring. The area surrounding Mayfield is farming country. In Graves County as in many other Southern counties, tobacco was a primary crop. Tobacco was one of the first industries of Mayfield, and one of the longest-lived. Ten miles out from Mayfield, on a fifty-acre tobacco farm, September 6, 1935, Paul Thurman Yandell was born.

In our family we say "Yandell" like "handle" but everyone else says yanDELL so I just let it ride. I grew up on a fifty-acre tobacco farm. My daddy tried to make a living farming. He never was a good farmer but we didn't know the difference. We were poor as Job's turkey. I thought we had a hard life at the time but now it doesn't seem like it was so bad.

The Yandells, Paul's father, Ted and his mother, Imogene, had a fifty-acre tobacco farm. To help make ends meet, Ted and Imogene worked for Merit Manufacturing Company in Mayfield. Ted pressed suits

Yandell family farmhouse near Mayfield, KY. As of 2013, the property was still in Yandell family possession and was regularly visited by Paul's family as a "country retreat." It is no longer used to farm tobacco. *Photo courtesy of YFA* and Imogene sewed sleeves onto suits. It was piecework for both of them. Instead of getting paid by the hour, piecework paid according to actual count of how many suits were pressed or sleeves were sewn as tallied at the end of day. This was in addition to having to run a farm.

Paul was the oldest of three kids. He had a sister, Yvonne, four years younger, and brother Forrest, ten years his junior. Paul and his siblings were working the farm with their parents from an early age. In a farm family everyone works, even the kids, almost from the time they can walk.

The modern twenty-first century farm, compared to its mid-thirties forerunners, is likely to be a dedicated agribusiness running all of one particular crop or meat animal and utilizing a lot of acreage in the process. The agribusiness farm is a marvel of machinery, all cold efficiency and, as a rule, little room is allowed for human amenities. The agribusiness of today is more like a factory than a farm.

The rural farm in Paul's day was a home operation in every sense of the word.

The Yandell farm consisted of two sections of land. The homestead, being the house, a barn, for their animals and a tobacco-curing barn, along with the meat smokehouse, was on the larger, thirty-two-acre sector. The other twenty acres were dedicated to tobacco and corn. The corn was primarily raised to feed the livestock.

The Yandells did not have a tractor for plowing or towing other farming machinery. They had a horse and a mule for that kind of thing. Generally, two cows were kept for milk. Breeding them periodically was required to keep the animals lactating. This also provided calves that could be raised and sold. The cows required a twice a day milking. With no refrigeration the milk had to be processed fairly quickly. Things that were perishable were often kept cool in the well if a farm did not have a springhouse. Butter was made in a churn and milk was taken directly from the cows in the barn to the family table. There was no money for such things or a store to buy them from out in the country.

In the rural farms of the day, families raised what they ate. They would have a truck patch for vegetables. Canning and preserving vegetables for winter was part of the farm routine. Poor people did not eat much beef. Raising a steer to full growth was expensive. Livestock on a farm needed to earn their own keep. The fodder they would require was better given to work animals and milk cows than to beef. Calves were raised until they were weaned, then sold off. Meat for the table came from pigs and chickens. The Yandells, like so many other farm families, kept a brood sow that had two litters a year. Most of the piglets were sold for a few dollars each to hog lots when they were about four months old. Some pigs, usually about four animals, were fed and fattened until the fall, around Thanksgiving. Farmers waited until after the first frost, when the nights were predictably cold. At that time the small community of neighboring farmers would gather for the ritual of hog slaughtering. This annual process had its own special needs, a scalding barrel or cauldron and certain tools specially used in the preparation of the fresh killed animals. The extra hands of the community were welcome as the animals were butchered and the meat washed and cleaned.

The resulting meat was carefully smoked in the family smokehouse for winter consumption. Nothing was wasted.

When the fields didn't need tending, fishing brought variety to the table. Sometimes small game was added to table fare—groundhogs, rabbits, and squirrels.

> Paul enjoyed shooting any kind of gun. Daddy had a single shot .22-caliber Winchester rifle. He taught Paul and me how to shoot. He always said 'if you can't shoot a squirrel in the head, don't shoot it at all.' Paul and I honed our skill by sticking matches into a board in the back yard and shooting the heads of the matches.
> — Forrest Yandell

Every farm had chickens kept for eggs for the table. A chicken dinner now and then never did anyone any harm. Milking, tending to the chickens and finding eggs in the morning were usually the earliest chores most farm kids remember. Also included on the kids' work list was slopping the hogs with leftover table scraps and milk products that had gone over. Nothing on a farm was wasted. Everybody worked. They were farmers after all.

Tobacco Farming

Tobacco farming was the main cash crop in that part of Kentucky. In modern times a farmer is often paid to raise certain types of tobacco. They are usually guaranteed a price per pound of good crop. But back in Paul's day, tobacco was sold at auction at the end of the growing season. There were no guarantees to the small farmer in the thirties.

The growing season varied depending on what part of the country tobacco was grown but it roughly went from May through October. Tobacco farming was labor intensive. In a farm family everyone pitched in to make a crop. Seedlings needed to be nurtured and planted. Fertilizer was applied. Weeds were taken out. Plants needed to be topped. The flower bud at the top of the plants needed to be removed to stimulate leaf growth. Next, the resulting growth, the "suckers" needed to be removed. This was done to force the remaining leaf to grow larger. The lower leaves were removed for the same reason suckers were removed to force the plant to develop a larger leaf for the final harvest.

Each plant is scrutinized for tobacco worms. Tobacco hornworms, the larva of the hawk moth, needed to be found and killed. They were large, plump caterpillars that could grow as long as four inches. They were removed by hand. Farm kids as young as five or six could be put to work pulling worms.

> When we pulled the worms off the tobacco plant we simply twisted and crushed their head between our thumb and index finger.
> — Forrest Yandell

The farmer had to watch for plant disease and mold damage through the entire process. Of course he needed the weather to cooperate. A bad hailstorm could ruin a crop as well as too much or too little rain. There were no guarantees in tobacco farming.

At harvest time the plants were cut close to the ground to be gathered up for drying and curing. There were different methods of curing tobacco. The Yandells cured their tobacco in a well-ventilated barn (air curing). This method produced cigar tobacco.

We used tobacco knives to split the stalk, starting from the top. We split to about two thirds of the way down the stalk and then cut the stalk off close to the ground. It had to be a hot, sunny day in order for the tobacco to wilt and become pliable for loading onto the wagon. If it was not wilted, the leaves would break off the stalk.

In the late afternoon we would spear the tobacco on tobacco drying sticks, load it on the wagon and take it to the drying barn. Inside the barn the temperature could reach well over 100 degrees (and usually did) especially at the top of the barn. The sticks would be placed about fourteen inches apart on horizontal beams arranged in tiers. Care was taken that the leaves were not touching to allow for air circulation. Many times it would be dark before the job was done and kerosene lanterns would be placed in the barn for light.

During the curing process the tobacco had to be constantly monitored for fungus, especially if there was a lot of rain. After the tobacco had cured and turned brown, the stripping process would start. The tobacco would be taken out of the barn, loaded onto a wagon and taken to either a stripping shed (one room small building) or if there was no stripping shed it would be taken to the back porch of a house to be stripped. We didn't have a stripping shed so we used our back porch.
— Forrest Yandell

The stripping process was very important as there are three grades of tobacco called the tips, leaf, and lugs. The tips are the short leaves at the top of the stalk. Leaf is from the main body and lugs are from the bottom of the stalk. The selling price for the leaf is the highest followed by the tips and then the lugs.

Tying the tobacco "hands." This is the process by which leaves of the same grade are placed together in your hand with the stems remaining at the top. When the diameter of the stems reach about two inches a tobacco leaf is folded, wrapped around the stems and secured by opening the tobacco hand and pulling the wrapping leaf through the tobacco hand.

Each grade, lugs, leaf and tips, is stored in a grade pile as not to mix the grades. After the stripping process is completed the tobacco is then arranged and stored in the bulk. The bulk is the final step in the process. Bulking is placing the tobacco hands in a pile. In each layer of the bulk the tobacco hands are rotated ninety degrees for uniformity. When the tobacco is delivered to the warehouse for sale the same process is used.

> Mayfield was a small town and only had two auction warehouses. At harvest time a band of roving gypsies would come into town and set up a small carnival. All the stores around the town square would put their wares on sale during this time. Daddy and his cousin would always celebrate the end of the season by going to a local bootlegger and buying some moonshine. Mother was a strict Baptist and didn't allow any booze in the house. Daddy kept it stored out in the smoke house.
> I remember one year was very dry with little rain. When daddy sold the tobacco crop his profit was $18. Normally, we would get $125-$150 per year. We were poor but us kids didn't know it because everyone was poor. But we were happy.
> — Forrest Yandell

They had no choice but to accept the auctioned price behind them and get ready to manage the next crop so they could do it all over again. They were farmers after all.

Farming people were rural, country folk. They lived away from towns, stores and the bustling bright lights of cities. Electricity was scarce, an impossible luxury to most farmers during the Depression. Indoor plumbing was for cities and towns. Farms didn't have faucets. They had wells and buckets. They used kerosene for lighting at night. They wistfully leafed through the mail order catalogs, wishing they could buy some of the things on those pages, knowing that their wishes were largely fantasies.

For news and entertainment they listened to battery operated radios. Some folks couldn't afford even that small luxury and used crystal sets instead. Some listened to local stations. It seemed like all small towns had a radio station and Mayfield was no exception with its own WNGO. Paul sometimes listened to WCKY out of Cincinnati. It seemed like everyone listened to the Saturday night Grand Ole Opry broadcast by WSM's clear-channel station in Nashville.

The radio took them away from the farm for a little bit of time. Before the days of television, radio required them to use their imagination to visualize what they were hearing. Many a rural youngster heard the singers and musicians on the radio, and dreamed of someday leaving the farm to become rich and famous, as actors, announcers, or playing music … being on the Opry. Paul was no different.

In the immediate Yandell family only Paul ever showed any real interest in learning to play an instrument professionally. Brother Forrest sang in a quartet and played a little guitar, while his sister, Yvonne, played piano in church. Paul was the one who actually focused on playing an instrument for a living but that notion was not to happen until he was almost in his teens.

Out in farm country there wasn't much for people to do to entertain themselves. Most families belonged to a church and some socializing was done there. An occasional "dinner on the ground" would be held. In nice weather, people would bring quilts to spread on the grass, bringing favorite dishes to share. Northern folk called these types of social gatherings picnics and they were often held at the local church.

In young Paul's life there was a more enjoyable custom. In rural communities people would gather at neighbors' houses to make music on whatever instruments were at hand. These gatherings were called "play parties." There were all kinds of instruments. Some were homemade, some were store-bought. Many were acquired through mail order catalogs. Fiddles, guitars, banjos and harmonicas. People brought what they had, gathering to make music, taking a break from the monotony of farm work. Young Paul would go to some of these play parties to hear them make music but he had no musical instrument of his own nor the understanding of how to play one.

When I was a kid in West Kentucky all we had for entertainment was the radio. There was a group that played on the radio in Mayfield, Kentucky, about ten miles from where we lived. They played country music and would go around to the schoolhouses to play shows. One night they came to a school about a mile from us so we went. I saw a young boy, "Little" Bobby Pugh, was what they called him, playing guitar. I'll never forget him. I thought to myself "I should get a guitar." I even asked my mother "Can I get a guitar?" Just around that time my parents had given me a calf to raise. When it got big enough we sold it and I got part of the money. I bought a baseball glove and a Stella guitar with my part of the money.

That Stella cost him thirteen dollars. There is something about the smell of that first new guitar when a youngster opens the box. There's not a guitarist alive who can forget that first new guitar aroma and its promise. Paul no doubt inhaled the aroma deeply when he brought the instrument home. Unbeknownst to him, that aroma had seeped into his very soul never ever to release him. It's one thing to have a guitar, quite another to play it. Paul didn't have much to go on as far as actually learning the guitar until one day a neighbor lady happened to be visiting after he got his new guitar.

"Miss Wanda" was a lady who lived across the field from us with her husband "Mr. Wes." Gunn was their last name. She was one of the greatest people I've ever known. I remember she wore a bonnet all the time. She used to walk over to our house to meet the peddler who came down the road once a week. He had a truck. It was like a grocery store to us.

The peddler truck would come every Saturday. It was a panel truck. Nowadays it would be called a van, but that was before the vans came out. The truck was lined with pots, pans, kitchen supplies, candy, a few small toys and a few staples such as flour and sugar. The driver would accept either cash or barter items such as eggs, chickens or ducks. I never had any money so I would trade eggs for candy. We looked forward to Saturday wondering if there would be new items in the truck.

He stopped coming around about 1955. I can't remember why. Maybe he died.

— Forrest Yandell

One day, when Miss Wanda was at our house, Mama or I mentioned my guitar. Miss Wanda told us she used to play when she was a young girl. One thing led to another and she started giving me lessons once a week. I would walk across the field and she would show me something. She played with her fingers, the old fashioned way. My first formal lessons were out of a Broadman Hymnal. She would mark the changes on tunes like "In The Garden" and things like that. That's how I really learned my first chords and got my first ear training. She had played at play parties when she was a young girl. She played with her fingers … no pick. I never saw anybody with a straight pick when I was learning to play.

After my lessons, I'd walk back home across that twenty-acre field, but I'd always stop under a big tree that stood right in the middle of it. I'd sit down in its shade and practice what she had shown me that day so that I wouldn't forget it. I remember one day after a lesson I had forgotten it already, and I sat there under that tree and cried.

As the years passed, I would get back home from time to time for visits, and I would always be sure to see Miss Wanda. The last time I saw her was in 1995. I had gone home with my family for Christmas, and by then, Miss Wanda was living at a rest home, her husband having passed away many years before. They had been married for seventy years. She seemed so happy to see us, and she told us a wonderful story. She was a hundred years old. She was frail, and her sight was failing, but she was as sharp as a tack. As we got up to say goodbye, she stopped me to tell me she wanted me to have her old guitar. It was over at her sister's house; we should stop by to get it.

We went to her sister's home, and she brought the guitar out to me in a pillowcase. Amazingly, it still had the same strings that were on it when I was a young boy taking lessons from her all those years ago. Miss Wanda had owned that guitar since she was ten years old. I don't know what kind it is. She said her Mother paid three dollars for it.

Today, that old guitar hangs on a wall in my music room. And every time I look at it, I think of the days when I was so excited to learn something that Miss Wanda had played on it. It is a treasure.

It is remarkable how one person can affect your life when you're young and learning about life. Sometimes someone will put you on a path that takes you through it ... you look back and know you owe them so much. She lived to be 103 years old. If there is anyone in Heaven Miss Wanda is one of them.

The next phase of learning guitar, (along with hours of practice) was to attend the play-parties.

Miss Wanda's guitar. Guitar owned by "Miss Wanda" Gunn, Paul's first guitar teacher. According to Paul, it still has the original strings Miss Wanda used on it. *Photo courtesy of Derek Rhodes*

CHAPTER 2

TUNING UP

There wasn't any television or anything, so on Saturday night people that could play would go to somebody's house. Back then they were called "play parties." It would be a different house every Saturday. That was my first introduction to people playing music together. It was really exciting for all of us. They would get in the living room and everybody would sit in a chair in a circle with their guitars or mandolins or whatever they had. That's how I started out.

These kinds of parties were make-or-break schools for many a young musician. If they wanted to play at these events they had to be quick to learn what they needed to know. Sometimes the older players would show a chord that the novice didn't know but much of the time the new player just had to figure it out as they went along.

For some reason this brought to mind when I was young I someway got a paper Nick Lucas chord wheel. You could turn it and find every chord you wanted. Of course back then I didn't want too many. I think I may still have it somewhere.

The play party is an ancient tradition that still goes on. Today the play party is arranged by phone and it goes something like this: "You want to come over to my house Saturday and jam with me and the guy next door?" Saturday will roll around, the musicians and their friends will come over, form a circle and play what they know. It's what musicians have done since they first started thumping hollow logs.

Now, in guitar history it is said Kennedy Jones, with his neighbor and friend, Mose Rager were the fathers of a certain infectious guitar style. At their own play parties the two men developed a style of playing rhythm with the right thumb and simultaneously playing the melody with the right hand's index finger. They called it thumb-style playing. They lived around Muhlenberg County that was east of Graves County; in coal mining country. Those two men inspired Merle Travis to learn the fascinating style and Merle brought it to the cities. It is now generally referred to as "Travis Style" guitar playing. A local war veteran learned the style from the men in Muhlenberg County. He visited a play party near Mayfield and had a tremendous impact on Paul. He was the first man Paul ever saw actually playing thumb-style.

When I first started trying to learn to play I didn't know enough to play other than second, as they said back then. Edwin Tynes came one night. Edwin had been hurt in WWII. I think a tank had run over him. I still think of that night when Mr. Tynes, who lived just up the road, changed my life. I was just about fourteen years old at the time. He played "A Shanty In Old Shanty Town." Boy that tore me up! I knew at that moment what I wanted to do. I thought it was the prettiest thing I'd ever heard. I couldn't believe how he could use his thumb to keep the rhythm going and play the melody. I hadn't heard of Chet or Merle Travis. I tried to play like that. That is what got me started on that style. From then on I wanted to be a fingerpicker!

While Paul enjoyed playing guitar he definitely did not enjoy the prospect of tobacco farming with all its hot, dusty ways. Paul wanted to find a way of making a living doing something that wasn't so backbreaking and speculative. He had other skills he once thought might be a way to get into something other than farming. Those ideas got set aside when he heard a young guitarist playing a song on Cincinnati radio station WCKY.

When I was young I could draw pretty good. I had a dream of being an artist but that all changed. I discovered Chet Atkins when I was about thirteen or fourteen years old. The first Chet song I ever heard was "I've been Working on the Guitar." I had been playing for a few years but when I heard Chet I knew that was the way to play a guitar. Almost every minute of the day I thought about him and worked on playing guitar. Working in that tobacco patch is the reason I practiced so hard. When I found out I could make money as a musician I practiced night and day just to stay out of that tobacco patch. It is backbreaking work and you will practice your butt off to get away from it.

When I was young I was in ill health. I had what they called Bright's Disease. It is a kidney disease. I couldn't do anything to exert myself. This was in my early teens. By then all I ever wanted to do was to come to Nashville to play the Grand Ole' Opry. That was my dream, night and day. The dream eventually came true.

Over the years I've been able to record with Chet, Les Paul, and Jerry Reed. I've played with Lenny Breau, Les Paul, Merle Travis ... all my heroes. What more can a guy want? Then to work for Chet later in life, well, that was the greatest blessing I could have.

Sooner or later you have to make up your mind whether it's really worth it to you or not. I mean, is it worth it to me to spend my whole life playing music?

It's no easy thing. It ain't a money thing like, "I'm gonna make all kinds of money." You have to love it enough, I think. You have to love it to the point where it means everything to you.

— Lenny Breau
(from a Breau seminar video)

Paul didn't have the luxury of today's teaching tools or the extensive audio/visual aids available to the modern guitar student. But they had a radio. Brother Forrest says they had a battery powered radio at home when Paul was about fifteen.

On Saturday night daddy would pour water on the ground where the ground rod was to get a better signal in order to listen to the Grand Ole' Opry.

I was too young to remember at the time but when I was older Paul told me he made a "potato radio." It was based on the "cat whisker" crystal radio principle. An Irish potato was substituted for the crystal which, due to lack of funds, Paul was unable to purchase.

Crystal radios are the simplest type of radio receiver and could be handmade with a few inexpensive parts, like an antenna wire, a tuning coil of copper wire, a crystal detector (in this case a potato) and earphones. They are distinct from ordinary radios because they are passive receivers, while other radios use a separate source of electric power such as a battery or the main power to amplify the weak radio signal from the antenna so it is louder.

Thus crystal/potato sets produce rather weak sound and must be listened to with earphones, and can only pick up stations within a limited range. Paul used an old set of army surplus headphones someone had given him. I have no idea where he got the idea. I didn't believe him so I built one myself and it worked!

— Forrest Yandell

For much of Paul's young life the Yandell farm didn't have electricity. Even a simple record player was out of the question in a household that depended on kerosene lamps for light after sundown.

All you could get were those crank-up things because there was no electricity. We were just really poor and couldn't afford anything like that.

Paul started looking for more Chet Atkins music on the radio intensifying his practice as he learned what would come to be known as thumb-style or finger-style guitar. Like many poor country boys he even made his own thumb picks out of celluloid toothbrush handles, a process involving heating the celluloid handle in boiling hot water and bending the material to fit.

It's been so long I don't remember where I first got a thumb pick. I know that I would try to make one out of a toothbrush handle like Chet said one time.

Needless to say I was 'eat up' with it! I went crazy just playing that way, trying anything to learn.

Back in those days they would have fiddler's contests every year at different schools to raise money. They would have different categories. After a few years I had a mandolin, a fiddle and a harmonica. I could play a little bit on everything. I could even play banjo a little bit. You could enter the different categories at the fiddler's contests. I got so I would win almost every one of them. For prizes you'd get dishes or a free oil change ... all this stuff that merchants would donate. My wife, Marie, has a set of FireKing Tulip bowls and a set of red His and Hers towels that I won when I played in some of those contests. My mother saved them and gave them to Marie. I got pretty hot down in there.

At one of these contests one year Paul won first place as Best Guitar, Best Mandolin, Best Harmonica and Youngest Fiddler. He was making a name for himself in the area.

Paul was to meet someone at one of those fiddle contests who would become one of his dearest friends, Odell Martin. Odell was a big Merle Travis fan and Paul was more into Chet which worked out well for the two of them. Initially Paul wasn't impressed with Merle Travis because Paul pegged him as a singer rather than a guitarist. As he got older that view changed as he became more aware of Merle's guitar skills. Both young men had the same dream ... to play the Opry.

Paul and Odell Martin. A rare photo of the two young men together. That is Paul's first Gretsch 6120 judging from the distinctive Gretsch case. The amp is a Fender Deluxe. Paul used that combination with the Louvins. *Photo courtesy of YFA*

Odell Martin was from Allegree in Todd County. That county is a little south of Muhlenberg County where Merle Travis came from. We lived about fifty miles apart up in Kentucky. Odell Martin and I met when we both were in high school. When we actually met we hit it off like crazy. We became friends that day.

I think that was my last year in High School. Odell had one year left. He and I played many a night at some person or others house and had a great time.

We were both in the FFA (Future Farmer's of America). They had a statewide fiddle contest every year. Out in the country that's Big Stuff. Every year at the state high school contests he'd win at his school and I'd win at mine. Both of us went on to the state finals. I was in one category, Odell was in another. You had to keep going up through the districts and all that until you got to state level just like basketball tournaments today. When you competed at a state level you won fifty dollars or a trophy or whatever.

Paul entered playing guitar in the "Novelty" category and Odell entered in the "Music" category. The difference was the music category was only open to those who could read music, which Odell could not. In fact neither boy could read music but that didn't stop Odell!

We didn't play against each other but they were having those competitions at a hotel somewhere in Louisville. It was real funny. I forget what I played. It was probably "Cannonball Rag" or "Dark Eyes." Odell played "St. Louis Blues" and played it so pretty. He had his cousin or nephew stand on the side and hold the music up in front of him. This was typical Odell Martin. He couldn't read a note! He just faked it.

When I started with the Louvins, Odell was still in school. After I was with the Louvins about a year, Bill Carlisle was looking for a guitar player and I recommended Odell. He came down and got the job.

Both of us wanted to come to Nashville to the Grand Ole' Opry. I came down first, then he came down. We roomed together for about four years until I went into the Army. All we did when we were in town was play and try to learn something new.

Then we both got married and that changed everything!

We were like brothers. Odell was a great player. One of the best thumbpickers ever. He loved Merle Travis and really worked on his thumb. I was more into

Chet. Odell was a great person. Everyone who knew him loved him. He was one of the best fingerpickers around. If he were alive today he would be a hot topic at any gathering of finger-style guitarists. He didn't record much but there are some homemade tapes of him playing floating around.

In 1985 Odell died in a car wreck early one morning a few miles from his home in Todd County Kentucky. It almost broke my heart ... it was a great waste. Guitar picking in Kentucky hasn't ever been the same since Odell died. There's just something missing. Everybody has Odell on their mind when they get together and play. I think of him every day.

Odell had a better ear than I did. I could do some things better than he could and he could do some things better than I could. He liked Merle Travis, being from that part of Kentucky, where I didn't try to play Merle's stuff. I was just all Chet Atkins. Nothing against Merle but that's just the way it was. I started hearing Merle Travis on the radio and reached a crossroad in my playing.

When you begin to play guitar, especially finger-style or 'thumb-style', as we called it in Kentucky, you get to a point where you have to decide are you going to play like Merle Travis or are you going to play like Chet Atkins. Some people go the Travis direction, some go the Atkins direction. I don't know what causes one to go in either direction but you have to commit yourself. I don't know of any guitar player who can play like Merle and play like Chet. They are totally different styles, different chords, different time figures and a totally different outlook on guitar. I went with Chet. You have to get on one thing and ride it out. If you want to be a stylist you have to make up your mind what you want to do. You can never be good at anything by changing all the time.

Interlude 1: Mose Rager

What can be said of a certain coal miner and sometime barber, Mose Rager? Mose and his friend, Kennedy Jones, are considered by many musical historians to be the founding fathers of the Kentucky thumbpicking style. In the liner notes of Merle Travis' album *Travis!*, Merle penned, "... I tried to play "Tiger Rag" as much like Mose Rager as I could."

Merle Travis learned guitar from people like Mose Rager and Kennedy Jones. The question then could be raised, would there have been a Merle Travis if there had not been a Mose Rager? And beyond that, would there have been a Chet Atkins as we know him without Merle Travis inspiring him?

I kept hearing about this guitar player who lived in Paducah, Kentucky, Mose Rager. I went to a fiddler's contest in Paducah. Mose was there. He played "Tiger Rag." I watched from backstage. I thought that was the most unbelievable thing I had ever heard. The audience went wild! That was the first time I'd heard Mose play. At the time I thought he was the greatest guitar player alive.

Later, when Odell Martin and I were young kids, we would go up to Mose's and play. It was hard to get Mose to pick a tune. For a while he got religion. He thought he shouldn't play but we would stay after him. He finally would pick a few. He was one of the funniest persons I've ever known. He knew all kind of stories. For a while he cut hair. I remember he broke one of the earpieces on his glasses. He had it taped up with white tape.

There wasn't ever anyone quite like him.

For Paul it still meant hours and hours and hours of practice. It took more than just seeing a person, like Edwin Tynes or Mose Rager play a particular way to learn it. It required sometimes monotonous focus to bring the music out of the instrument the way he wanted.

It was a little tough back in those days. There was only radio. No TV. I had to learn from other people but there just weren't too many people who played lead. If you didn't live around somebody who could play a little bit to show you something, then that was it if you lived in the country. Of course they had phonographs but we were so poor that we didn't have one so I couldn't get any records. I had to just learn from other people. There weren't too many people down there who played lead.

I played eight hours a day. I would get up in the morning, milk the cows and whatever else I had to do before getting ready for school. Then I'd sit on the front porch and play guitar, looking up the road until the school bus came. When I got home at night I'd start playing again. I like to ran my mother crazy. But when you play that much, if you've got any talent, you can really improve.

Radio was popular in the rural south and, like Chet before him, Paul got a job playing on the radio. Sixteen-year-old Paul's first radio job was with a band on *The Fonzie Davis Show* which aired at 10 a.m. on WNGO in Mayfield. It paid fifteen dollars a week, which was excellent money for the time, particularly in that area. This also helped his learning process because now he had access to the station's library of records. Best of all, he was able to hear the latest Chet Atkins records as they arrived.

Paul was also sixteen when electricity finally came to the Yandell farm around 1950. A local jack-of-all-trades, Lowell Smith, rigged the farm for electricity. That same year a green record player was purchased for his sister, Yvonne. Paul's dad got it at the "Melody Maker" music store in the basement of a hotel in Mayfield.

> While he was in high school he got a job at the local radio station playing on early morning shows and weekends. He played with three or four bands and was making more money than his Mother and Daddy who both worked at Merritt Clothing Factory (a factory that made men's suits for places like J.C. Penny's) in Mayfield, Kentucky.
>
> Sometimes on weekends, he and some of the local musicians would play in a little wooded park like the area out behind Dairy Hill in Mayfield. 'Dairy Hill' was their local hamburger, hot dog, Dairy Queen type place.
> — Marie Yandell

It wasn't that I was so good. There just wasn't anybody else around.

Now that the Yandell household had a record player Paul acquired every Chet Atkins record he could find and learned the songs from those records. But as he was absorbing Chet's style he also studied being a good rhythm guitarist. It was plain to him that there was a need for a solid rhythm guitarist and this had a great bearing on his career. He absorbed Chet's songs and could play them with accuracy but he saw himself as a support musician.

I've never been a lead player. It was always rhythm. There's always a demand for it as everybody else wants to be the "hot" player. I'm always happy just keeping things going, providing the base for the music. I always wanted to be a good rhythm player. I've spent many hours working on timing and learning chords. I taught myself how to play arch top rhythm listening to Django and Homer and Jethro records.

Note: "Arch top," (sometimes called "orchestral" guitar) is a term that refers to carved top guitars like the Gibson L-5 or the D'Angelico instruments that were used in orchestra rhythm sections before amplification freed the guitar for playing melody.

The guitarist playing "arch top rhythm" primarily plays down strokes on the beat. The left (chording) hand makes a six-string chord that utilizes all the strings (or mutes unused strings) in the chord forms applied. This allows the guitarist to control how long strings are allowed to sound after the down stroke giving the guitar an almost percussive effect.

It's hard to be a good musician if you can't play a steady beat. Not playing with other players as you're learning isn't easy. When one records you have to play with a steady beat, in time. I practiced many hours with a drum machine. Keeping time is one of the things a player must learn to do.

Interlude 2: Instrumental Evolution

Here is a brief list of some of the significant guitars Paul owned from his first Stella to his 6120 he used with the Louvins. As time went on (and a surprisingly short span of time at that) Paul upgraded his instruments. His first true electric guitar, his Telecaster, he bought when he was still a teenager. He went through several different models until finally he upgraded to his first Gretsch when he hired on with the Louvins. It is an demonstration of his increasing skill and, at the same time, a indication of how his personal fortunes picked up due to earning money by playing guitar to even be able to afford the upgrades.

My first guitar was a Stella. My first really good guitar was a Gibson flattop, a sunburst J-50 type I got in 1950. I remember when I got my first electric guitar as a boy. I didn't have an amplifier because I couldn't afford one at the time. I asked a fellow if I could plug my guitar into his amp to see how my guitar sounded. He wouldn't let me do it. From that day on I promised myself I would never turn down anyone that needed help or advice. I've never forgotten that. Sometimes musicians are a jealous lot.

My next really good guitar after that was a Fender Telecaster. I wish I had it now but that's another story. I got a job at a radio station. I was playing with three or four different bands by then and on the radio a lot of the time. From the Telecaster I went to a Stratocaster.

A lot of the country musicians used Telecasters in the fifties and even today the Telecaster is most often the instrument of choice for the working country musician. When Paul was starting out the Fender solid bodies were less expensive than the big Gibson's and D'Angelico hollow bodied guitars that some of the better known guitarists were using.

I went to a Gibson three pickup model (The Gibson ES-5 Switchmaster). That's what I was using when I auditioned for the Louvins. When they hired me the first thing I did was to go to Kendall's music store and got a 1955 Gretsch 6120. I did a lot of modification on that guitar.

I was always changing my guitar back then. I had someone in Nashville redo the fingerboard and peghead. I had the neck reworked

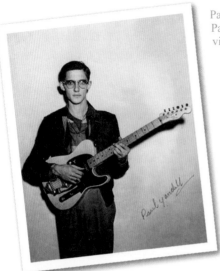

Paul's first electric. A Fender Telecaster. Paul ordered and installed the Bigsby vibrato himself. *Photo courtesy of YFA*

with different inlays. I thought it looked pretty good back then but it looks goofy now.

I changed the neck pickup in my 6120 about 1958 to a Bigsby. I think I got that Bigsby pickup from Jimmy Capps. I got the best sound out of that set up. Then I used a P-90 pickup. Odell and I rigged up some kind of handle for the vibrato. I remember going to the Oldsmobile dealership to get a turn signal handle and putting it on there some way. Eventually the neck broke on it in transit and I bought a Country Gentleman.

Back in Mayfield the teenaged Paul played music with everyone he could. This increased his ability to adapt to any musical situation that gave him familiarity in playing with and in front of others. Playing live on local radio shows taught him to focus on getting it right the first time. He had experiences similar to Chet's playing in the cramped radio studios of the day.

Playing on the radio could be a trying experience due to conditions in those days. Chet did the best he could with the equipment he had. He told me that on the (Gibson) L-12 that he is using on those shows the first string would sometimes fall off when he did pull-offs so he had to be careful when he played. He tells in the Cochran book (*Me and My Guitars*) about having to stand on a chair to reach the mic when he played. They only had one mic that was set to favor singers and fiddlers. I can understand those shows because when I was young at my hometown, I played with a

band on the local radio station. We were on every Saturday morning. I sat my amp up in a chair back against the wall. There was only one microphone ... it was a great time in my life.

His radio performances and local live music shows increased his confidence onstage. He learned rocklike stability that helped immensely when he later hired on with well-known acts. His focus, along with his growing musical facility, eventually led him to be part of the A-list of Nashville studio musicians. All of these experiences were factors that later qualified him to work with Jerry Reed and Chet Atkins.

Even in high school Paul was looking for a way to hire on with a known act. The trip from Mayfield to Nashville was about three hours in those days. An enterprising young guitarist could make the trip, knock on doors hoping for auditions, and still make it home in time for supper. Sometimes Fonzie Davis, who loved Paul's playing and looked out for him, would drive him—other times he took the Greyhound bus. He would not own his own car until he started working with the Louvins when he bought a used Studebaker Golden Hawk. From time to time Paul would make that trek to Nashville looking for an opening, a foot in the door. It was on one of these trips when he first met Chet Atkins.

When I was in high school I had just one dream: to come to Nashville and play in the Grand Old Opry ... to play with Bill Carlisle or someone like that.

Paul's first radio band. L to R: Pat Summers on bass; Charles Riley with Martin guitar; Paul, of course, (eighteen-years-old); and Bud Hailey on fiddle. Marie Yandell said, "Their band, called 'The Sunshine Boys,' was formed in 1953. They all played together for about three years. They played every week at Radio Station WNGO (which stood for We Need God Only) in Mayfield, KY. They did not get paid but played for their own enjoyment and for people who enjoyed country music."
Photo courtesy of YFA

At that time "The Solemn Old Judge," George D. Hay, held auditions every Wednesday afternoon about two o'clock. One week I came down with a friend of mine. I guess school was out that day. Back then they had a studio called 'Studio C' at the corner of 5th and Union where Judge Hay had his auditions. At the same time, also in Studio C, they held rehearsals for the *Prince Albert Show*, which was a network show on Saturday nights at nine o'clock. Of course Chet was on that show.

There were a number of people around because Judge Hay was auditioning that day. When it came time for me to play he said "Son, I've got just five minutes left." I wasn't quite ready. Being a kid, I was unprepared. I told him my guitar and amp were down in the car. He said, "Well I don't have time for you to go get it."

Now, Chet was on break, standing out in the hallway. He overheard the conversation. He came up to me and said, "You can borrow my guitar and use it if you want." That scared the hell out of me! Chet went back into the studio to get his amp, I think it was a little Fender Deluxe. He brought it out along with his guitar. It was a 6121, the one that looks like a solid body. He plugged it all in, handed it to me and walked away.

I played a couple tunes. After I was done, Judge Hay said, "Well son, we'll call you." But I knew that he wouldn't. I didn't really care anymore because I got to meet Chet Atkins and play his guitar! Chet didn't remember that day but it was the greatest thing that ever happened to me. It gave me so much encouragement.

When I was nineteen, I guess it was in 1954, I came to Nashville to see what was happening. At that time WSM had the Friday Night Frolics in the National Life Insurance building in Studio C. As I was roaming up and down the hallway I saw Chet taking a smoking break. I went up to him and asked him for his autograph. He had just started playing Gretsch. I was sort of upset because of the change in his tone and sound going from his D'Angelico to Gretsch. I said to him, "Chet, I don't think that Gretsch guitar sounds as good as your D'Angelico."

Chet replied, "I like it."

I didn't say anything else. I still have his autograph from that meeting. He signed it in green ink.

None of the early trips to Nashville landed him the work or attention he sought but he kept practicing, playing at every opportunity. He focused primarily on playing as much like Chet Atkins as he could, as well as improving his rhythm playing. Eventually, after high school, he caught a job playing with a small band in a club in Michigan when he got a phone call that was to change his life.

Not long after he graduated from high school, he begin playing with a band that went to Detroit and played in a nightclub there for several months before getting hired by the Louvin Brothers.
— Marie Yandell.

CHAPTER 3

THE LOUVIN BROTHERS

I really enjoyed working with the Louvin Brothers. I didn't make a lot of money but they didn't either back in those days. They were nice to me and let me record with them which got my name in front of the public.

The Loudermilk brothers, Ira and Charlie, were born in Alabama in the mid-nineteen twenties. Ira, the oldest by three years, was born in 1924, Charlie in 1927. The brothers started singing together at an early age, influenced by the Delmore Brothers and most heavily by Blue Sky Boys, a mandolin/guitar duet. "There is something special about the vocal harmony when brothers sing." Phil Everly once said, "A lot of it had to do with brothers using the same manner of pronouncing words that made the harmonies a little tighter."

Charlie had the lower tenor voice with Ira taking the high tenor lines. Ira's voice had a magnificent quality, so clear and clean that even his falsetto had body. Over the years they learned to switch off on who sang the lead and who sang the harmony as they shaped their sound.

Charlie played a solid rhythm guitar and Ira was very proficient as a mandolin player. They primarily sang gospel music, having been brought up in a strict Christian fundamentalist home. Gospel music was loved by rural farm folks who needed God's help to make their crops and to help make the harsh life of hardscrabble farming bearable. They needed a God who also provided some joyful, gospel music.

Radio was the dominant entertainment medium as the boys grew up. They played on radio as often as they could. They sometimes had their own radio show at a local level. It was hard to make a living working out of small radio stations. They booked themselves within the range of the radio stations they played but often would "play out," or saturate an area finding they had to move on. They had a hard time catching a break and a harder time breaking into the all-important Grand Ole Opry. They often had to quit music as the necessities of life required that they take day jobs to feed themselves and their families.

Both of them had their turn in the army having come of draft age in the forties. Very near the end of WWII they changed their name from "Loudermilk" to "Louvin." "Loudermilk" was awkward to deal with for some. It was spelled wrong quite a bit according to Charlie so they took the "Lou" of Loudermilk and added the "vin." Or so the story goes …

The Louvins never gave up, graduating to bigger and better radio shows. Eventually they made it to Springfield, Missouri, and KWTO. ("Keep Watching the Ozarks") They played the Midday Merry Go Round, a very popular radio show. But it wasn't the Grand Ole Opry and the Grand Ole Opry was what they wanted.

Finally things started to come together for Ira and Charlie. Their bookings started to pick up. They got signed with Capitol Records and they started to make records that were getting noticed. On one of these records made in Nashville was "Love Thy Neighbor." They used thumb-style guitarist Chester Reason on the cut. The record was released in January of 1955 and got some traction and airplay. "Love Thy Neighbor" was the first song they sang on the Grand Ole Opry. They had finally made it into the Mother Church of country music.

Their guitarist, Chester Reason, fit the bill musically but suddenly Reason's commitment was getting shaky. His wife did not want to leave Alabama and move to Nashville. The boys knew they'd soon be needing another guitarist to replicate the sound they had decided worked best for them. The old adage of "Play it like the record" could be a double-edged sword when they had to find someone who played an uncommon guitar style to fit their act.

That first night on the Opry, when they sang "Love Thy Neighbor," Chet Atkins instead of Chester Reason backed them up. They got an encore at the Ryman! Suddenly they were getting more attention.

Chet Atkins' approach to guitar was fast becoming a popular style with audiences. Chet's guitar style was new and fresh. Ira and Charlie liked the sound Chet's guitar playing gave to their music so they made their next few records with Chet doing the guitar parts in the studio.

> They were a fine country duet as you know, and Ira wrote some great songs, but Ira was a little difficult to work with … he had a terrible temper. He didn't like anything you did. He'd get a smirk on his face and say "Well, I guess that'll do if you can't find anything better."
> — Chet Atkins
> (from a Hank Wanford UK television series)

The brothers wanted to capitalize on the success of their hit record and this meant they needed to find a guitarist well grounded in finger-style guitar. They knew their fans wanted to hear the songs that had featured Chet to sound just like the record. But there was a problem. Chet Atkins didn't want to travel. He was making excellent money working less for the Carters and more for Fred Rose and Steve Sholes at RCA, producing and playing in recording sessions there. Chet often got extra pay as session leader. He also played several local radio spots. He was quite comfortable staying home after a life of moving all around the country in his rise to guitar prominence

Chet was working some with Fred Rose at Acuff-Rose doing sessions. Fred was one of the greatest music people Nashville ever knew. Chet told me

that once Fred told him that he should stop trying to play so many Django licks and come up with some of his own. Chet said after that he did and after a while things started to happen with his playing. Chet had great ability to arrange tunes. His early records prove that. He was a Natural.

By that time Paul had polished his approach to Chet's style, gaining a reputation for both his excellent foundation and his ability to copy his idol. In the spring of 1955 the Louvins were booked in Kentucky and Mayfield deejay Fonzie Davis heard they were looking for a guitarist. Fonzie knew Paul very well and saw an opportunity.

I was playing around my home with about three different bands. I was fairly popular at one time. This guy, Fonzie Davis I used to work with, had a radio show I played on. I quit him to work in Detroit with a steel player.

The Louvin Brothers had come to Mayfield. They had booked a week of shows. They were looking for a guitar player. Fonzie Davis called me to ask me to come back, saying that I could probably get the job. So I quit and came back home.

Fonzie Davis contacted the Louvins telling them about Paul. He told them that Paul played "everything that Chet recorded!" As a bonus, Paul, as a fan of the Louvins, was able to play all of their material too! The Louvins were interested and asked Fonzie to send Paul to them for an audition. Paul got the word and immediately headed home. Fonzie drove him to Nashville to audition for the Louvin Brothers backstage at the Opry the very next Saturday.

I believe they sang "Born Again" for the audition. It was one of their songs I had learned. Chet had recorded all their songs so I knew their stuff from trying to learn Chet's licks off their records. That gave me an inside track. I really impressed them when I played their tunes note for note.

They liked my playing, but this other guy they were using hadn't quit yet. His name was Chester Reason. He was from Alabama. They had just come to the Opry but his wife didn't like Nashville and she wasn't going to move. He had recorded "Love Thy Neighbor" with them. He played with picks on his fingers. If you listen to him on that record you can hear those fingerpicks clicking on the strings.

As it happened, Grandpa Jones heard Paul's Louvin Brothers audition and when it finished, "Pa" offered Paul a job on a tour of the Pacific Northwest. Paul couldn't help but to have a wry memory of that turn of events.

It was funny. I had been trying so hard to get to Nashville and here Grandpa Jones was offering me a job to play in Alaska!

I went back home and the following Monday morning Fonzie Davis came to the house to tell me that the Louvin Brothers had called. Chester Reason had quit and could I meet them in Prestonsburg, Kentucky, which is practically in West Virginia.

The next Saturday night I played the Opry for the first time. I'll never forget it. I was thrilled. Chet was on the Opry that night, too. My dream had come true. I was twenty years old when I started working with them, fresh off a tobacco farm in West Kentucky when I started living my dream of going to the Grand Ole Opry.

The Louvins were very pleased with Paul. All his years of focus and practice gave them a guitarist that sounded so much like Chet Atkins it is difficult to tell, even today, which Louvin Brothers tracks used Chet and which were using Paul. They wasted no time using Paul on their next recording session. Paul bought a Gretsch 6120 "Chet Atkins" hollow body guitar just a day or two prior to that first recording session with the Louvins at Castle Studio. Castle Studio was a room at the Tulane Hotel in Nashville. Chet once described it as a big room with primitive, but permanent recording equipment in it. There wasn't much else in Nashville at the time.

From the liner notes to *When I Stop Dreaming: The Best of the Louvin Brothers*. Charlie Louvin, at right, in the heyday of the Louvin Brothers. With him, left to right, are Smiley Wilson, brother Ira Louvin, Paul Yandell, Chet Atkins, and Merle Travis. *Razor and Tie compilation*

Their first recording produced a song, now revered as a Louvin Brother's classic, "When I Stop Dreaming" featuring Paul playing his excellent thumb-style guitar on it. It was Paul's debut as a sideman on a record.

I traded for my 6120 on Saturday at Kendall's Music Store (which later became Hank Snow's Music Store). The session was the next day on Sunday. October 29, 1955. If I remember correctly Eddie Hill played rhythm, and either Lightning Chance or Ernie Newton played bass Marvin Hughes played piano. We recorded four sides, including I "Don't Believe You've Met My Baby." The first album session I worked on was "Tragic Songs of Life" in the Spring of 1956. On those records I sound a little like Chet but I really don't. I knew I should try and sound like myself. That was a big day in my life.

> Paul had a lot of respect for a lot of different types of music. He once told me that he thought "Rock Around the Clock" was one of the best songs ever recorded and he loved the guitar solo in it. The guy who played the solo on the recording was named Danny Cedrone. Paul said that Cedrone tragically fell down a flight of stairs and was killed just shortly after the song was recorded
> — Robbie Jones

Here's side note about the 6120 I used in the early days. My first 6120 didn't have much output for some reason. It was tough to play the Opry because I wasn't loud enough.

One Saturday night I asked Chet about it. He invited me out to his house and said he would take a look at my guitar. I went the next day which was Sunday. He was living in the house where the picture was taken of the *Chet Atkins at Home* album cover, on Lincoln Court. It was a great thrill to go to Chet's house.

He looked at my guitar but couldn't find anything wrong with it. I traded it for another 6120 which I used throughout my years with Ira and Charlie. On most of the records I did with the Louvins I used a Fender Pro amplifier. For one session I borrowed Buddy Emmons' Standel.

On that 6120 that I used with the Louvins I had the neck reworked with different inlays. I changed the neck pickup to a Bigsby pickup that I had then later I changed it to a P-90.

I had it sent to me when I went in the Army. I was stationed about twenty miles from the Framus factory. I had seen Chet's solid top 6120

A 1955 Gretsch catalog page. This is how Paul's first Gretsch (the 6120) was priced and described when he bought it. *Photo courtesy of Fred Gretsch Mfg.*

CHET ATKINS with his thumb pick and his four fingers plays in his inimitable 'modern-country' style to produce a tone that delights the listener. It's so tasteful, so melodic, so enhanced by Chet's own clever improvisations! Every Chet Atkins appearance, whether in person or on T-V (you should see and hear his reception at Grand Ol' Opry!) and every new album he cuts for RCA Victor, wins new admirers to swell the vast army of Chet Atkins fans.

CHET ATKINS ELECTRIC GUITARS by GRETSCH

Chet Atkins' own ideas combine with Gretsch 'know how' to produce these two truly distinctive guitars. For real country-style tone, for exceptional playing convenience and comfort, and for regular he-man good looks, it's m ghty hard to match them—*anywhere!* In both models you f nd every one of these important construction features:

- Deep cut-away bodies for easy fingering of the en.ire scale;
- Twin, built-in Gretsch-Dynasonic pickups (no others come even close for sensitivity, fide.ity, and power) with five controls, including two-way, finger-tip switch to cut out either pickup or combine them—*instantly*;
- Built-in Vibrato tailpiece for exciting tonal effects; single tones or full chords sustain with beautiful tremolo under manipulation of the lever;
- Metal bridge saddle and nut, perfect for real cowboy and country-style tone;
- Special thin-gauge strings;
- Chet Atkins-designed shorter scale;
- Oval rosewood fingerboard with pearl positions engraved in Western motifs, on fast-playing Gretsch 'Miracle Neck';
- Individual machines with slip-proof metal buttons;
- Metal parts heavily gold plated.

CHET ATKINS SOLID BODY GUITAR

Compact 13½" body and neck of selected brown mahogany, hand polished finish. The slim 'Miracle Neck' joining at the 16th fret and the deep cutaway help you get those highs in brilliant fashion. Western style decorations including carved saddle leather body binding and shoulder strap. For ultra-fine tone projection and sustaining power, this is your guitar! (Illustration "A")

PX6121—Chet Atkins Solid Body Electric Guitar **$385.00**

CHET ATKINS HOLLOW BODY GUITAR

Conventional style but a little narrower (15½") and a little thinner (2¾") to give you that Gretsch new look, new feel, new playing comfort. Body and neck are choice curly maple finished Western-style in amber-red, highly polished by hand. The neck joins at the 14th fret. Complete with carved saddle leather shoulder strap. Here's a wonderful combination of mellow tone with brilliance when you want it! (Illustration "B")

PX6120—Chet Atkins Hollow Body Electric Guitar **$385.00**

(See Page 16 for Chet Atkins Guitar Cases.)

DELUXE 8 AND 6 STEEL GUITARS

The Deluxe Steel Guitar is one of the finest single neck instruments available on today's market and is highly recommended for both professional and non-professional use. It incorporates many of the same outstanding features found on Stringmaster guitars.

It employs the counterbalanced dual pickups with mixing control, the Fender adjustable bridge for correction of intonation variations and the precision grooved nut of case hardened steel, assuring level strings at all times. These special features, plus excellent playing qualities and unique body design, combine to make the Deluxe model guitar outstanding among present day instruments.

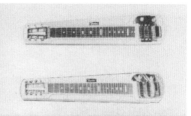

BANDMASTER AMP

Recommended where high performance at moderate cost is important. Flexible tone control system of this amplifier makes it extremely useful for any electrical musical instrument. Chrome plated chassis, on-and-off switch, ground switch, standby switch, bass, treble and presence tone controls, two volume controls and four input jacks. It employs three heavy duty 10" Jensen speakers for un-distorted high-fidelity output. A favorite of hundreds of professional and non-professional musicians.

Size: Height, 21½"; Width, 22½"; Depth, 10¾".

PRO AMP

The Pro Amp is practically a fixture in the world of amplified musical instruments. It is as equally adaptable for steel or standard guitar amplification as it is for piano, vocals or announcing. Its rugged dependability is well known to countless musicians throughout the world.

It features the solid wood lock jointed cabinet, covered with the regular Fender brown and white diagonal stripe luggage linen; chrome plated chassis, 15" heavy duty Jensen speaker, ground switch, standby switch, on-and-off switch, bass, treble and presence tone controls, two volume controls and four input jacks.

Size: Height, 20"; Width, 22"; Depth, 10".

DELUXE AMP

The Deluxe Amp is as modern as tomorrow and will give long lasting satisfaction to the owner. This amplifier is outstanding in its class and embodies the follow-ing features: top mounted chrome plated chassis, heavy duty 12" Jensen speaker; ground switch, on-and-off switch, panel mounted fuse holder, bull's-eye pilot light; tone control, two volume controls, three input jacks. It also has the extension speaker jack mounted on the chassis and wired for instant use. It is an exceptional performer, both for tone and for volume in its price class, and represents one of the finest values available.

Size: Height, 16¾"; Width, 20"; Depth, 9½".

Leon McAuliffe   Alvino Rey

Compare Fender...you'll agree they're the Finest

Fender Catalog page describing Pro and Deluxe amplifiers. These were very common amps, popular in the days of radio and used by Paul as well as many other guitarists. *Photo courtesy of Fender Musical Instruments*

Paul onstage with his 6120. His modified Bigsby handle and the modified fingerboard and headstock inlays can be seen on this guitar. *Photo courtesy of YFA*

Paul with re-topped 6120. Paul had a new top installed by the Framu guitar company while he was in Germany in the army. This instrument was broken during its return trip home. Paul and Odell eventually had it repaired. *Photo courtesy of YFA*

when he played it on the Opry so I had Framus replace the top on mine with a solid top. They did a good job on it. I didn't change the wiring on it at all. When I came back it got damaged in shipment so I just got a new Country Gentleman.

Between the two of them Paul and Odell Martin fixed the damaged guitar. Odell took charge of it, using it for a while on the road. Paul later reminisced about this instrument.

Odell Martin owned my guitar and later gave it to a friend of his. I tried to get it back but he wouldn't give it up. I don't know where it is now.

The Louvins were nice to me and started using me on their recordings on their next session. I was very lucky to come along when the Louvins needed a guitar player. They let me play what I wanted to on their records. Everything I played was a mix of Chet and Merle. We recorded for Capitol Records. It was easy to get a good tone with them. Ira wrote the songs and Charlie took care of the business end. They were the greatest duo ever, I think. No one could write songs better than Ira.

GRETSCH GUITARS

CHET ATKINS "COUNTRY GENTLEMAN" GUITAR

This handsome showpiece has slim 17" closed body with simulated inlaid "F" holes. Grover 16-to-1 ratio enclosed gears. Bigsby Tremolo and Tailpiece. Adjustable rod—Actionflo neck. Satin ebony Neo-Classic fingerboard. Heavy 24-karat gold plating and rich mahogany-grained country style finish. Gretsch Filter'Tron twin electronic heads. Trim, fine-quality leather shoulder strap.

PX6122 Chet Atkins "Country Gentleman"
Electric Guitar........................ **$525.00**

No one can compare with Chet Atkins...

Get Chet Atkins' Own Guitar Method, diagramming Chet's unique finger styling: #9363, ea. $3.00B.

His name is famous all over the world...so is his unique playing style. Every tune Chet arranges and plays delights the ear with its tasteful, melodic interpretations. Each RCA Victor album Chet records (you'll find several new ones every year) swells his army of enthusiastic admirers.

...no other guitars can match Chet Atkins electric guitars by Gretsch

Chet Atkins is an engineer, too. His own ideas about the special features and styling of the guitars he plays have been translated by skilled Gretsch guitar specialists into the four fine instruments seen here.

CHET ATKINS HOLLOW BODY GUITAR

Still the most popular Chet Atkins guitar made. Slim 16" cutaway body. Bigsby Tremolo and Tailpiece. Gretsch Filter'Tron twin electronic heads. Adjustable rod—Actionflo neck. Curly maple body and neck beautifully finished in amber red, highly polished. Satin ebony Neo-Classic fingerboard. Carved saddle leather shoulder strap. Gold-plated metal parts.

PX6120 Chet Atkins Hollow Body Electric Guitar..... **$425.00**

A 1960 Gretsch catalog page. This is how Paul's first Gretsch Country Gentleman guitar was listed when he bought it in 1960. *Photo courtesy of Fred Gretsch Mfg. Used with permission*

After Paul went to work with the Louvin Brothers he stayed in Nashville. To begin with, he rented a room at a home, like a boarding house, where a lot of musicians and entertainers stayed. Then he and Ira rented a place together for a short time when Ira's wife left him.

Finally he and Odell Martin rented an apartment from Ms. Mamie Sullivan who was on Gallatin Road in Nashville. After he pulled his two year hitch in the army, he rented a room at Ms. Sullivan's again and stayed there until we married in 1961.

— Marie Yandell

Odell and I rented an apartment and stayed together for about five years until I went in the service. We'd sit up until three o'clock in the morning trying to figure out what Chet was doing.

The Opry

Samuel Porter Jones, born in 1857, became a converted Christian after leading a wastrel's life. He "got the call" at the age of twenty-five, becoming a travelling evangelist rising to be very famous in his day. In one of his travels he happened to do a revival in Nashville. One of the attendees was Thomas G. Ryman an owner of several gambling riverboats and saloons. It was Ryman's intention to attend the revival and heckle Jones. Instead, Ryman found himself converted and so thoroughly converted that he built the Union Gospel Tabernacle in Nashville specifically for preacher Jones.

After Ryman's death the building was renamed Ryman Auditorium. With an eventual capacity of over 2,300 people it functioned primarily as a revival hall but was also leased for various other venues over the years. The building had remarkably good acoustics that rivaled any auditorium or theater in the world and was sometimes called the "Carnegie Hall of the South."

The Grand Ole Opry was started in 1925 by George D. Hay the "Solemn Old Judge" on the fifth floor studio of the National Life and Accident Company. The show was originally called the WSM Barn Dance. In 1927 he renamed it the Grand Ole Opry. After several relocations, due to increasing space demands, the Opry finally settled at the Ryman auditorium in 1943 where it became the Mecca for country music fans until 1974 when the GOO (Grand Ole Opry) venue was moved to a larger, more modern building in Opryland USA.

One of the most popular shows out of WSM was the Friday Night Frolic. But Saturday night was the pinnacle, the actual Grand Ole Opry and fans from all around the country and the world queued up to see the shows which were broadcast live.

Patrons sat on hard oak church pew style benches on the ground floor or in the "Confederate Gallery" balcony. The balcony was paid for by Civil War Confederate veterans in gratitude for having the hall made available to them for one of their reunions in 1897. The attendance was so large that it was necessary to increase seating capacity. A balcony was built and called the Confederate Gallery in their honor.

The building's remarkably good acoustics meant there were no dead spots in the hall. Every note could be heard anywhere in the building, which was appreciated by all. When electronic amplification was first brought in even the simpler forms of the new medium worked very well in that room.

The building had no air conditioning, which meant in summer it could get oppressively hot but it didn't matter to the fans. To even be there was like the end of a pilgrimage to a holy place. They were there for the music! This was The Opry!

During the shows in the all-radio days, the audience saw the large stage as a beehive of activity. By the late fifties there were two pedal steel guitars set up on the front edge of the stage, each with different tunings so the steel players could slip into the chair of the instrument with their required tuning and play. There was a microphone at center stage for the singers to use and backdrop curtains were changed as required to display the sponsor's names for all to see.

At one end of the stage was a simple piece of paper tacked to a post that had the lineup of who was to play when. It was long-time stage manager, Vito Pellettieri, who made out the list. Vito was part of the management of the show from the early days. It was he who segmented the show for better sponsor marketing and logged the songs for airplay records for BMI and ASCAP.

At stage center was the main mic (abbreviation for microphone. Pronounced "mike"). Whoever was up used the main mic and their sidemen were right behind them as they performed their songs. Meanwhile, the stage was full of activity as the next performers waited to step up and fill his or her spot. Elsewhere on the stage performers, and sometimes family, would be milling around. While it looked chaotic to the visitor, it was all kept together by Vito Pellettieri's little sheet of paper tacked in its spot just offstage.

None of this was visible to the radio audience of course. This meant that the Ryman attending audience was treated to the exciting "ins" of How Things Worked. They also got to see the costumes, everything from Minnie Pearl's straw hat with the price tag dangling from the brim and Stringbean's exaggeratedly short-legged outfit, to the stunning sequined outfits made by "Nudie the Tailor" glittering in the spotlights.

All performers were paid pretty much the same money. No one got rich playing the Opry. In the fifties and sixties the Opry paid something less than ten dollars for the first at-mic appearance on a given Saturday night and if they played a second spot on the same night they were paid half that fee for the second spot. Playing the Opry often meant sacrificing a higher paying gig on the road, certainly for the stars if not the sidemen. The acts were required to play the Opry at least twenty-six times a year to be able to claim membership in the Opry and sometimes this caused hardship. Every GOO act has a harrowing story of dangerous chances taken on the road to get back to Nashville on a Saturday night to fulfill the requirement for membership. A performer did not necessarily have to be a member to play the Opry. Chet Atkins was never a member of the Opry yet he played it often as a soloist or as a backup guitarist for the Carter girls or sometimes the Louvin Brothers or other groups. He stopped when he finally started making a good living working for RCA as a producer and session chief.

Chet told me once he didn't like to play the Opry much because while he was playing some guy would be down in front of the stage yelling about selling popcorn. Chet was never a member of the Opry. He just played on it. He had a solo spot on the show for a while. He told me that the people in New York called down to WSM and told them to get rid of "that guitar player" on the Prince Albert Network Show. When they did that he quit working the Opry altogether. While Chet was playing the Opry they had a Saturday night show at the Ryman. The Friday night show (Friday Night Frolic) was up in the National Life Building.

What, then, were the advantages, of being a "member" of the Grand Ole Opry? It certainly wasn't the pay. Musicians can't make a living on one Saturday night gig even if it paid well, which the Opry did not. Being a member meant the artists got to sign their autographs with a "goo" (indicating membership) alongside their name. There doesn't seem to be any real advantage in this. To a fan, an autograph is an autograph.

The true advantage of being a member was exposure. It was easier to get onto the schedule list to play on Saturday night if they were a member. The Saturday show was by far the most listened to show. If they played on the Opry they got heard by a vast nationwide listenership and through this they could get the all-important bookings to play the road. Playing the road went a long way to making a living (such as it was) in the country music business. It still does.

The Opry even had its own post office, which helped immensely in the pre-Internet days when listeners sent fan letters and postcards and booking requests to their favorite stars. Nevertheless, it got frantic, sometimes, for artists to make it back to Nashville to make one of the twenty-six show commitments required to maintain "membership" but, grueling as it was, artists did it to keep their radio presence alive. The Opry was a plateau. The Opry was a milestone and to some it meant survival. To Paul, playing the Opry meant he had arrived.

Reflections on the Opry

Playing the Opry in those days was interesting from a guitarist's standpoint.
WSM's Ryman Auditorium had a box connected to the floor. It had, I think, four inputs for electric guitars to plug into. Right above it, about eight

feet high, hanging down, was the monitor speaker. So when you played you plugged in the box and then stood under the speaker.

I remember when I was with the Louvin Brothers on the Opry Chet would be on the show too. I made sure I never missed when he played. I would go to the Opry early to watch him because sometimes he would plug in an amp backstage, tune up and play a little. I would be sure to be there when he did. I would stand over at Stage Right so I could watch him when he played onstage. So would the other guitar players.

I remember when Chet started playing that solid top 6120 with the prototype Filter-Tron pickups. I had never seen anything like that before. Nobody had. Chet was light years ahead of everybody back then and he still is. He was always nice to me backstage. He would stop and ask me how I was getting along.

As I remember, the Opry really sounded good. There was an engineer in the booth over at Stage Left listening to WSM over the radio to hear how the mix was. It would be a lot better today if they still did it that way. Surprisingly, there was never a sound check. No one had heard of such a thing in those days. Nobody knew what they were.

Someone (Al Gannaway) issued a DVD of some color films of Chet playing in what looked like a Grand Ole Opry setting. Those videos were done about 1955 [Author: actually 1955–1957]. I remember being on the Opry with the Louvins at the time. I did some of those films with the Louvin Brothers. Chet would be on an early show then maybe a 10:00 pm show. I was there when he was playing that solid top 6120 and the black 6120 seen on the "Dark Eyes" video.

Those films were kind of like what it was like at the Ryman on Saturday night. They used one or two cameras. When those films were made they were originally shown at movie theaters in between a double feature. Later, when TV came along, they cut the films up to make different shows.

They have a million dollar sound system at the Opry house now and it sounds like crap. The sound people know nothing about mixing. The TV cuing is no better. Many times I've seen, on the TV portion, how the fiddle player would take a break on a song and the camera would be on the steel player.

About 1960 or so, a few of the musicians, who are now the staff band, talked the Opry people into using a house band. I think that was the worst thing that ever happened to the Opry! Other players like myself and Hank

Garland and Grady Martin had to stop working the Opry. It put a lot of people out of work. It made the show boring to have the same licks and musicians every weekend.

Some of them are good musicians, but once there was a drummer in the staff band who got his brother on there playing rhythm who was the worse you ever saw.

Nowadays they have a young guy running the Opry who knows nothing about show business.

When I came to Nashville the Opry was a big deal. An artist had to be somebody to join. At one time it was really a great thing. Nowadays it's not as important as it once was. As time went along they started putting people on the Opry who had never even had a hit record and in a sense that dumbed it down.

On the Opry today, the musicians play so loud on stage it's terrible. The bass is always three times louder than it should be. A friend of mine who does the Opry told me they have the mixing board set but they won't allow anyone to adjust the mics. This is an outfit that has a million dollars invested in equipment.

There's hardly any humor anymore; it's all singers now. The TV show is a showcase for unknowns. The artists sing the same songs every Friday and Saturday night. I very seldom ever listen to it anymore, but that's the world we live in. It's like the movies they make today.

WSM, TNN and the modern Opry have always had a problem with the sound. When I was working with Chet we would often do a show on TNN. Sometimes the sound guys couldn't tell when I was playing and would have me louder than Chet or have the camera on Chet while I played my part.

There's not many left of the great 1950s Nashville musicians. All the great stars were young and in their prime then. Hank Garland was playing the Opry with different artists as was Grady Martin. Chet was on every Friday and Saturday night. It seemed almost every week or two Chet would be playing a new Gretsch guitar. I remember one Saturday night Hank Garland showing Odell Martin and myself how to play "Sugarfoot Rag."

Working with the Louvins on and off the Opry things started to happen. Paul's guitar playing became an integral part of the Louvins' sound. But even caught in the headiness of being part of one of country music's better known acts didn't change the fact that, as noted earlier, Paul didn't make much money playing with them.

There is an advantage to using a finger-style guitarist on the road. The technique of sounding like two guitarists at once by playing both rhythm and melody made for a fuller, more interesting backup. Best of all, they could get by without having to hire a bass player. They saved money.

At one time they had me and a bass and rhythm guitarist, but most of the time it was just them and me.

Initially he contracted with them for less than two hundred dollars a week but Paul didn't care for the working conditions in that arrangement. He chose the *per diem* (pay by the day or per show) method of payment instead. It meant less money—about twenty five dollars a day when they played. "When they played" is just what it says. On days they did not play there was no money unless Paul could catch a spot with another act or work a recording session. Still, Paul's guitar work became part of the Louvin Brothers sound. So much so that when Paul got drafted in 1958 a few years later, the Louvins had to find a guitarist that played that distinctive guitar style.

My last session with the Louvins was on August 10, 1958, for the "Satan Is Real" LP. We recorded three tunes, including "There's A Higher Power." In December of 1958, I got drafted into the Army and that ended my working with them. Jimmy Capps took my job right after that.

Paul, and guitarists like Odell Martin, were part of the faceless but necessary cadre of musicians that are usually better players than the hobby guitarist or saloon guitarist. They worked the sessions. They worked the road and were largely unrecognized. They were professional musicians ... they were sidemen.

CHAPTER 4

PROFESSIONAL MUSICIANSHIP

Just what is a "Professional Musician"?

Be reliable and easy to work with. Show up on time and be prepared. In music, as in any field, those who work the hardest and are the most dedicated, stand the best chance of succeeding. — Musician's Union (AFM) Guidelines

In Nashville, every day, two symbolic buses are in motion. One bus, the arrival bus, has, as a passenger, the New Kid, come to town to "set the woods on fire" as the saying goes.

The other bus, the departure bus, is leaving, carrying last week's New Kid, headed back to the farm because he couldn't get any fire going at all.

It is very hard to make a living nowadays playing guitar. It sometimes seems like the only people interested in guitarists are other guitar players. I used to play in a Top Forty band when Chet was in town and we were off the road. Most of the people in nightclubs are looking for a one-night stand and by quitting time they are higher than a pine cone. If you are playing in a group you sometimes have to play at brain damage level to be heard. They aren't interested in what the band is doing. You could play wrong notes all the time and no one would know or care.

Really, I wouldn't advise anyone to do it for a living now. In the long run it would be better to have a good livelihood and play for a hobby. Since I have been in the music business trying to make a living I would say that 75% of musicians that I have known lived from hand to mouth, as they use to say in Kentucky. Unfortunately, if you try to make a living playing finger-style you'll soon be on food stamps nowadays. I don't particularly like it but there it is.

A short definition of professional musician would be anyone who gets paid for making music. This could range from the summertime street musician or the twenty dollars a night neighborhood saloon musician, to a classical or symphony first chair making thousands of dollars a year. Some people, when they think "professional musician," think of the last live concert they saw, the last musical star whose show they attended, or perhaps it was that live music club they went to. They, particularly the non-musicians, might think being a professional musician means living a freewheeling, exciting life of bright lights and travel.

It's a tough business, this professional musician stuff, and the thing is, the ones that get the work aren't always as highly paid as the attending public thinks they are. After all, most of them work *per diem*, meaning by the day or by the show. There are very few acts working five shows a week. Most of the work is on weekends.

Once a performer (usually a singer) becomes popular and makes a record that gets traction and airplay, they find that their public expects certain things of them. First and foremost, if there is a hit song or hit album, the ticket buyers expect to hear that song played and they expect it to sound just like the record they bought. The familiarity of the piece reinforces the fan's opinion of themselves as musical connoisseurs. Too much divergence from the recorded piece seems almost threatening to some fans. If the song strays too far from the original record they may feel cheated because the song on the stage does not sound like the record at home.

This means the travelling professional musician, the sideman hired by a star performer, is expected to play it like it is on the record at every stop on the tour. Free improvisation is not only discouraged but is often grounds for termination.

Today, while CDs have replaced vinyl records, technology constantly changes. With the evolution of the PC there is now the ability to make complete musical offerings digitally by computer and it is possible to do this with the musicians never seeing each other.

Incredible as it may seem, starting in the late fifties, the record itself was probably not even made by using the singer's band. It was most likely made by a team of musical specialists in a studio and the only participant that the fan can be sure of being at the session was the star-singer.

After the record was made and released it was left to the singer's band to learn the parts on the finished record and learn them well enough so that when the singer was on the road the audience heard exactly what was on the record. If the road band musician couldn't learn to duplicate the recorded riffs the solution was simple. The star would simply hire someone else. Enter the professional musician.

The performer, the star, had a show to deliver. First and foremost one of the main things they required was that the musicians were not to distract the star. One way for the star to get distracted was for someone in the band to make a mistake, or throw the rhythm off. Even today, the intervals in the vocals where a sideman is allowed to "take a break" and play a part of the melody must be structured with little in the way of true improvisation. To make such a musical error that causes the audience's attention to waver from the star for any reason except for designated solos is intolerable.

In many cases errors mean rapid replacement of the musician. Sometimes the offender might be given a chance to redeem themselves but a musician, no matter how good he may be most of the time, is not good enough if, for the same price, the star can hire one who gets it right every time. The reason is, that in most cases, the audience pays little attention to who is actually in the band. Individual musicians are virtually invisible, interchangeable and expendable, particularly if they are dressed in band outfits. One guy wearing a western shirt playing guitar looks pretty much like the next guy wearing a western shirt and playing guitar. To the audience, the star is all that matters. Never fear, in many cases, the star feels the same way. "Get it right!" or they'd get someone else.

There is seldom any problem finding a replacement. In Nashville there is always a line of people who have just gotten off the bus who think they play as good if not better than the musicians they see onstage and they are dying to prove it. Even today the road band musicians usually get paid by the day avoiding the need for having complicated contracts. Getting fired is a quick, easy bit of business if it happens and finding a replacement ready to step in is a minor inconvenience. Since no contracts are involved, a notice is not required making termination of a player a fairly easy thing to execute.

Playing the road can be very restricting to a guitar player if they're just a sideman. The headliner/star keeps a tight rein on how much "shine" the musicians are allowed to add to a show, usually limiting the musicians to one solo instrumental per set.

It was hard for the thumb-style players. The sidemen usually only got one chance to "pick one for the folks" in a show. When the guitarist made their selection they had to choose something that the steel player and fiddler could play, too so they also could "take a ride on the song." This could put a crimp in their repertoire. A good thumb player may have learned one of Chet's more challenging songs but odds are the rest of the band might not be up to it in ability.

— Gayle Moseley

Most times the star didn't really care. The guitar player or steel player or fiddler gets to play an instrumental because it's part of the show and gives the singer's voice a little rest. Some filler that pads out the show time.

One of the exceptions was in Ernest Tubb's band, called the "Texas Troubadours." Ernest Tubb liked to keep a consistent band. To keep a consistent band usually meant they had to keep them working and ET booked 200 dates a year for most of his life.

Ernest's music tended to be a steady paced, almost simplistic I-IV-V three chord sequence as he scooped into his trademark vocal phrasing. The audience could always count on a five-note signature lick created by Billy Byrd but forever associated with Tubb, to end every guitar break/solo in almost every song Ernest sang. The audience liked that. He was sure to name the musician about to take an instrumental break. The audience liked this homey touch. He even did it on recordings. The audience liked that, too. They looked for it. It was part of the Ernest Tubb presentation!

For several years Ernest employed some of the best sidemen Nashville had to offer. Two were top-flight musicians, steeler Buddy Charleton and guitarist Leon Rhodes hired in the early sixties. When it came time to "pick one for the folks" those two men were *ready*! They were all too briefly and furiously free. They fired off some fabulous, tightly harmonized flurries of notes. The audience sat stunned through this avalanche of brilliantly executed works of musical art, more jazz than country. The audience no doubt loved it but at the same time they knew that when the exercise was over Buddy and Leon would settle down and go back to steadily paced three chord tunes, playing "real" country, doing exactly what they were paid to do. Backing Ernest Tubb and endlessly tagging the songs with the five-note signature guitar lick. Just like it was on the record. Because they were professional musicians. Besides, the fans are here to see the star, not the guitar players. This is aptly described by Gayle Moseley.

I was friends with Odell long before I ever met Paul. After Odell went to work with Faron Young we were all interested in seeing him live on those Saturday afternoon TV shows.

I noticed he wasn't burnin' up the fretboard as he used to do when he played with us on our club dates. He told us that after he had worked about two jobs with Faron, he was called over to the side one night while they were having intermission.

Faron said, "Son, you're a fine guitar player, but when you're on the stage with me, I am the only star up there … always remember that if you want a long career in the music business!"

Even back then, you were fighting a battle getting a job with a big star if you were a thumbpicker. You usually started with somebody who liked the style, Grandpa Jones, Cousin Jody, etc. Paul used to say that Billy Byrd told him he'd better "throw that damn thumb pick away" if he wanted longevity in Nashville!

It's a shame that such great players as Odell never got more publicity, but it's a tough business. Those stars don't want any competition on stage, and most all the session players used straight picks and got that clean single note sound. When you played backup that's what the singer wanted to hear. "Play what's on the record, boy!"
— Gayle Moseley

When a star performer went on the road they tried to get the best musicians they could. It was always an employer's advantage. There were usually more musicians than there were jobs available so the star could hire people who were very often overqualified players. But the star didn't care. They wanted consistency. They wanted those who played exactly as rehearsed. Players like Paul Yandell and Odell Martin would get hired to go on the road with people like Faron Young or Kitty Wells or the Louvins or the Wilburn Brothers and others because they were solid, accurate, and dependable. Perhaps more importantly, being young, lean and hungry, they would take all the rigors of the road for surprisingly little money.

Being a professional musician is actually more restricting than being an at-home musician. At home they're free to play whatever they want with no pressure. Musicians playing in a local bar get forgiven, mistakes can be laughed off. However, on the road as part of a stage show or TV show, their job is to keep their stunning musical ability in check. Their job was to make the star sound like their record at each show, free of mistakes, as well as be their own roadie and sometimes be the band bus driver.

> The pay of a professional musician doesn't compensate for the time expended. By the time you consider the hours of practice required to keep your chops sharp, the hours of rehearsal that makes for a top-flight group, the pay you get for this show or that show does not really pay enough for all those hours you put in.
> — Kevin Jarvis

> I'm just starting to make money and I've been playing guitar for thirty years. I'm just starting to make a decent living.
> — Lenny Breau

That's show business; more work than glamour actually. But it's hard to spend glamour at a grocery store. Having said all that, some professional musicians did well enough to become prime hires. Some, like Billy Byrd, gained sideman recognition for their own sake. Steel players like Curley Chalker gained some status of their own. Some people who may have started as sidemen became stars themselves; Bob Wills for one, Glenn Campbell for another.

As already noted, the studio musicians had the best gig. Scale for studio recording in the late fifties and sixties was around $40 (up from the $25 of 1954) for a three hour recording session with some musicians and the session leader (a position Chet often held) making double scale. They were spared the rigors and danger of the road. They could go home at night.

Studio work had its own pressure and there they really *were* invisible. For many years the sidemen were rarely listed on liner notes of an album. Until the late sixties, the fan had no idea who was playing on that hit record they just bought. They knew who the singer was but that was about it. But, anonymous or not, studio work was excellent if a musician could get it.

Paul Yandell was one of those who got to work with some of the better acts. They saw him work in the recording sessions delivering what was demanded of him without complaint and with cold efficiency. They heard him back up well known artists with skill and taste. He didn't make mistakes. He didn't have any substance abuse issues. They knew he wasn't a prima donna with an ego. He was an excellent instrument mechanic. For these reasons he got to work with some of the finest acts around.

However, the meager pay given to musicians in a road band didn't go far when they had a wife and child at home. Even though he worked with some of the best known acts he and his family had financial hardship. He would get burnt out from being on the road and the pressure from studio work. He eventually quit the road for a steady, stay-home job with the post office. Eating regularly and seeing his wife on a daily basis had its good points.

But the hunger and excitement of playing for an audience was still there. As one musician put it, "playing in the spotlight is a disease they didn't want to be cured of."

Later in life Paul mused about what the professional musician's life was.

I know some great players who spend half their lives in beer joints. I was one of the lucky ones. I always seemed to have a good job as I went through life. I just think it's better to get an education and play for a hobby. Before you know it you're ready to retire and it takes more than Social Security to do that.

Some folks ask me if I miss going on the road ... No I don't miss it at all. When you are on the road you always have to catch an early plane so that leaves out any sightseeing. I was on the road for about fifty years and that is enough bad food, bad rooms in motels and hotels ... little sleep ... crying babies on the planes. I get offers from time to time to play around the country, mostly fingerpicking clubs, but I did the road for almost fifty years so I don't do it anymore.

There is a pause as Paul considers what his life has been as a musician. Almost as a comparison he muses about his son Micah with great pride.

My son, Micah plays. He plays guitar for a hobby. He's pretty good, has a good thumb and a good ear. He plays pretty much like I do, of course, because I taught him. We play together about once a week. We have recorded a couple of tunes for fun. Micah loves to play and it's great to have a son to share music with.

I'm very proud of Micah. He is a fine person. I'm glad he didn't want to be a musician because there's not much future in it. He's a director at Southern Hills Hospital here in Nashville. We get together every now and then to play some but I'm glad he didn't become a musician. It's a crummy life.

Crummy life, or no, young Paul, for the moment was still enjoying working with Ira and Charlie. It was fun and exciting playing the Opry and playing package shows with the Louvins and people like Johnny Cash and occasionally the new guy, Elvis Presley. Playing with the Louvins was a heady, exciting period for the young guitarist. Paul was also doing recording sessions with others when he could because he needed to make a living and sessions paid pretty well. While the general public may not recognize the sidemen so much, the working musicians did. The good ones got hired for sessions when they were not on the road.

The sidemen, the guys who worked in the recording studios, all knew each other and for the most part got along well with each other. Paul talks of the great Hank Garland.

About 1957, when I was with the Louvin Brothers, they decided to use two electric guitars doing harmony parts for a couple of songs. "River Of Jordan" was one of them. They chose Hank Garland.

I knew Hank from playing the Opry. At that time he and Grady Martin were the two top session guitarists of the day. Hank treated me with the utmost kindness and didn't try to outplay me. He let me do the fills just like I always had, then we would do a twin guitar part when it was called for. I think he was using a blond Epiphone with two Bigsby pickups. Both of us had Fender Pro amps. I remember we had sessions on two different days.

After the first session, Hank suggested that I let him take my amp home with him so he could do some work on it. I don't remember what was wrong with it, maybe it had some hum, but he brought it back the next day and I used it on the session.

Paul had a lot of respect for Hank Garland. During a recording session Hank took Paul's amplifier home for a night and doctored on it and brought it back the next day to the session. Paul said it was a Fender Pro amp. He said, "I don't know what he did to it but it sure did help it."
— Robbie Jones

One of the best tunes he and I did together was that "River of Jordan." Of all the tunes I did with the Louvins I think I played that one the best. Hank played great on it. Hank was a fine person, a player's player. Chet used Hank on a lot of sessions. If he had been difficult to work with, Chet wouldn't have used him.

I did several sessions with Hank. I never met anyone nicer. He was ten times the player I was but he always tried to help me. The Epiphone, with the Bigsby pickups and the "Sugarfoot" pickguard, is the guitar he loaned me once when I got to work three or four days with Faron Young and Roger Miller.

At that time, Chet, Odell Martin, Joe Edwards, Jackie Phelps and myself were the only ones using a thumb pick on the Opry. I remember taking a lot of kidding about using one. Billy Byrd used to give me the business about it. He told me I'd better 'throw that damn thumb pick away!' That really got next to me because I thought I was doing right. Anyway, as I got older, I realized what they thought didn't make much difference in the long run, because now I think there are as many players using thumb picks as straight picks.

We did some tours with Ernest Tubb's band when I was with the Louvins. Billy was with Ernest at that time. We all had a great time. Billy was a big poker player and liked to have one now and then but most everyone did back then. I don't remember anyone who wasn't a nice person who worked the Opry. It was like a big family.

Years ago before I started working with Jerry Reed I used to go out with Carl Smith, mostly on weekends. It was just he and I on those shows. He was very nice to me. I really enjoyed working with him.

One day I went out to his farm for some reason. I pulled up in his drive and stopped, turning my motor off. A giant Great Dane ran up to my car. I had the window down so he stuck his head right into the car! It scared the hell out of me! Carl came to the back door and saw it and had a big laugh.

Carl had some kind of thin Super 400 he played back then. He was a good businessman. He had a five hundred acre farm and later sold it for about three million dollars. In the 1950s, he had the best band around ... Dale Potter on fiddle, Junior Husky on bass, Buddy Harman on drums and Johnny Sibert on steel. They all wore those greatest Nudie suits.

Paul working with Carl Smith was probably in the 1970s. Carl's steel player, Johnny Sibert and his wife, Gayle, were really good friends to us as well as being neighbors on our street.

I remember seeing that dog that Paul talks about, He really was as tall as the car! Gayle and I, along with our sons, went out to Franklin to their farm one Sunday afternoon to visit and eat with Goldie Hill (Carl's wife.) We had the same experience with the dog. The dog was harmless. He would come up to the car and stick his head in the window (just being friendly).

When Johnny Sibert and Gayle were married, Paul and I helped to hide Johnny's vehicle in my sister-in-law's garage to keep attendees from painting it up with shoe polish. After the reception, they jumped in our car and we sped away to the hiding place. It was a great plan!

We all use to take in the "Figure 8" car races together at the Nashville Speedway whenever they were racing. Johnny, Paul and Micah got into the model car racing at one time spending a lot of afternoons racing their model cars in places.

Johnny also played steel guitar with Kitty Wells and Johnny Wright. He and Paul were the best of friends.

The weekends working with Carl Smith that Paul talks about were not a regular thing. If Carl had some bookings, he would occasionally call Paul to work with him. Of course if Paul was already booked to record or work with someone else, he couldn't do it. Carl would have to find another guitar player. Johnny Sibert played on all of Carl's dates.
— Marie Yandell

In the course of working different kinds of shows, Paul naturally met different people that became household names in show business.

Then There Was Elvis

Tom Parker (The Colonel) had been a promoter for, among others, Eddy Arnold. In the early 1950s, Parker got involved with Hank Snow and formed some touring package shows with him featuring country acts, starring (who else?) Hank Snow. Some of those shows even included Chet Atkins on occasion. The roster would change from time to time but popular country acts like Johnny Cash and the Louvin Brothers would also be in the lineup. Paul Yandell had signed on with the Louvins about the same time The Colonel had set the hook in Elvis. The Colonel added Presley to his package shows and used him as the closing act.

To say Elvis Presley was a phenomenon is a gross understatement. His impact on the musical scene was unprecedented and to date, unequaled. The closest to it would be the Beatles but they rank a pale second.

No one was prepared for Elvis. As the crowds for Parker's travelling package show swelled, it soon became evident that the main reason fans, particularly the female fans, were buying the tickets, was to see Elvis Presley. The impatience of the fans to get the other acts to move on so Elvis could appear often translated to fan rudeness, which bruised the sometimes delicate egos of some of the other performers.

Some of the acts turned hostile to the newcomer. Ira Louvin was one of these. According to legend Ira confronted Elvis in an ugly fashion that may or may not have had the end result that Presley never recorded a single Louvin

Brother's song. This may not sound like much on the surface but the fact remains, if Elvis recorded a song, it made money and had he recorded any Louvin Brothers music everyone's bank accounts would have increased.

Paul was not involved in any of that. He was a sideman with no star ambitions. To him, Elvis was one of the guys in the show. Paul saw nothing unusual about going and getting something to eat with the new guy.

I was on the road a lot in the fifties working with the Louvins. Col. Tom Parker and others got a large package together of country acts along with Elvis. We did three different tours up and down the east coast, generally doing two shows a day.

When I was with the Louvins, about 1956, we were playing one of those package shows on a Sunday afternoon in Norfolk, Virginia. The show was being held at the convention center there. We pulled up in the parking lot. As we started to get out, a yellow Cadillac Coupe Deville roared right up next to us, rocks flying everywhere! We looked around and Elvis got out. He was on the bill also. Scotty Moore and Bill Black were with him too.

As I remember, Elvis closed the show. There were a number of artists on the show. It was a country music show but most everyone came to see Elvis. The girls kept screaming for Elvis. The other acts didn't like that very much. It was quite a day.

Back then the PAs and sound systems were terrible in the buildings. Nobody knew to put mics on the amps. It really didn't matter. When Elvis was on stage the noise from the crowd was so deafening that the only thing you heard was when Elvis started the song and when he said a few words in between the songs.

Once, in between shows, I went with Elvis and his cousin Red, Elvis's bodyguard, to eat. We sat in a booth. I was on the inside, Elvis was next to me and Red was across the table. We all ordered cheeseburgers. When Elvis and Red got theirs, they started cutting up ... spitting their food across at each other. They would also thump each other on the forehead. I know it sounds immature but remember we were almost teenagers.

Elvis went into the Army about six months before I did. Elvis was in the Third Armored Division while I was in the Second Armored Division. We both were out in the field on training maneuvers and we actually met at a PX once.

Paul told me on one of the dates they played with Elvis the microphone cable ran through a hole in the floor directly below the microphone stand then over to the mixer off-stage. The stage was elevated about five feet.

While Elvis was singing Paul eased over to the side of the stage and started pulling on the microphone cable. This in turn started lowering the microphone. Elvis noticed it and pulled it back up. Paul then repeated the devious act and Elvis, not to be outdone by a defective microphone stand, started bending lower toward the microphone. Finally, Paul gave a big jerk on the cable and the microphone went all the way down to the floor.
— Forrest Yandell

My sister and I and some friends went to one of Col. Tom Parker's package shows in the fifties. The Louvin Brothers were on the show as well as Elvis Presley. Paul was playing with the Louvins then but I had no idea who he was, nor was I interested.

They had us, as kids, sitting over to the side of the stage and when Elvis finished his performance, he came over to the side of the stage where we were sitting and grabbed my youngest sister, who is six years younger than me. He squatted down and lifted her to sit on his knees. She hopped up from his knees immediately! She had watched him dance around, perform, and shake his legs on the stage and she was afraid of him. We laugh about it today but that's her claim to fame...sitting in Elvis' lap.
— Marie Yandell

Guitarist Scotty Moore and drummer Bill Black were the two musicians who were Elvis' sidemen from the absolute beginning, starting with that first fateful recording at Sun Studio in Memphis. It was once reported that the most Scotty and Bill made working with Elvis was $250 a week. How accurate that sum was is not known for certain. The amount could be a straight salary or it might have been an averaging out of a per-show payment.

By 1955, sources indicate Elvis was often booked for five or more venues a week and some of those may have been two shows a day. Five venues, two shows each. Ten shows a week. $25 a show, $50 a day (minimum wage in 1955 was ¢75; Eight hour day at ¢75, $6; let's say skilled labor $2.50 an hour, $20 for an eight hour day). So the sideman rate at Moore's peak with Elvis was actually pretty good money for the period, particularly since they didn't need to work an eight-hour day. It seems more likely that the Colonel would have contracted Moore to a weekly guarantee to keep him from seeking greener pastures. It is said that there were some rumblings about money. $250 a week wasn't a lot when you put it up against what Elvis himself was drawing from those venues.

All things must end and the association Elvis had with his main sidemen wound down and pretty much stopped when Elvis went into the army. There was an occasional reunion appearance but those were rare.

Scotty got involved in studio work at the control board and producer level and probably was glad to be off the road. He was quietly successful in the recording industry behind the scenes drawing on years of hands-on experience.

Bill Black formed his own group and had some minor hits but died in 1965 of a brain tumor.

Elvis got re-invented when he got out of the army and went on to impressive musical sales. He was, and still is, being very profitably marketed, even after his death.

Elvis was a good guy. He just got too much fame, too soon.

Merle Travis

Merle Travis, of course, is a touchstone to Paul Yandell and Chet Atkins. Born and raised in a coal mining community in Kentucky, Travis learned thumb-style from Kennedy Jones, Ike Everly, and Mose Rager. Of the three, only Merle ever attained any national recognition, mostly due to his songwriting. Hearing his singing and playing on the radio, even spottily, was enough to focus Chet Atkins on finger-style guitar. That alone did the guitar world a service but Merle inspired countless other guitarists too. Merle had a charismatic stage presence and was a good entertainer who seemed to leave good impressions on anyone who came in contact with him.

I was lucky to have been around Merle Travis a few times. Back in the 1980s, I went with some guys up to a place in Ohio on the 4th of July to be in a backup band. Merle Travis was on the show. He asked me to play bass for him. He was using a MusicMan 130 with one fifteen-inch speaker at the time. I never heard anyone play so loud! His amp was almost bouncing off the floor! It's a memory I'll never forget. Later Merle asked me to go eat with him and his wife.

Merle had a great thumb...sounded like a pile driver. And he didn't keep straight time. He'd rush a little bit, but that's one of the things that made him exciting. There was so much energy in his playing.

He was really a unique individual. He and Mose Rager were a lot alike ... same personalities ... "full of devilment" as they used to say. Merle was a great writer, songwriter, poet, cartoonist ... there wasn't anything he couldn't do. I don't know if people are aware of it but he wrote the folk music section for the Encyclopedia Britannica. Great player. I always loved his playing. What would we have done without Merle Travis? He was one of those people like Chet and Jerry Reed that, when you were with him, you got excited just because you were there. He was a most interesting person to hear talk ... always telling great stories about other stars and saying witty things.

I think Merle Travis had one set of P-90 pickups that he liked the sound of so well he moved them from guitar to guitar when he was using Super 400s. Merle was like Chet in that a lot of the soul on his recordings was in his touch. Chet told me once if I wanted to sound like Merle to use large gauge strings and record direct.

I'll tell you a true story. Back in the 1950s, I was working with the Louvin Brothers during the time they still had the Prince Albert network radio show on Saturday nights at nine o'clock. They would hold the rehearsal at the old studio C at 5th and Union on Saturday afternoon. I used to go watch because Chet was on the Prince Albert show.

One week Merle was the guest artist. He was playing his Super 400, the Gibson Special with all the pearl inlay on the head and his name down the fingerboard. When I arrived he was tuning up and as he did, the plastic knob on the third string key broke so he couldn't turn it. Somebody went and got a set of pliers and he managed to turn the key with them to get tuned up. I always thought that was sort of a funny happening. "Those were the days" as they say.

While we're on the subject of Merle and his music, I went up for the grand opening of the Merle Travis Music Center at Paradise Park in Muhlenberg Kentucky in November 2007. The building is excellent and as good a sounding room as I've ever played. The building is built so they can expand it at some point. Whoever designed it has done it before. It has a large dressing room area.

The display of the guitars is great! A number of things that were Merle's are there. I asked the Gretsch Guitar Company to donate a 6120 in honor of Chet which they did and there are a few things that belonged to Chet around his guitar, too. To sum up, it's a great place to play and I think everyone will want to go and play there. I'm glad I was a part of it. As I have said before some people should live forever. Merle, Chet and Jerry were three of those people.

Porter Wagoner

A few days ago I was watching the Porter Wagoner show on RFD-TV. It brought back some memories of when I used to record for him. I liked Porter, but he was a tyrant when he was recording! He would tell you every note to play. He didn't want you to suggest anything. I did an album with Dolly that he was producing once and he wore me out. I never was so glad to be finished with a session as I was that day. I always hated it when he would call me to do a session. Porter was a strange one. Sometimes he would lock the studio doors when the session started. You couldn't go get a coffee or go to the restroom.

Porter was all right, he was just very hard to work for. A fellow named Little Jack Little used to work for him. I think he played bass. He told me once that they were on the road and were returning to Nashville. Porter told Little Jack to empty the trash baskets on the bus when they got in. Well, Jack forgot to do it. They left again in a couple of days. When they got about fifty miles out of Nashville Porter noticed the trash baskets hadn't been cleaned so he fired Little Jack.

Buddy Killen (Tree Publishing) was another tough one to work for. Most of the producers have a group of musicians they use all of the time. When they had to use someone new they gave them the business. Most of the producers I worked for were nice to me and the other musicians.

One time when he was recording at RCA for a Dolly Parton session, they were taking a break and Paul went over to the side of the studio and lay down and closed his eyes to relax. He dozed off a little. Dolly came over and lay down beside him and gave him a big surprise when he realized someone was laying beside him. Chet, the engineer and the other musicians in the studio had a big laugh when they saw Paul's reaction.
— Marie Yandell

Marie

Paul worked with the Louvins from 1955 to 1958. A whole lot of things happened in 1958. Paul got drafted into the army in 1958. Hell on Wheels Second Armored Division based in Fort Hood, Texas. He was home on leave right after basic training and was visiting Ira Louvin. It happened that Ira knew a girl he wanted Paul to meet. Ira Louvin lived not too far from Little Jimmie Dickens. Jimmie's wife at the time had a sister, Marie, that Ira thought would be right for Paul. Marie, a petite, pretty little blonde, was in the area to go to college. Ira arranged the meeting. They got on well and for their first date, being a guitar player, he did what any guitar player does on a first date. He took his date to a gig!
Marie Yandell tells it:

Fortunately, my parents were somewhat familiar with the music business before Paul and I met. My brother was married to Helen (the oldest daughter of Mother Maybelle Carter). In fact, when I was in high school, the Carter family was on a package show in Waycross, Georgia and Helen and Mother Maybelle came to our home in Baxley, Georgia and picked us up and took us to the show. This was probably 1955 or 1956. The Louvin Brothers were on the same show as well as Elvis Presley. Paul was playing with the Louvins then but I had no idea who he was, nor was I interested.

Later, after I graduated from high school, I came to Nashville to live with my sister, Ernestine, (who was married to Little Jimmy Dickens) and attend Belmont College. Jimmy and my sister lived about a half-mile from Ira and Faye Louvin and I was well acquainted with them. In fact, I babysat their little girl from time to time.

When Paul was home from six weeks of basic training in the army, in between Christmas and New Years of 1958, he came to visit Ira and Faye on Friday night and Ira thought about me and wanted me to meet Paul and came to my sister's and picked me up to go to their home. Paul was playing the Opry on Saturday night with Cousin Jody and he asked me to go with him, which I did.

After he played a couple of spots on the Opry, he wanted to go to a drive-in movie … and that was a BIG Mistake. He had more hands than an octopus and I couldn't wait to get back home that night and had no desire to see him again!

As I was getting out of the car, he asked me to write to him and I responded, "OK, but you can write too." Then, he was off to Ft. Hood, Texas and then on to Munich, Germany for two years. He didn't bother to get my address so sometime later, he wrote Ira and Faye and asked for my address and the first letter I got from him was addressed to Mary Jones (not Marie). I felt sorry for him, as a soldier away from home, and began corresponding with him and I guess you could say that we fell in love with each other thru letter writing. He came home from Germany in November 1960 and we were married on February 26, 1961.

Paul's version of the tale is a little bit shorter:

We met sort of on a blind date. We fell in love, and married while I was in the service.

Paul got drafted when he was working with the Louvins. Guitarist Jimmy Capps took over his spot on Paul's recommendation. When he got out two years later he found the Louvin Brothers were quite satisfied with Jimmy Capps.

Paul and Marie's wedding. This marriage was to last fifty years ... Paul was a wise man. February 26, 1961. *Photo courtesy of YFA*

Interlude 3: The Grand Ole Opry Tent Show

It is unknown whether Paul ever played a Grand Ole Opry tent show but they were an early version, a precursor, of what today's grand touring stage shows would eventually be. They were a way for a touring group to book themselves and have more freedom since they didn't have to commit to (or pay rent on) a fixed venue building. They actually did use tents and portable stages and usually featured a headliner and secondary act and a "girl singer" of some sort to round the show out.

Shows like this were still touring in the late fifties even as they were being driven into extinction by shows like Kitty Wells and Johnny Wright's bus tours. They, and other artists, were changing the country music landscape. Band busses were the coming thing. Kitty Wells, and acts like hers, depended on the venue providing the stage. The tent show brought their own.

You could see it ... it was an actual tent just like a medium-to-small sized circus-type tent. It had the same yellow/brown color as a circus tent. The part where the top joined the sides had a strip running around it with Grand Ole Opry repeated again and again in blue letters. This one had the sides rolled up because it was late summer and humid. It gets that way in August in the Midwest. The air gets still, with barely a breeze. Crickets and mosquitoes vie for attention, the mosquitoes having a slight edge in that contest.

Roy Acuff, "King of Country Music" was the headliner, Roy, as always, being backed by Beecher, "Oswald" Kirby. Second bill was The Wilburn Brothers, Teddy and Doyle.

They had their obligatory "girl singer" but instead of it being banjo plunking Rachel Veach they had "a pretty little thing" (and she was!). June Webb.

June was petite … all big blue eyes and pretty lips. She wasn't allowed to look too sexy because, after all, this is a moral show and it was still the fifties. Still, she was very pretty and a portent of what the future would bring in female vocalists. But at this time the rule was still no cleavage and a full skirt with petticoats.

The tent and stage was nicely made. It was not new but not tattered, either. It had a real wooden stage that raised the performers about two feet above the ground. There was a wooden rail which kept the ravenous fans at bay and also transmit the idea you were seeing a real show, not just a bunch of musicians in a vacant lot or campground, which, truth be told, they kind of were.

Roy and his people did the first show in typical Roy Acuff fashion. Roy sang his hits and played some fiddle and when it came time to "pick one for the folks," Oswald obliged with (what else?) "Wabash Cannonball" well played on his Dobro.

Then The Wilburn Brothers, resplendent in their powder blue Nudie suits, did a quick number as a teaser and an intermission was called. Roy, Oswald, Teddy,and Doyle were soon out there, talking to the fans.

There were a couple of unnamed sidemen who retired to where the cars were parked, probably going in hiding to have a smoke. You *know* Roy wouldn't permit any hint of endorsing smoking by any of his crew.

Now, perhaps June Webb didn't feel all that well known so she might have thought it safe to tiptoe off to where the sidemen were hiding. Maybe to have a smoke, maybe she was sweet on one of them. History has left the "why" for other minds to ponder.

What does happen is that Roy saw her starting to sidle away. Roy's "Happy Country Boy" visage went frosty for a second and he said (in a *pay attention* voice …) "Git on over here, Junie! These people are wantin' to talk to you!"

So she meekly came to where the mingling is going on and, poor lass, no one approached her. The boys were shy and tongue tied … maybe a little embarrassed to have witnessed her chastisement. The women just gave her icy glares … jealous because she really *was* a "pretty little thing" who had just better stay away from their menfolk if she knew what was good for her.

The second half of the show was great. The Wilburns once again were glittering under the floodlights as they did their greatest hits, June Webb sang her song. The sidemen "picked one for the folks" and otherwise acquitted themselves as true pros. Everyone went home happy.

Who were the sidemen? Who knows?. They were just sidemen … a guitar player and a bass player. The guitar player was pretty good but we've already forgotten what he played. Some sidemen don't even have names, or so it seemed. Because nobody asked. Sometimes no one bothered to "introduce them to the folks as individuals." They were often just "The Boys."

CHAPTER 5

KITTY, THE BUS, AND THE ROAD

Paul was released from the army (the first time) in 1960. A shipping disaster forced him to get a guitar upgrade, then it was back to scrambling for a living, looking for a steady gig.

When I went in the army in December 1958, I was stationed in Germany so I had the Gretsch 6120 sent to me. When I came back home two years later I had my guitar shipped back. It came by boat and took about six or seven weeks. Unfortunately, it got broken in transit. I didn't know it would arrive broken so I didn't have a guitar.

Meanwhile, I didn't have a job, and Marie and I were wanting to get married. I was back about three weeks when I ran into Faron Young. He asked me to go to South Carolina to play three days with him. I told him I would if I could find a guitar and amp. I went over to RCA to see Chet. I ran into Hank Garland in the lobby. I got to telling him about my problem. Hank said he had a guitar he would lend me. It was an Epiphone with Bigsby pickups, the one he cut "Sugarfoot Rag" with.

I took it on the job but I was so dumb! When I got back I noticed I had scratched the back of the guitar with my belt buckle! I was sick, friends! I have never forgotten that! I hated so badly to take that guitar back to him. He didn't get upset about it, or he didn't act like it. By the way, Roger Miller went on that job with Faron Young on drums! I bought a Country Gentleman.

Now a civilian and engaged to Marie at the time, his soon-to-be brother-in-law, Jimmie Dickens, got him a job with Kitty Wells. He worked with her for about a year when he was called back into the service.

This second tour of duty was during the 1961 "Berlin Crisis" that saw the building of the infamous Berlin Wall during John F. Kennedy's presidency. The administration had a temporary call-up of troops so Paul was back in uniform. This time he remained stateside and did not have to go back to Germany.

He and Marie got married (February 2, 1961) while he was stationed in Fort Benning, Georgia. He only had to spend a year on active duty. The army released him but kept him in the reserves. He went home to a wife who would soon be a mother.

Kitty Wells and Johnny Wright hired him back. He applied to the army to be excused from regularly scheduled reserve meetings due to the unpredictability of his band schedule. Permission was granted and his final discharge came through in 1964.

After I got discharged the first time, Little Jimmy Dickens helped me get a job with Kitty Wells. That was in 1960. I worked with her band until I got called back into the service in 1961. That was a one-year break. I got hired back after that. We stayed on the road 200 days a year. I worked for her for about ten years.

The pay was better with Kitty than it had been with the Louvins. Kitty's group started him out at fifty dollars a show and bumped that to seventy-five dollars a show when he helped by driving the bus. He got paid for travel days but it was less than it was for the show dates. Paul was not contracted but he was considered a "Tennessee Mountain Boy" band member. This meant when Kitty Wells and Johnny Wright hit the road Paul was expected to go along. Kitty Wells booked a lot of dates. Marie Yandell said Paul was gone for a month or more at a stretch.

> After the show and/or concert, the band sold records, tapes, pictures and books for Kitty and Johnny and they paid the band members a small percentage on what they sold.
>
> Kitty and Johnny played a lot of dates in Canada. Johnny tried to keep customs from knowing what they were bringing into Canada to sell to save money and make a bigger profit.
>
> One particular trip into Canada, Johnny Wright had hidden a bunch of stuff on the bus that they were going to sell and when customs asked him about what he was bringing into the country to sell, he didn't declare it. That night, when they began selling the records, tapes and such, someone from customs was at the show and they got caught! Their bus almost got taken away from them because of Johnny not declaring the goods they were selling.
> — Marie Yandell

People think working the road is exciting but everybody just thinks about getting back home. The best time you have is that hour and a half that you spend on stage. That's where all the fun is. It's not in the going and coming. That's what wears your butt out. But it's better than hauling gravel or working in a tobacco patch.

After over ten years on the road with acts like the Louvins and Kitty Wells, I really don't like the road anymore. The only reason I work with Chet is because it is a blast to go on gigs with him, to just be around such a

super talent. Those kinds of road jobs are fun, not work. It was a lot like that with Jerry Reed too. Most entertainers spend over 275 days on the road each year playing bars, fairs and general road shows. Jerry only spent 100 days a year on the road because he had to stay close to Nashville. He was involved in writing songs for himself and numerous other artists, then he always had to cut new records since his hits were so successful. As a result, when we did go on the road it was always a good time.

Here's an idea of how hard road life could be. I saw Odell Martin every now and then when he was working with Donna Fargo. It was a tough job. He was playing one or two shows, then driving the bus to the next date. When Odell and I worked with Kitty Wells he and I did the same thing. I tell you folks, it's rough to play two shows, get behind the wheel of a bus at midnight and drive until daylight. I did it many times. When I started with Jerry Reed and found out he flew everywhere it was like heaven.

Speaking of driving a bus, in steel guitar circles this story is attributed to steeler Ben Keith telling about when he was working in Faron Young's band with Odell Martin:

> "Country Girl" was a big hit, and we were up in Michigan one time. Me and Odell and a bunch of us were on the bus. It was after a show and we'd all had a couple of beers.
>
> I was driving the bus. I had lost one of the lenses to my sunglasses. I was pretty well looped, so I wore them anyway and had them on cockeyed.
>
> I got pulled over and the cop approached me. I looked at him with my one lens out, and he said, "Well, I'm gonna have to arrest you. You're drunk."
>
> I said, "You can't arrest me. I played on '"Country Girl.'"
>
> He said, "I don't give a damn if you played on the 'Star Spangled Banner,' you're going to jail!" He finally let us go. He let Odell drive, and I think Odell was in worse shape than I was.

The Bus

In the early days everyone would pile into cars loaded with gear or they would tow little trailers with their gear. The road was a dangerous place, particularly before the big interstate highways were laid down. Every year the road would claim some musicians in crashes. Odds got worse if they worked two hundred dates a year, or so it seemed. Some, like Earl Scruggs and Hank Thompson learned to fly and were well off enough to buy and fly small aircraft to minimize their actual road time.

When busses became popular, sometimes the musicians themselves had to double as bus drivers as they went from one date to another, eating when they could and hoping to stay awake long enough to make the next play date on time. They got paid a little more money doing this but the time behind the wheel took its toll on the driver/musician. Paul remarked once that on one leg they drove from Norfolk, Virginia, to Vancouver, British Columbia (a road distance of over 3,000 miles) in three days.

The Kitty Wells show bus was a good example of the modern tour vehicle used in the sixties and seventies. Prior to getting a bus the band would travel, usually in at least two cars. A bus has greater cargo carrying capacity so they could get to the next gig knowing the band and the equipment is arriving at the same time. Having said that there is the story of Kitty going shopping during one of the rest stops and the bus taking off without her. They had gone about a hundred miles before they realized she wasn't on the bus and went back to fetch her. She never panicked. She just made herself comfortable and waited. After all … it was her name on the side of the bus.

They had more than one bus over the years but the one they had in the early sixties started out as a twenty-nine-passenger bus remodeled to suit a travelling band. It had eight seats, two couch-like affairs that could convert to bunks, closet space and a private room in the back for Kitty and her husband, Johnny Wright. This area had beds (upper and lower), closet space and a dressing table. Of course the entire bus had overhead shelving and space efficient storage nooks. It was carpeted nicely, insulated against weather and excess noise. A bus offered the physical protection of sheer mass that an auto could not.

Johnny Wright was an intuitive mechanic. He had Paul's admiration for his ability to keep the bus running and even he did some of the driving. Paul put in many a mile driving that bus.

It was during the Kitty Wells period that Paul bought another guitar like Chet's. A brief tale of gain and loss:

D'Angelico's were the number one guitar back then.

I had a D'Angelico Excel back in the 1960s that I bought from John D'Angelico. Odell and I were with Kitty Wells at the time. We were playing Madison Square Garden. One morning Odell and I went down to the Bowery where D'Angelico's shop was located. He had this beautiful sunburst Excel with a small repair in the top. I bought it. I think I paid him about $650 for it.

It had a narrow neck which I didn't care for but I bought it anyway. I took a couple of Johnny Smith pickups and fixed them to the pickguard so I wouldn't have to cut any holes in the top. I didn't put sound posts in it

like Chet did with his. It didn't sound like Chet's mainly because of those two Johnny Smith pickups. I had a gold Bigsby on it too.

Odell Martin bought a D'Angelico too. I was with Odell Martin when he ordered his. Before it was finished, John D'Angelico died. John had seven or eight unfinished guitars left to do when he died. Jimmy D'Aquisto finished Odell's and the others. Odell kept his for a year or two when he then sold it to Don Gibson. I never played it but I saw Don on the Opry with it once. I'm sure it was a good one.

I kept my D'Angelico for about two years but when my wife and I were having a tough time making ends meet I sold it to Kelly Simms in Chattanooga, Tennessee. I think later he sold it to a music store in Atlanta.

I regret selling that guitar, but we were poor and I wound up having to sell it ... something that has bothered me ever since. The downside about selling a good guitar or amp is that soon the money is gone, the guitar or amp is gone and all you have is a memory.

I read some years ago Johnny Smith sold his D'Angelico guitar for $50,000 to a collector. When I sold my D'Angelico Excel back in the 1960s I sold it for $750.00. Now Excel's are worth around $40,000. I've thought a lot about that in years past. I regret not still having that guitar. The music business can be tough.

Paul loved to tinker and was more than willing to educate himself in electronics and the technology of the day. It certainly came in handy when he was on the road with Chet.

> After Paul's time in the army and after we were married, he took advantage of the GI Bill for education and took an electronic course which he completed. He was always interested in electronics and how things worked. Then when he became interested in Ham Radio, he built his first unit (a HeathKit transceiver and transmitter) to use. He always loved challenges and he would stay awake all hours of the night so that he could "work" (communicate in Morse code) ham operators all over the world. His goal was to work all countries and it was a challenge to him. Chet was a Ham Operator too. He gave Paul his Collins Radio some years ago.
> — Marie Yandell

In 1965 I got my amateur radio license. I then gave Paul the test and he received his license. Paul and I attended the Ham convention in Dayton, Ohio yearly. We would speak on the ham radio almost every

night for many years when he was not on the road. He liked to use Morse code rather than the mic. We joined the ARRL (American Radio Relay League) and Paul got his 25 words per minute code proficiency certificate plus the advanced class certificate. Even in his final months he liked to turn on his radio and copy code. Paul's call sign was WB4KVB.
— Forrest Yandell

Things seemed to be going well enough when Paul and Marie got married in 1961. It was a good, lifelong match up. They celebrated their fiftieth anniversary on February, 26, 2011. Nevertheless, in the beginning, times were hard. Paul just wasn't making enough money and he and Marie were having a tough time of it. Being away from home and the rigors of the road started to wear away at him. Playing the road as a sideman in a show like the Kitty Wells/Johnny Wright group got to be mind numbingly monotonous.

A star like Kitty Wells has an established list she sings with little change over the years.

What the fan fails to realize is they are attending a travelling show. Since it *is* a travelling show, the jokes and songs the fresh audience enjoyed were being heard by the band again and again … and again. Paul loved and respected Kitty but the routine was just too much for too little.

Playing with Kitty Wells you'd play the same ten or twelve songs every night and finally I really got bored with the whole thing. After ten years of Kitty Wells I needed a break so I went with George Hamilton IV for about six months. I just got tired of playing … feeling like I'd gone as far as I could go with it so I quit for a year. I went about six months without even playing at all. It was just too hard to make ends meet with a wife and child so I took a job with the Post Office and really intended to give it all up. That's the worst place in the world to work. I couldn't stand it.

He settled into his day job but kept his chops up. He kept working on Chet Atkins' tunes. Having to work for the post office did not diminish his desire or ability to play guitar in the least.

Bobby Wright, who at one time was an actor on *McHale's Navy* and was the son of Kitty and Johnny, actually went out on his own for a short period of time and tried to make it as a solo artist. Paul played with him during that time. After that, he went to work with George Hamilton, IV and worked for him for a short time before he quit and went to work in the post office. He worked there about a year and hated every minute of it. He realized how much he missed playing his guitar during his time with the post office. He would occasionally go out with

other artists and play gigs on weekends. Bob Luman was one entertainer that he sometimes traveled and played dates with on weekends.
— Marie Yandell

That might have been the end of it. Paul could have been one of hundreds of musicians who made the trek to Nashville and found that music and money do not always go together for all participants and ended up another faded musical memory. Then Jerry Reed happened.

CHAPTER 6

JERRY REED

Guitars are nothin' to me but somethin' to use. Paul Yandell was in my band, and boy, you'd think his guitar was made out of gold, man. I mean, it was like one of his children. And I'm throwin' mine against a wall, lettin' it flop against a chair. [laughs] He was always puttin' it up, wipin' his strings, polishin' it up. — Jerry Reed, *Country Weekly*

Born in Atlanta, Georgia, in 1937, Jerry Reed Hubbard took to the guitar at a very early age, around seven years old, he has said. He told of just focusing on guitar playing very young in life simply because that was what he wanted to do. He knew he wanted to be an entertainer and in high school he dabbled in theater and acting as well. But his musical talent caught the eye and ear of some Capitol scouts and music became his primary calling. He was a good songwriter, signing on with a publisher and cutting his first record when he was only eighteen.

He, like Paul, had a stint in the military but never lost his focus on being a musician. He had developed a wildly syncopated guitar style that stunned other musicians but it was his songwriting that got the attention. Some of his songs were getting picked up by various artists. But he, himself, wasn't getting much notice.

Things connect for one reason or another. One night, Jerry happened to be playing in a club when sax player Boots Randolph heard him. Boots knew exactly what to do with this kid. He told Chet Atkins about him.

Chet liked what he heard. He recorded one of Jerry's tunes, delighting in the new approach to finger-style guitar Jerry had created. Chet suggested that Jerry move to Nashville. Chet felt he could put him to work in the local studios. Chet signed Jerry to an RCA recording contract. Jerry moved to Nashville and soon he was doing four sessions a day working the studios, eventually branching out to television, most notably the *Glenn Campbell Goodtime Hour*. This got him a lot of exposure so he started booking himself on the road having become a very popular act.

It has already been pointed out that the headliner on the road does not want to have to worry about his backup musicians. The headliner wants to be able to announce his next number and just know that his sidemen will be there with exactly the right support. Jerry wanted someone who would "do his homework" and be absolutely rock solid on rhythm. If the man played finger-style guitar he would probably be better suited to deliver what Jerry wanted.

He knew just the guy to do it, Paul Yandell. He'd seen him work on the road and he'd seen him work in the studio. But Paul was working in the post office, soured on the music business. To get Paul to sign on with him meant some persuasion was in order.

Jerry had been doing well on the *Glenn Campbell Goodtime Hour* on TV and he was getting personal bookings so he needed a backup band. By that time I had been working in the post office for about a year. I had gotten burned out with the road and just quit playing for a while.

Bob Luman called me and asked me to play the Saturday show at the Belle Meade Country Club. Jerry happened to be on the show. At that time he had "When You're Hot You're Hot" out so he was looking for musicians to form a band. It took some time, about two weeks, for Jerry to talk me into doing it. He hired Larrie Londin on drums and Steve Schaefer on bass to fill out his combo.

To be honest I wasn't a very good player. I was a terrible musician when I started with him. I don't think I was a very good guitar player. Not that I am now, but I was really bad until I went to work with Jerry. I had always played country music. Playing with Kitty Wells didn't challenge me. I didn't have the opportunity to do anything. Going with Jerry was like going to College. If I hadn't worked for Jerry first I don't think I would have been good enough to work for Chet.

Anyone who works with Jerry Reed comes away being a lot better musician. He really gave me an education. I couldn't count time. I didn't know where beat one was. He taught me to read numbers.

Paul with Jerry Reed in the early seventies. *Photo courtesy of YFA*

Note: "read numbers" refers to the Nashville Number System, a powerful shorthand method used by session musicians in Nashville to indicate chords and chord changes in a song.

I'd sit with the radio on and a tablet of paper and write numbers for the chord changes I heard on the songs. I'd do that sometimes two hours a day.

Jerry and I had been friends for years, back when I was working with the Louvin Brothers. I knew Jerry when he was first getting started in Georgia, when he was doing mostly singing, before he even got into guitar playing much. In fact, once he asked me to show him one of Chet's licks. Little did I know he would turn out to be one of the world's greats.

Jerry lived in Atlanta when he wrote "Down Home" and sent it to Chet. Of course Chet was knocked out by it. He called Jerry and told him he should write some more tunes. Chet named "Down Home" because Jerry hadn't put a name to it and recorded it. After Chet recorded "Down Home" Jerry's name became a hot item in Nashville. I remember when I first heard "Down Home." I was in the Army and driving back to Ft. Benning, Georgia. I pulled over to the side of the road and listened to it. I had never heard anything like it. From that recording Chet started recording different kinds of tunes, a lot of them written by Jerry or suggested by Jerry. I think Jerry and Chet did more for finger-style than anyone.

As time went by Chet told Jerry he should move to Nashville, that he would use him on sessions to help him get started. Jerry did, and you know the rest of the story. Jerry Reed was the one person that Chet was the most proud of because he had helped him and signed him to RCA.

Jerry Reed had started off just playing clubs. When he came out of Atlanta with all that soul, I, like everyone else, knew Jerry Reed was on his way to being a big star.

At the time Jerry moved to town there were a couple of local live TV shows on the air that Jerry would be on about once a week. Chet started using him on sessions so he could make a living.

Jerry turned Nashville on its ear. He was all that people in the music business wanted to talk about. He wore that little golfing hat, played his nylon string, and did those great tunes he'd worked up. Everybody went and bought a classical guitar to start playing his licks! Chet started taking Jerry out with him when he did the Chet, Floyd and Boots Festival of Music. Jerry would come out with his Baldwin and that little old golfing hat and sit on a stool and wear it out! Sometime after that Jerry had the hit "Amos Moses" and formed the band which I was lucky to be a part of with Steve Schaefer and Larrie Londin.

Chet and Jerry Reed were the best two guitar players to ever play together. Each had his own style and they played off each other. They both had great ideas and they loved each other. Jerry was Chet's son he never had. He always bragged on Jerry, telling him how great he was. Jerry, of course, denied it. It was Jerry's idea for Chet to do "Yacketey Axe" and it was Jerry's arrangement Chet used on "Music To Watch Girls By." Two geniuses at work and there I was, in the middle of all that.

One thing about Jerry, he was always bored with his own playing. When he recorded he would have a studio full of guitar players and he would be trying to show them what he wanted them to play rather than doing it himself. But no one could play it as well as he could to begin with.

Working with creative guys like Chet and Jerry you play their ideas.

Those guys are the Thomas Edison's of guitar. The rest of us play catch-up.

When I worked with Jerry and Chet, my objective was to play just what was necessary and stay out of their way. You have to learn your place, complimenting what they do and not upstage them.

"You have to learn your place." This is the essence, the core of what makes a good sideman. They may have musical skills equal to and often surpassing the main performer but to keep working as a sideman you "learned your place" and didn't stray from it. It almost sounds subservient but in itself it is a vital, valuable skill. Some felt restricted by being a sideman but Paul thrived on it.

For the most part Chet and Jerry knew what they wanted. Having followed their leads for so long it's like being married to someone for forty years. You know what they're going to say before they say it. It's the same way with Chet and Jerry. You get so you can anticipate what they'll do. People who are stylists basically have a formula. If you listened to Jerry, he has a rhythmic theme, with certain variations, that runs all the way through his tunes.

Jerry cranked out tunes like a coffee grinder. He'd get up real early in the morning and write. That's the best time, if you're a creative person, because your mind is fresh and open ... no cares from the previous day.

I never knew for sure if Jerry read music but he understood it. He could talk to a conductor and tell him what he wanted. Jerry was one of those people who could do whatever he set his head to! I have never known anyone who had the talent Jerry had. There are people who come in this world like Chet and Jerry who show the rest of us how it's done. How lucky we are to have lived when they did.

I still don't know why he hired me. I guess he thought I was better than I was. I owe Jerry a lot. Working with Jerry was the greatest thing that happened up to that point in my career because I learned so much from him. I worked with him for about four years.

The pay situation vastly improved working for Jerry. Having said that, there was another unsung champion in Paul's corner. It was his wife, Marie. She had come to Nashville to go to college when she met Paul and she ended up in the banking industry and over time did well, steadily advancing in her profession. Paul was quick to tell people if it had not been for Marie they would truly have starved. She helped keep the bills paid while Paul did what he loved. Even Chet acknowledged her at a CAAS gathering asking her to stand and telling the attendees that Paul had told him, 'If you're going to play guitar for a living, you'd better make sure that you marry a woman that will work and keep a job.' The crowd loved his remark. There's a whole lot of truth in what he said. Paul Yandell was a lucky man and he knew it.

But along with that, Jerry just paid better. Jerry paid him for the dates they worked plus he paid him a weekly salary for work in the studio. Paul would get paid more for actual show dates. Paul was forever grateful to Jerry for the new lease on his musical life and the gratitude wasn't all financial. Not by a long shot.

Jerry gave me so much and made me a better musician. We had many great times and working with him was one of the greatest things you could ever do. After I left him and went with Chet we stayed close friends and I recorded with him every now and then. Jerry was always doing something new and would have a rehearsal at a moment's notice which caused some problems with my wife.

It was just a little bone of contention from time to time. Jerry was a very spur of the moment person. Many times, Paul, Micah and I would have something planned and we'd have to cancel our plans so that Paul could meet Jerry and rehearse or do whatever it was Jerry was wanting to do. Whatever Jerry wanted to do came first. I might have complained to Paul about it a little but I also understood why he felt obligated.
— Marie Yandell

We had a lot of rehearsals. I had to learn Jerry's guitar parts. He showed me what to play on all his tunes. He just sang and played rhythm on an Ovation with a Prismatone pickup. I used a Telecaster and a Baldwin nylon string. Jerry used a Telecaster a lot so I did too.

He was in his prime. He was writing tunes, it seemed like every other day. Jerry didn't listen to other guitar players because he didn't want to be influenced by them. This is not to say he didn't like other guitarists. He liked some of the guitarist he worked with in the studio. Jerry was into himself and that was it.

He had an office in an old building on 18th Avenue. Chet loaned him a tape recorder that he set up in a studio which I tried to run. I didn't know much about all that back then. Chet had loaned him his Ampex eight-track machine. It was fun to use. Each track had a large VU meter and I learned a lot by operating it. I don't know what Jerry ever did with it.

We traveled all over the country and stayed a lot in California. It was a great time.

Jerry was, without a doubt, one of the greatest guitar players that's ever been. There might be some people who would take me to task for saying that. Jerry was a great composer. He has written some of the greatest tunes that's ever been written for the guitar. He had a different outlook on writing for the guitar.

I think a lot of his style, came from piano playing. Piano players play lot of lines with their left hand against a melody … counterpoint, things like that. I always thought maybe that was where Jerry got his ideas for a lot of those things in that style.

After I left Jerry to go with Chet he changed his band completely. He hired Paul Franklin, Grady Martin and two or three others. Jerry got into George Benson and started using a straight pick. I got onto him about it. That tune he wrote "Nervous Rag" was with a straight pick. I hated to see him doing that because he was such a great finger-picker.

He finally got it out of his system and went back to finger picking. Jerry was always searching for answers. But if he never played another lick he contributed more as a writer for the guitar than anybody I know in this generation.

Jerry is so talented not even he can realize his full powers. His mind is so creative and his hands are so coordinated there's nothing he can't do with a guitar. All that aside, however, the major thing that I admire about

Jerry is that he was the first guitarist to come along in at least ten years with a completely new style of guitar playing.

Just as you can pick out Les Paul's style of picking or Chet's style you can listen to a Jerry Reed guitar instrumental and say "That's Reed!" His claw-hammer method of picking on an amplified nylon string guitar really set him apart.

It's so complicated he has to show you because you could never figure it out listening to his records. Jerry never borrows leads from anyone. His runs come straight out of his head. His technique is very classical in one respect, because he makes tremendous use of the low bass strings for lengthy runs. In another respect it's bluegrassy, in that he got those high tinny-sounding leads from his high strings.

It was Chet who convinced Jerry to start picking a gut string guitar and, sure enough, it enhanced Jerry's individual technique. Shortly after Jerry started using a nylon string guitar Baldwin came out with their line of nylon string classical guitars amplified with a Prismatone pickup. Jerry got one and made it an extension of himself.

Jerry wasn't much for expensive guitars. When I started working with him he had an old beat up Telecaster that he recorded with. He loved the Baldwin guitars. His love affair with those Baldwin guitars started at a NAMM show in Chicago that Jerry and Chet attended. It was before I started working for either one of them.

Jerry came back with one of the Baldwin classicals at that time. It really wasn't all that good of a guitar but it had a Prismatone pickup in it. The combination of Jerry and that guitar was one of a kind. It really sent him on his way because that's when Jerry got his sound. He would tune up in a G tuning and capo up to A and do "Mule Skinner Blues" or some other 'Clawing' song. Jerry liked to tune below standard pitch. He thought it sounded great!

When he started using that guitar it made everyone crazy wanting one.

People would make him guitars but he always went back to those two old ones. Jerry had many guitars over the years and the ones he didn't like he gave them away or sold them.

He took to using his middle and ring finger rather than his index and middle finger on his right hand for a while. He said it was because a person's middle finger and ring finger are almost the same length so you don't have to reach so to speak as you do with your index finger. He felt like he could play much faster that way. He made that change a short time before he recorded "Lightning Rod." I did about four or five albums with him. I did the clawing on "Jerry's Breakdown" and "Lord Mister Ford" and others I can't remember.

I was young and playing pretty good and I was always excited when we got to the studio with the other musicians but it was a trip to record with Jerry! Jerry was the best in the studio I ever saw. He played better when the red light went on than when it was off. When I was recording with Jerry Reed most of the time it was with a group. Jerry would run the song down and you had to learn it quick. It was a lot of fun.

He would make the drummer set up in the middle of the floor, not in the drum booth. He didn't want anyone to write a number or chord chart! Everyone had to learn it. He thought everyone could play with more feeling that way. But (steel guitarist) Pete Wade always wrote a number chart.

When I was with Jerry RCA had an in-house Fender Twin Reverb amp in Studio A. The engineer would set it in a chair and Jerry would use that. He'd just plug into it that was it. I don't remember him ever going direct. He may have after I left him but I doubt it.

A lot of musicians are bothered when the red light goes on and the tape machine is rolling but Jerry played better when the Recording light was on. He wasn't afraid of anything! He was a great leader in the studio. Those two guys, Chet and Jerry, did things that will never be done again.

Chet didn't like to do over two takes on a tune. Jerry Reed was the same way. Back then Jerry Reed was writing a lot and Chet was always doing one of his tunes. The greatest thing about Jerry was he wrote tunes that others play. I don't think there will ever be anyone who can do what Jerry did. Jerry was like Chet in that respect. There will never be another.

One day Jerry called me and said 'I want to give you my Baldwin guitar. I think you would appreciate it better than anybody.' So we met for lunch and he gave me the guitar. It's the one he wrote and recorded all his instrumentals with ... "Jerry's Breakdown," "The Claw," "Amos Moses"... All his early records and TV shows were done on that guitar. Jerry's guitar is one of those guitars that comes down the pike and is a cut above the rest. I had two or three Baldwins back in the old days. Jerry's was much better than any I had, but what else could it be, belonging to Jerry and having all of those great tunes written on it. At one point he had Gene Martin, who worked at Sho-Bud, to do a cutaway on it. He did a terrible job on it, just cutting out a section of the lower upper bout.

When Jerry gave me his old Baldwin guitar. It was in pretty bad shape. The bridge and original Prismatone pickup were gone and the top was in pretty rough shape. I think Jerry might have thought it was beyond repair but me being me, I got it going. I didn't have a Prismatone pickup at that time and the top was weak where the bridge had been removed so I used a Gibson CE bridge and pickup. I would like to have put a Prismatone on it but I originally didn't think it would be good for the guitar considering its age.

Eventually I decided to go ahead and put a Prismatone pickup back on it. Mark Piper down in Spring Hill did it for me. Mark Thorton and I went and got it and I put the wiring back in it and it works fine. It sounds pretty good as is but as far as sounding like it did when Jerry had it that would be hard to do. I've let Craig Dobbins use it a couple of times at CAAS but I don't loan it out.

It looks like it did when Jerry was playing it. It brought tears to my eyes as I held it. It's sort of an icon now. I gave it back to Jerry's family in February of 2010.

We lost Jerry Reed the first of September in 2008. When Jerry died it meant that I lost two of my greatest friends in Chet and Jerry.

Jerry's Baldwin classical guitar restored by Paul. Paul kept it for a while and returned it to the Jerry Reed family after Jerry passed on. *Photo credit YFA*

What everyone needs to understand about the last seven or eight years of Jerry's life he had many health issues, some of them affected his ability to play. He did the best he could. He kept writing tunes but it was difficult for him to play them.

> Jerry's had bad trouble with his hands for about five years. It's called Essential Tremors. It's not Parkinson's disease. I think it's hereditary. His hand started doing this (shakes) … both his hands started doing this. It got so bad he couldn't drink a cup of coffee. He called about a week ago and the doctors gave him some medicine that seemed to stabilize him so he hopes he'll be able to play again.
> — Excerpt from Paul talking at a CAAS meeting.

It wasn't Jerry's fault that he couldn't play like he once could any more than it's my fault that I can't play as well as I use to. It's easy to put someone down when you don't have any compassion for them. Jerry had nothing to apologize for. Some folks may think I'm a little touchy about this but Jerry and Chet were my best friends and both of them were tremendously important in my life.

I kept Jerry's CD "Pickin'" in my car and I listened to it a lot. I think it's one of the best things he ever did. The rhythm licks are outstanding and "My Gypsy Heart" is one of his best. The sound he got was the best. It brings tears to my eyes when I listen to that CD. I loved Jerry. He was a great friend.

One more little thing … when I was with Jerry Reed, Porter's office was down the street from Jerry's on 18th. One day Porter called Jerry's office and told Jerry's office lady to tell me to come down to his office. I went down and Porter wanted me to leave Jerry and go to work with him. I told him thanks, but I was happy working with Jerry. When I got back to Jerry's office I told him about it, and Jerry and I had a good laugh.

After Paul passed, Marie Yandell made some observations about Jerry and Paul's relationship; observations that underscored Jerry's complete and absolute trust in Paul's integrity.

> When Paul worked with Jerry, Paul took care of collecting the money at the end of their performances. Many times Jerry was paid in cash and Paul would be walking around airports with wads of cash in his boots or briefcase. When they would get back to Nashville, Paul would take all of what he had collected in to Jerry's secretary and/or office

manager for them to make deposits. Jerry relied on Paul a lot. Working on his and Jerry's equipment, lining up transportation at the venues where they were performing.
— Marie Yandell

There can be no doubt that Jerry told Chet about how he relied on Paul and there can be no doubt Chet took all this into consideration when Paul applied for a job as second to Mister Guitar.

CHAPTER 7

THE BUSINESS OF RECORDING

"You went in the studio to cut four songs in three hours and you'd better have 'em!"
— Eddy Arnold

There is another factor closely related to the "play it like it is on the record" rule. It involves the creation of the actual recording of the song the public buys (that the sideman needs to copy). In many cases the touring band had little or nothing to do with the song as it was heard on the hit record.

That is because studio time is extremely valuable. In the "golden era" of recording, the mid-fifties through the eighties, the Nashville studios were pretty much set on the principle that they went in to deliver four songs in a three hour session, each song more or less three minutes long.

All the musicians showed up in the same room on the same day. No time was expended on taking weeks to micromanage each separate track on the recording. No time was allotted for endless rehearsal so the artist can "find themselves." No sir! They did their rehearsing the day before the session. They went in with the idea of getting it done as quickly and efficiently as possible.

It got to the point in most cases the singer was the only participant from the show band allowed in the recording session. The singer's band, if they had one, was seldom asked to play on the session because frankly, they usually weren't good enough or spontaneous enough to actually create the "hooks" that make the hits. When the Louvins did their recording there was no "punching in" or fixing an error by addressing just the flaw. The Louvins recordings, when mistakes were made, were done over from the beginning.

Making records like the Louvins did, using Paul on the tracks instead of a house guitarist became an exception. The Louvins, Ira in particular, were very meticulous. Ira would insist on take after take after take to get it right.

This resulted in excellent records but it was use of time that the big studios chafed at. Time is, after all, money. Eventually the studios just hired musicians who could and would deliver the finished product in less time and with greater skill.

To accomplish this, the larger labels employed loosely knit groups of "hired guns," often called "The A-Team," or something similar. These groups of musicians were known for not making mistakes. There was no waiting for them to ponder learnedly about moods. The red recording light went on and in most cases a song was delivered, usually in no more than three takes. Then it was on to the next song, which may have a totally different mood altogether. It didn't matter. The musicians didn't sit around drinking coffee and patting themselves on the back because they were so good. Someone, usually the producer, would say "Ok, that's a keeper." They would all wait for the demo to be played for the next song, making shorthand notes about the chord progression, putting the song they just finished out of their mind. It was done. Move on to the next tune on the list. "Look at the time. Let's keep things moving along, folks."

In Nashville the "loosely knit group" was called "The 'A' Team" which, over the years included:

Bass: Bob Moore, Henry Strzelecki, Junior Huskey, Floyd "Lightnin'" Chance, Joe Osborne.
Drums: Buddy Harman, Jerry Carrigan, Ferris Coursey, Larrie Londin (1970s)
Keyboards: Floyd Cramer, Hargus "Pig" Robbins, Owen Bradley
Guitar: Grady Martin, Hank Garland, Ray Edenton (also mandolin, ukulele and banjo), Harold Bradley, Paul Yandell, Pete Wade, Jerry Kennedy, Norman Blake, Jimmy Capps, Fred Carter Jr., Jimmy Colvard, Velma Smith.
Fiddle: Tommy Jackson, Johnny Gimble, Buddy Spicher, Dale Potter, Vassar Clements, Brenton Banks
Steel Guitar: Pete Drake, Jerry Byrd, Buddy Emmons, Ralph Mooney, Lloyd Green, Buck West, Shot Jackson, Maurice Anderson
Saxophone: Boots Randolph
Harmonica: Charlie McCoy, Terry McMillan.
Harp: Mary Alice Hoepfinger
Backup singers: The Jordanaires, The Anita Kerr Singers, The Hardin Trio

Don't allow yourself to get emotionally involved if the music you're playing does not agree with you. Treat the day as a necessary evil. There is music and there is a music business. It is not too often that they will overlap. Get your fill of music outside of your work.
— Tommy Tedesco
(session guitarist)

The Recording Session: Homer and Jethro

They fool around a lot.
— Guitarist George Barnes in response when asked what he thought of Nashville recording sessions compared to those in New York, Chicago, or Los Angeles.

A recording studio, from the mid-fifties onward, was a building housing what was usually one large room dedicated to recording audio media. There is usually one section closed off, the control room, which had a large window looking out into the area used by the musicians. The control room was where the tape machines and controls were manipulated by recording engineers. There was always a control board that had volume and tone controls for each microphone. Traditionally, slide switches were used instead of rotary knobs.

Before the recording renaissance of the fifties there weren't many recording studios in Nashville and none were dedicated constructions. Some, like Castle Studio, were based in hotel rooms. RCA used a facility run by a church. There were very few real recording studios.

In 1952, Owen Bradley built a small studio in his barn outside Nashville. "Bradley's Barn" started having good luck recording some local talent so he moved his operation to a large Quonset hut on 17th Avenue South in Nashville. Decca and Columbia record companies started using the facility. The seed for Nashville's "Music Row" was planted.

Steve Sholes, who had taken note of the increasing studio activity in Nashville, convinced New York to build a studio in Nashville. It was built and in operation by 1957. It was the first building in Nashville specifically constructed from the ground up to be used as a recording studio. Sholes put Chet Atkins in charge of it.

Called simply "RCA Studio," the name was changed to "Studio B" when RCA added a larger, better designed, studio close by. The smaller facility was called "Studio B," the larger one "Studio A."

Studio B was initially run by Chet Atkins where he was cast as an "in house" producer, meaning he was salaried and received no extra pay for producing artists for RCA. Later, as an acknowledgment of his talent and contribution, RCA gave him one-third ownership in a building in Nashville that generated steady rental income.

Studio B was not quite what they had hoped as far as the room ambiance was concerned. They had room resonance problems at times. Getting a good placement for the bass was tricky. Many of the problems were finally cured when engineer Bill Porter came on board in 1959. He created what were known as "Porter's Pyramids." These were pyramid shaped panels made of soundproof material suspended from the ceiling at various heights. That helped the situation immensely. He also marked ideal spots for the basses to be placed on the floor itself. They found work-arounds for the acoustic issues and Studio B gained a reputation as a "lucky" studio as hit after hit was recorded there. It was kept in high demand because of this "mojo" factor.

RCA built Studio A in 1964, very close to Studio B. Benefiting from lessons learned at Studio B, RCA built a more comprehensive and better room for recording. This studio too, became the source of record hits and remained a popular recording facility. Chet and Jerry used both studios for their own projects. Chet did most of his personal recording at home but sometimes used the resources at RCA to acquire backup tracks that he was able to add to at home using a compatible taping system.

It is interesting that the building formerly known as "Studio A" is still doing business as a recording studio. For many years, over the meters on one of the control consoles, was a strip of masking tape. On it, in what looked like a blue Sharpie pen was this testament to Chet's affect on the industry.

It read: "W.W.C.D.? What Would Chet Do?"

Studio A and Studio B are the only studios referred to in this book but Nashville soon had hundreds of studios in its greater metropolitan area, which is part of the reason Nashville became "Music City," a name that did not go over well with the city intelligentsia who would rather Nashville be known as "Athens of the South" but it's hard to argue about the money the industry brought in.

The way things were done in the so-called golden era of analog (tape) recording was to record four songs in a three-hour session. Most songs were expected to last around three minutes. Marty Robbins and his brilliant masterpiece, the near perfect, "El Paso," at four minutes and thirty eight seconds raised concerns because the suits were worried it would get little airplay due to its length. This proved not to be the case of course and it became a milestone in breaking recording limitation barriers because of its success.

In most cases the studios were booked at 10:00 am, 2:00 pm and 6:00 pm There were some exceptions and night sessions were sometimes booked. Elvis, for one, liked to do night sessions for privacy's sake and because there were fewer time constraints.

Those time frames allowed for teardown and setup of equipment although some musicians on the "A teams" had amenities. Grady Martin had an easy chair he liked to use on sessions kept in Studio B. "A" Team drummer, Buddy Harman, had a drum set permanently in place in several of the better studios.

Every recording session was different but by the same token there was sameness to them as there was in any industry requiring skilled workers. The session was usually run by the producer. He was ordered by the company to deliver the final product and usually called the shots.

Some producers were, like Chet Atkins, musicians, some were not. Every producer had his own way. Some, like Chet, had a quiet but firm way of getting the best from the singer. Some producers could be extremely demanding. Some were outright tyrants.

Most times one of the musicians was designated as session leader. He actually directed the band. Session leaders usually got paid double scale. There were engineers in the control room to monitor the board for sound levels and manipulate tape machines. Some of them became legends in their own time and a good one would often mix the session as it was recorded.

Booking a Session

What can you say about Ray Edenton? He is a sideman's sideman. After working on the road with various acts he started doing demo sessions for Acuff-Rose publishing company. Starting in 1953, he moved to full studio sessions helped by his friendship with Chet Atkins.

This put him on the ground floor of the golden age of analog country recording and part of the driving force that created the "Nashville Sound" as a long-time member of the "A-Team." He received NARAS (National Association of Recording Arts and Sciences) awards for the most valuable player for rhythm guitar for several years and, not surprisingly, is in the Musician's Hall of Fame.

So how did a sought after sideman get booked for a recording session? There may have been minor variations but here is how it was done at RCA when Chet Atkins was producer.

Ray's wife, Polly, was Chet's receptionist. She worked closely with Juanita Jones, Chet's secretary for many years. Juanita was Chet's secretary until around 1983 when she was tapped to run the Nashville ASCAP office. Polly was kind enough to provide a brief overview how session musicians were booked.

> Chet and the artist he was recording decided which musicians they wanted on the session and Juanita or I called them.
>
> Ray and the other musicians carried their date books with them at all times. In Ray's case, his sister had one at home also, as most of the secretaries called the home phones.
>
> — Polly Edenton

RCA favored the group called "The 'A' Team," using them on a steady basis. The musicians were not directly contracted to the studio but sometimes were given perks (such as paying double scale) to keep them available. Grady Martin kept a personal easy chair at Studio B and drummer Buddy Harmon kept a drumset there also for his convenience.

If the star has a band his or her band was not invited to the session. Only the singer's presence was required. The song was presented to the group usually by a demo tape or an acetate disk. The musicians made chording notes, using the "Nashville Shorthand" as the Nashville Numbering System was called, as the demo was played. There was some discussion of how the song was to be performed, beginnings and endings are suggested and a run-through was tried, adjustments, if any, made and the red "recording" light went on for the take.

Homer and Jethro made an album called "Songs My Mother Never Sang," produced by Chet Atkins, had the engineers run a little more tape at the beginning of the tracks and included them on the final LP so the listener could get an audio glimpse of how a session could sound.

On one cut ("In the Shade of the Old Apple Tree") it sounded like utter chaos. One person was being coached for a gag line in a spoken part. The Anita Kerr Singers were on board but they sounded like they were just having coffee and yakking. Chet could be heard on the talk-back mic indicating readiness in the control room. Suddenly, all activity stopped. The Anita Kerr singers sang a short chorus, an ending to the song they were about to do, probably to set mic levels, and the chatter started up again.

Then Homer turned to a guitarist, very possibly George Barnes, and said "Hey … Gimmie a wild intro in arpeggio style … on the guitar, ya' know? Big buncha chords and wind up in "E" (here Jethro added "wing-ding style"). "Just ad lib," Homer finished.

With no hesitation whatsoever, the guitarist served up a dazzlingly beautiful intro, a combination of single notes and chords that clearly impacted everyone in the room. There was a little discussion as the guitarist absently played a little flourish of chords. After Chet and Jethro had a final second or two of banter, there was a pause. Homer softly said "Take it southpaw" … and the intro, similar to, but not identical to, the warm-up, flew off the guitarist's fingers, no doubt ending up in "E" as required, sounding as if he had been working on it for days. Homer and Jethro and the Anita Kerr Singers, along with the rest of the crew, delivered the song flawlessly. After all the opening silliness it was an impressive education of what professionalism was.

The album had one cut where the singers had two false starts but again, the third one launched perfectly. On some of the cuts Chet's voice could be heard on the talk-back mic indicating readiness or in at least one instance, chanting the take number and brief data pertaining to a given cut. Sometimes all you heard was Chet saying "Rolling." Listening to that track could make a person almost see that the red "recording" light was surely on.

The guitarist in question and the bass player are unknown. They are not listed on the album sleeve. Homer was probably playing rhythm guitar. He should have been. He was unsurpassed as a rhythm guitarist. As pointed out, it was pretty certain George Barnes was a guitarist on the session. George Barnes was a jazz guitar legend but even legends have to work for a living. Barnes was actually the rhythm guitarist for Chet's first RCA session. Chet found this a little intimidating at the time. When Chet later recorded *Chet Atkins in Hollywood,* jazz great Howard Roberts was there with a music stand in front of him doing rhythm guitar honors, just another face in the Dennis Faron Orchestra.

All of the great jazzmen worked sessions if they could. On sessions like this they were sidemen. It was part of making a living as a professional. Who they were, except for being good at what they did, was unimportant at the time. The custom of listing all the sidemen by name that contributed to a song session did not start until the early seventies.

The producer tends to focus on the singer. Keep them relaxed and willing to do it one more time if he thinks it's necessary. Chet was very good at this. He would get on the talk-back and gently ask, "Do you think you can do it again, a little better?" With Eddy Arnold, Chet would invite some pretty girls to watch the session because he knew Eddie liked to sing to people, pretty women in particular. Other singers wanted no one in the room except such personnel as were absolutely required.

Nobody worried too much about the musicians, the sidemen. They wouldn't even be in the room if the producer didn't think they could deliver. Excellence was expected of them and if they didn't deliver their name would drop down a notch on the "first call" list. Some could be dropped off the list altogether.

Paul Comments on Recording

This is a series of observations Paul made about recording and studio work. Recording with Chet and Jerry is touched on elsewhere. These comments are not made pertaining to any one period of Paul's life and are no way chronological. They reflect his overview of studio work.

Recording in those earlier days, the fifties, was very different. When I recorded with the Louvins, back then, studios were different ... no effects, no reverb, nothing. All I had was a Gretsch 6120 and a Fender Pro amp with a fifteen-inch speaker in it. It was miked with an RCA-44 microphone. They were ribbon microphones. You got a big, fat, sound with them. They used that mic a lot back then.

Back then there wasn't anything like punching in to fix an error. If someone made a mistake you stopped and started over. If anyone thinks it's easy doing a live session they should try it sometime. When I was with the Louvins sometimes we would do twenty takes on tunes to get it right.

In early recording you didn't have much time to do anything like they do nowadays. I know it's hard to believe, but back then you would rehearse the day before the session then go in and do it. Back in the 1960s the engineer mixed the song as it was recorded which meant everyone had to almost play perfect. Digital recording is too clean and cold. The warmth is gone.

When I came to Nashville on a full time basis I discovered that I had to have more versatility if I planned to keep working steadily. I began to practice speed flatpicking and bluegrass lead material. Doing sessions you had to learn to play rock and roll so I had gone out and bought a bunch of blues records, Allman Brothers records. Doing contemporary stuff like the Doobie Brothers and all that. It gave me the depth I needed. After a while it sort of gets ingrained.

When you make records you try to do something different. That's the main reason you do something like double a tune; to give it a sound that calls attention to it. If I remember rightly, Jerry doubled "Lightning Rod." I don't know anybody around today that can come close to doing what

Jerry has done. You can't argue with genius. Jerry Reed has recorded some of the greatest records ever made and each one was different.

Note: "Doubling." What Jerry would do was to play his main guitar track. Then, on a separate track, he would play it again, as close to matching the first track as he could. During the mix those two tracks could be run together. The notes would all be just a little bit out of sync which gave his overall guitar sound a remarkable quality. Sometimes he would retune his guitar up or down just a little for the second track when he doubled. A "hook." Something extra to catch the listener's ear and possibly increase sales or airplay.

I didn't do studio work near as much as some of the musicians in Nashville. There are about 10% of the players here who get about 75% of the sessions and rightly so because they're good. Everybody copies who the most recorded lead man is. This can be a problem. It used to be everybody copied Grady Martin. They played Grady Martin's stuff so much they just burned it out and Grady had to leave town. He became a parody of himself.

That's the thing about studio work. It's hard to be an individual because if you've got anything going that is a little different you're not going to have it long. People will rob you blind. That's because studio work is so competitive. Whatever's selling today, man, everybody will have it tomorrow.

When you played a rhythm in a session in Nashville they always wanted you to double it ... overdub another rhythm part which really spreads the rhythm section out. So maybe you capo up a few frets and do it from there or use a "high string" guitar. There are different ways of playing rhythm. There's the open strumming kind that is used on country records, the arch top type used in jazz, and the kind I played with Chet and Jerry. A player should be good at all of them. Sometimes you use a straight pick, other times a thumb pick. You learned to adapt to what was required.

On "doubling the rhythm tracks." Some studios did this kind of thing for a specific reason. After listening to the playback on the big state of the art studio monitors, some producers also listened to the song on a system similar to a good car stereo rig.

The reasoning was that their target marketing demographic might be more inclined to hear the song in their car before they heard it at home in a more sophisticated system. Many producers felt that beefing up the rhythm tracks made for a better tone on a car radio. Some would even "double" the bass guitar line with a standard guitar to give it more clarity on a car speaker.

The people who own the record companies in Nashville are interested in making hit records. As such, guys like myself perform for commercial appeal. I don't go into a session with the goal of trying to impress all the other musicians around me. What good do I serve trying to jazz up a straight country session? I've got to work and we all have a boss to please. Sure I'm commercial, but it also means I'm a professional. I go in with the idea of plugging in the formula ... that is, giving the session producer exactly what he wants to hear. Session players do it so much that it becomes easy. A lot of songs can tend to sound alike so they can record them pretty quick. I've made a lot of records. Some were hits ... most of them were not.

When you record you have to have variety in your guitars. Different sounding guitars, to play different types of music. In a session where you would do four songs sometimes they would all be unrelated styles.

What kind of guitar did you use in a recording session? It all depended on the session. When I was doing studio work I would carry a Martin D-28, an electric guitar and amp, an effects rack, sometimes a classical guitar. I've had various Fenders. I had a Tom Holmes double cutaway that I used on some TV shows. I've had three or four Les Pauls and even a Yamaha on loan for a while. I used to have a Strat that I recorded with a lot that I had a Distortion Plus and a Dyna Comp installed in it. That was real handy because I didn't have to haul around effects all of the time. Some people ask if I gave a lot of consideration about tonal qualities when I used one or another guitar in a given situation. I never thought about it. I just used what I had.

Later in my life I got to recording a lot for a while. When I was doing a lot of session work I played rhythm a lot. I would have a guitar in hand on the average of three hours a day at least. I never had to do much limbering up because it was my everyday work. I was always ready for that. Sometimes I would do three sessions a day ... 10am, 2pm, and 6pm. When I got home I was a nervous basket case and couldn't go to sleep for hours. I finally got tired of it. I stopped doing sessions. I would record with Chet and Jerry but that was it.

Paul on Making Independent CDs

People seem to think it's an easy thing to put out a CD. In some ways it is easier than it was when Chet was recording. Nowadays a person can do a lot of it at home with the new software they have out. There are things that need attention when using other people's material along with core costs for the actual CDs

The way it works on a thing like this is for every tune played on the final work, there must be a license bought, which is $105 each. The licensing deal is how the writer of the tune or song gets paid. The publisher gets 50% and the writer gets 50%. It's a business, not a charity. When I do a CD I have to buy a license for every tune except for the ones I write. If there are twenty-five or thirty tunes on the tape then you have around $2,500 or more for that.

Then you have to have the CDs made, which, depending on how many are made, can cost $1,500 or more. This does not include studio time and mixing. So you see, someone has to pay for all that up front and take a chance they will get their money back.

About the "free" (unlicensed) videos on YouTube and other streaming sites: I understand how we all feel about seeing the videos. I enjoy them too.

But the other side of it is that licensing is the way the writer of the tune or song gets paid. What point is there in writing a tune or song and not getting paid for doing it? These kids nowadays think they should get all the music free!

Interlude 4: Product Endorsement: On and Off the Record

When people hear a musical artist it is usually through audio media, be it analog or digital. It is via radio, records or whatever currently popular hand-held device a person may be using. The music they are listening to is, in most cases, recorded in a studio.

Not surprisingly, most well known guitarists use favorite guitars when they go into a studio to record, for obvious reasons. The chosen instrument plays better or has a certain sound. The instrument the public sees them using in the ad or on the television or on the album cover may be nothing at all like the guitar they used when they recorded the music that found its way into the record buyer's home. For example...here are three famous guitarists, each with "signature" or endorsed models made by various companies.

Everyone is familiar with the ubiquitous Les Paul guitar, first released in 1952. What is interesting is that, not only did Les Paul not design that guitar; he didn't use it in any of the immensely popular Les Paul and Mary Ford recordings from the mid fifties. He and Mary did use Les Paul guitars onstage once the endorsement contracts were signed but none of their hits were recorded using

Paul's Kiser Street studio. This is Paul's home recording setup in Hendersonville, Tennessee. *Photo courtesy of Derek Rhodes*

Gibson Les Paul guitars. His most used recording guitar was one that had started out as an acoustic archtop 1942 Epiphone Broadway model that didn't even have a cutaway. Les's guitars used low impedance pickups whereas commercial guitars use high impedance pickups. He had several of these heavily modified Epiphone guitars that he called "Klunkers" that he used for his recording experiments. They were made for function, not style, some with gaping holes cut in their backs so he could more easily rearrange the wiring and pickups.

Another famous guitarist, Barney Kessel, had various signature guitars made by different companies over the years. He tended to use a Gibson 1946/47 modified ES-350 when he needed to make an album or work the studio sessions. This guitar was an electrified version of the Gibson L-7 using a "Charlie Christian" pickup.

Gibson made a Johnny Smith model guitar that became quite famous in its own way but for most of his own recording and much of his public performance he favored his D'Angelico.

On the other hand, Chet Atkins was a little different. After years of changing guitars and upgrading, he finally was able to afford what is accepted as one of the finest guitars available at the time, the D'Angelico Excel. But that was hand-made to his specifications. He didn't actually endorse a guitar until Gretsch signed him in the mid fifties.

When Chet endorsed a company, (first Gretsch and later Gibson), with very rare exceptions, the electric guitars he used to record or to play in public were his endorsed models provided to him by the company he was contracted with. When he endorsed Gretsch, it was a Gretsch guitar with his name on it that he played onstage or on television. It was a Gretsch guitar he recorded with. When he endorsed Gibson the public only saw him with Gibsons designed for him. The exceptions were an occasional classical guitar or his DelVecchio resonator guitar played for contrast or used in special music.

The period from 1949 until about 1980 (his D'Angelico/Gretsch period) was his golden era in recording. This was when Chet made what are considered his most memorable records. He played, handled and was photographed with a lot of Gretsch guitars that the company sent to him during that period. A few he kept. Most of them he gave away. During that roughly thirty-year period, Chet Atkins did his electric guitar recording using the D'Angelico and two singular Gretsch guitars. One was a certain 6120, the other a certain Country Gentleman. All three instruments will be discussed separately.

CHAPTER 8

THE GENIUS OF PAUL BIGSBY

The Groundbreaking Merle Travis Bigsby Guitar

Although this is not one of Chet or Paul's guitars this instrument deserves a look due to the impact it had on the industry. Every working guitarist in the country, including Chet Atkins and Paul Yandell, was very aware of creations of Paul Bigsby.

Paul Bigsby was a patternmaker for the Crocker motorcycle company in Southern California. He also played steel guitar, making steel guitars in his home workshop. Those steel guitars were highly prized instruments and state-of-the-art in their day. Guitarist Merle Travis, who was living in Southern California at the time, rode motorcycles so between the motorcycles and their mutual love for country music it was only a matter of time before they met.

It struck Merle one day that he wanted a guitar that had the tuning keys on one side of the peghead. He saw it as a way to make changing strings easier. Who, other than his friend Paul Bigsby, would be up for such a task? He knew Bigsby liked a challenge so he not only requested such a peghead but also challenged him to make a solid body guitar. According to legend, much drawing on napkins ensued to design the finished unit. The first guitar didn't have that now famous peghead design but the second unit did.

Bigsby had, in fact, made an earlier solid body guitar but it had a much smaller lozenge-shaped body and had the standard three-to-the-side tuning pegs. Bigsby liked Birdseye Maple when he built his steels because, being a dense hardwood, it added to the sustain of his steel guitars. He used maple wood extensively on the guitars he built also. The Travis guitar was the first guitar Bigsby made of that type that looked more like a guitar as we understand them today.

The guitar that Travis used featured the peghead design that so strongly resembles the Fender peghead featured on some of their most well-known guitars and basses. Fender never officially admitted to copying the distinctive peg-head design. When asked about the similarity, most often the response was inconclusive double-speak. Still, it is known that Merle loaned the guitar to Leo Fender for about two weeks and not long after that Leo started building the now famous Fender guitars.

Meanwhile, Bigsby's hand-made guitars gained popularity with some of the Nashville high profile guitarists. The guitars were expensive for the time, made to order and tailored for the buyer. The pickups were extremely popular as an aftermarket add-on because of their excellent tone and their heavy shielding that made them quieter than competing units.

There was also a spate of "Bigsby-Necking" of acoustic guitars where Paul Bigsby would make a neck featuring his distinctive in-line tuners and peghead and attach it to an acoustic guitar provided by the buyer. The most famous (and no doubt the first) of these was the one owned by Merle Travis, which consisted of the distinctive in-line tuning peghead attached to the body of a Martin acoustic D-28 guitar.

The first Bigsby solid body guitar, made for Merle Travis in 1948, is kept at the Country Music Hall of Fame. It is more of a chambered solid body in that it appears to be a solid instrument but it is hollowed out to some degree, no doubt for weight considerations.

Early in 2003, I played Merle Travis's solid body Bigsby at the Hall of Fame. It is the only original Bigsby I played. It was Merle's, the very first one.

It has a neck about like a Martin flattop. It really sounds great ... a big full sound. It has a strange wiring setup. It has a lot of sustain and seems to be a really short scale neck. Fred Gretsch made some remakes of the Bigsby models but they couldn't figure out how Merle's was wired up. I knew a fellow at the Country Music Hall of Fame. He let me play Merle's guitar. I took a practice amp and headphones and hooked it up.

Merle's guitar has two volume controls, one tone control and a three way switch. One volume control was for rhythm, I would guess, for while

This is the first Bigsby guitar made with the in-line tuning pegs. The design was a collaboration between Paul Bigsby and Merle Travis. Variations of this guitar were soon appearing in Nashville studios being used by the top players. All were handmade. *Photo Courtesy of Fred Gretsch Enterprises* he was singing. The other volume control was for what Merle called "take off." He could set the volume for each pickup then just switch between them. The guitar really has a lot of sustain but it isn't balanced very well. It would take some getting used to play it.

The neck is pretty good, still straight after all these years. The position markers in the neck looked to me like they are clear plastic with aluminum foil underneath. I could be wrong about that. Paul Bigsby was far, far ahead of his time. Without him the guitar business as we know it would be very different.

Bigsby's Gadget: The Bigsby True Vibrato

Chet's electric guitars all had one thing in common. It was a device that amounted to being a gadget, properly called a vibrato tailpiece. Chet probably used the device more than any other guitarist certainly in his day. That gadget made such a strong contribution to the Chet Atkins sound it deserves its own discussion.

The device, quite common today, is referred to by several names, a Vibrola, a vibrato, "whammy bar," "wiggle stick" or some other name. It is a device attached to or built into a guitar down by the bridge. They are spring-loaded units manipulated with a handle. By moving the handle many novel effects can be had but its original intent was to emulate the vibrato heard when a good vocalist sings.

One of the most popular early manifestations of this device was the Kaufman "Vib-Rola" made and distributed by the Rickenbacker guitar company. It attached to the guitar by replacing the stock tailpiece. The strings were attached to the Vib-Rola then run over the bridge and attached to the tuning keys at the peghead in the normal way The spring loaded tailpiece, moved by its handle, could be used to make a quavering trill at the end of musical phrases. For a long time it was the most effective unit of its type available.

Chet Atkins bought one of these Kaufman units in 1945 and claimed to have paid about $5 for it when it was new. He transferred it to each guitar he acquired as an upgrade during his career. It eventually ended up on his D'Angelico. Use of the device had become an ingrained part of his recorded and public sound.

When Chet signed on with Gretsch he started using the Bigsby "True Vibrato" but even then the Vib-Rola would occasionally be seen on his Gretsch *du jour* 6120 guitars. Changing out a tailpiece, which was what it amounted to, was no big deal to a seasoned guitarist who had a bench and a couple of screwdrivers. With the proper tools it could be done in less than ten minutes. In most cases it just involved three screws where the device attached to the end of the guitar.

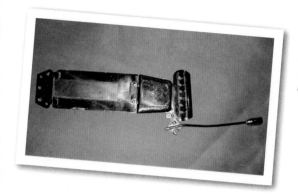

The Kaufman Vib-Rola. This is one of Paul's units. This was the most popular vibrato tailpiece available until the Bigsby was produced. *Photo courtesy of YFA*

The "Vib-Rola" vibrato unit on the D'Angelico doesn't work the same as a Bigsby. It works sideways ... if you pull it down toward the floor it lowers the pitch, if you pull it up toward the pickguard it raises the pitch. It stays in tune as well as a Bigsby but has a different sound when you work it. It's very difficult to get used to because it works sideways. You have to cup your hand in an odd way to use it. Those vibratos each have a different sound to them and I'm not sure why.

The Vib-Rola has a pin that holds the part that the strings go through. Chet told me once he always worried about the pin coming out while he was playing.

The Bigsby unit came to be made in this way. In the late forties Merle Travis was having trouble with his Kaufman Vib-Rola. Paul Bigsby, patternmaker, motorcycle engineer, steel guitar builder and player, boasted he could fix anything.

Even Bigsby couldn't get the Vib-Rola to work right so at Merle Travis' suggestion (or, some say, a dare) designed and built a vibrato unit from scratch. His unit, eventually called the Bigsby "True Vibrato," was a masterpiece of robust simplicity and design. Virtually indestructible, it could raise or lower individual notes or whole chords by almost a half tone and still return to in-tune status by intuitive manipulation of a handle/lever. The design went through developmental growing pains as any invention does. It was improved, finalized and, in 1954, the Bigsby "True Vibrato" reached a marketable form. It was released just in time for Gretsch to make it a part of the Chet Atkins line of signature guitars. It initially had a cast aluminum fixed handle and used a rubber plug in lieu of a spring in its design but soon had the more familiar swing away handle and steel spring application known the world over.

When I was a kid trying to learn to play I would listen to Chet on the Opry. At the end of his tunes he would do a wave with his vibrato. I couldn't understand how he was doing that ... It drove me nuts! I had never heard of a vibrato tailpiece. I thought Chet was bending the neck of his guitar!

Then, around 1953, the band I was playing with went to Union City, Tennessee to play on the 4th of July. Moon Mullins, who was a star on the Opry, was there. As I walked up to the stage Billy Byrd was standing there with his Bigsby guitar and it had a vibrato on it. I knew in a moment how Chet was doing that wave!

Billy gave me Bigsby's address and I ordered a vibrato for my Telecaster. I think I had one of the first vibratos in Kentucky. It was an early version. It didn't have a spring. It used a light blue piece of rubber the size of the spring that is used today.

Chet made Vibrato use a standard. Chet played with more feeling by using it. As he went down through the years he used his Bigsby less and did a finger vibrato. I think it was because he was playing the nylon string guitars more.

Chet was the only person I ever knew who could use a Bigsby and stay in tune. I never saw him put anything in the nut to lubricate it. I know he always had a bone nut which was a help. Merle Travis used a vibrato too, but not as much as Chet.

Basic Bigsby "True-Vibrato" with standard swing-away handle. *Photo courtesy of YFA*

The Bigsby "Chet handle" (sometimes referred to as a "wire handle") is an interesting story. The stationary bracket that Chet used since the 1950s is the second one Paul Bigsby made. Merle Travis got the first one. The first brackets were fixed with a large pin to the string bar and didn't attach with a set screw like they do today. Chet would just take his out of the Bigsby frame and put it in the unit on the guitar that he was using at that time. The actual handle he bent himself out of quarter inch cold rolled steel. He put the tip on it then had it chrome plated. This handle was eventually copied by the Bigsby people for those who wanted one like his.

The difference (and advantage) with those stationary brackets is they stay in the same position all the time. You don't have to keep reaching for the handle that way, but some folks find it is hard to get used to them. A swinging handle is always in the wrong position when you need it. It is much better to have it fixed like Chet and I did so you don't have to hunt for it. The original bracket Chet got and the handle he made for it is still on the '59 Gretsch Country Gentleman that he played for so long. On my original 6120 I used a turn signal arm from an Oldsmobile. I use a fixed handle on all my guitars. I have used them since the 1950s.

In February of 2009, Gretsch produced a great book about Paul Bigsby, his guitars and the vibrato tailpiece (*The Story Of Paul A. Bigsby: The Father*

Bigsby vibrato with a stationary bracket and a "Chet Handle" copied from Chet's personal unit. A swivel bracket for this handle was available but Chet, Paul, and many other finger style players preferred this version. *Photo courtesy of YFA*

Of The Modern Electric Solidbody Guitar, by Andy Babiuk). It has lots of pictures and history. In it, Les Paul was at it again. In the book Les tells how Paul Bigsby came over to his studio many times asking about how to build pickups and when Paul Bigsby built the vibrato he brought one over and implies they kept working on them until he got them worked out. Bigsby built the first one and gave it to Merle Travis. I don't think Paul Bigsby needed much help from anyone.

Chet always said Les took credit for everything.

Once they sent a Lear jet down to get Chet and me for the Merle Watson Festival. You can see it on the Rare Performances 1976–95 DVD. This was where he debuted "Young Thing." We only took our (Gibson Country Gentleman) electrics. He didn't take his nylon string guitar but he always played Young Thing on nylon strings. He had named the piece after Bill Young who was there with his family sitting behind us on the stage.

Some folks asked me what happened to Chet's guitar because on the video it looks like the Bigsby handle was bent to an extreme just before he played Young Thing.

When he went to play "Young Thing," the handle was in his way, so he turned it sideways to get it out of the way. After "Young Thing" he turned it back. You just can't see it real good on the tape. There's no way to actually bend one of those handles while it's on a guitar. It's a job to bend one when it's off the guitar.

Here's an interesting little aside about those stationary brackets used to attach the Chet handles to the Bigsby. Bill "Rip" Wilson was a dear friend of mine. He was one of the guys who worked with various acts as a sideman over the years. He played "take off guitar" as he called it. After he died (in 2010) I got to thinking about things we had done over the years. One thing that Bill should get credit for is getting Bigsby to start making the stationary bracket again. Back in the 1960s, Bill had a real nice Gretsch Country Gentleman. I borrowed it from time to time. He wanted to get one of those Chet handles so he contacted Bigsby. They told him that they did not make it any more. They had lost the casting mold for it but if he could send one to them, they would recast it and start producing it again. He did exactly that and that's how Bigsby got back to making the bracket again for the wire handle. It's a nice little story and I thought everyone would be interested in it.

Interlude 5: A Word about Sustain

"Sustain" is the ability of an instrument's notes to ring or sustain when it is played. There is a basic rule of thumb regarding sustain:

1. The denser and heavier the material that the bridge of an instrument sits on, the quieter the note will be, but the longer the sustain of the note will be.

If a note is played on a solid body guitar the note will ring for quite a long time although it will be hard to hear more than a few feet away if not plugged into an amplifier. This is because the energy from the vibration of the string tends to stay in the string and is not drained by the instrument. An extreme example of this would be to pick a note on a modern pedal steel guitar. As one wag put it, "You can pick a note on a steel guitar, go out for coffee, and it'll be ringing when you come back."

2. The lighter or thinner the material the bridge of an instrument sits on, the louder the note will be but the shorter the sustain will be.

The most extreme illustration of this principle would be to play a note on a banjo. It is loud but quickly fades. This is because that string vibration energy gets absorbed in moving the thin head of the banjo.

When guitars were first introduced into orchestras, volume, not sustain, was paramount. Orchestra leaders liked the softer tone of the guitar in the rhythm section over the strident tone of banjos. It was just a matter of getting the guitar to deliver some respectable volume.

Lloyd Loar, a designer for Gibson, came up with the idea of carving the guitar top out of a block of spruce. He carved an arch in the top using the violin design as a model. This approach produced the legendary Gibson L-5 in the 1920s.

These guitars had remarkable volume and projection. The style was copied by many builders of the day including John D'Angelico. These so-called "arch top" or "orchestral" guitars could actually be heard, in the rhythm section, if well and firmly played. With the emergence of this style of guitar construction, the relatively harsh banjo was retired from ballroom orchestras. True, the guitars lacked sustain but adding pickups and an amplifier opened new doors for the guitar. They could then be used to solo and play melodies.

Paul Bigsby, already making electric steel guitars, was making interesting inroads into the idea of electrifying a solid body instrument. Les Paul was experimenting with the solid body idea with his "Log" and aluminum-bodied experiments but it was the built-to-order Bigsby guitars that were first solid body guitars seen in Nashville studios in use by the elite recording and performing guitarists. From Bigsby custom solid bodies to Fender's plank and bolt-on neck instrument is a short leap but most electric guitars of the day still consisted of a guitar designed as an acoustic instrument that had electric pickups installed on it. Many times this installation was made by the owner of the guitar.

Chet Atkins had a lot of guitars pass through his hands over the years. Three of those guitars were of great significance to him. They were his D'Angelico Excel, a certain Gretsch 6120 and a certain Gretsch 6122 Country Gentleman.

Their significance was due to the remarkable tonal identity of his music when he used these particular instruments for recording. None are more remarkable than his D'Angelico guitar.

CHAPTER 9

THE D'ANGELICO

When he played the D'Angelico he first used a Fender tweed Deluxe amp. He used that setup on such great tunes as "Bells of St. Mary's," "Country Gentleman," "Kentucky Derby" and countless others.

Chet and his D'Angelico. This photo is as it looked when he finished installing the Bigsby pickup near the fingerboard, and a P-90 at the bridge position. Note the lever switch used as a pickup selector. Chet pulled this one from a recording console. For some reason Chet used this type instead of a toggle switch. Photo source RCA Victor LPM/LSP-2678 "Travelin'"

Chet, like many other guitarists, looked for more sustain in his guitars, starting with his first very important guitar, his D'Angelico Excel. Purchased in August of 1950 for $300, it was a very expensive guitar for the period. The Gibson L-5 (like Maybelle Carter's guitar) sold for $275 and Gibson's most expensive guitar, the Super 400, sold for $400.

Chet and I were discussing his D'Angelico once. He told me when he ordered it he asked John D'Angelico to make the neck wider at the nut. He had him space the top braces further apart because he planned to put pickups in it. He also had sound posts put in it to increase sustain. He had them under the bridge on each side about where the adjustment screws were in the bridge.

Sound Posts were simply dowels that connected the top (front) to the back of the guitar. This reduced the overall volume of the instrument by restricting the ability of the top to vibrate but it also notably increased the sustain and had some effect on cutting down annoying acoustic/electric feedback howl that sometimes happened when an electrified acoustic guitar was amplified.

The metal bridge on Chet's D'Angelico does not appear to be a common item. Frank Ford, of Gryphon Stringed Instruments, in Palo Alto, CA, thinks it is most likely an early Bigsby version. This is very possible since Chet installed a Bigsby pickup in this guitar. Getting one of Bigsby's bridges would have been an easy purchase. Bigsby guitars were becoming popular in Nashville and Chet would have seen variations on the bridges Bigsby made and used on his guitars. John D'Angelico sold his guitars with wooden bridges that wouldn't work well with a vibrato unit like the Kaufman. It would eventually need to be replaced. Chet would have favored a metal bridge for the added sustain and Bigsby was experimenting with different metal bridges at that time. The idea of the final bridge on the D'Angelico being a Bigsby is very logical.

His D'Angelico was, I think, his best sounding guitar. The tone, presence and sustain in this instrument was the greatest. Some of his finest recordings were played on it. He got it in August of 1950 paying around $300 for it. That was a lot of money for a guitar in 1950.

When Chet first got the D'Angelico he didn't have the Bigsby pickup. It's my guess that Chet put two P-90s at first in the guitar and he used it like that for awhile. When Paul Bigsby started making his electric guitars, Hank Garland and Grady Martin were using Bigsby guitars getting a great sound from them. Chet liked the sound of them so he got a Bigsby pickup to put in the neck position on his D'Angelico, leaving the P-90 in the bridge position.

The P-90 had a lot more output than the Bigsby had. Chet told me the P-90 had a great sound but he thought it wasn't too clean. The P-90 is about 7500 or 8 K ohms so it has pretty good output. Chet told me the P-90 had a different sound that he liked. I guess he wanted more highs and more output.

By today's standards, those Bigsby pickups are out of date, but because of their low output they had a smooth tone. The Bigsby pickup doesn't have a lot of highs because it is encased in aluminum. On the other hand, it is shielded well. It doesn't have a lot of the hum that is normal for a single coil pickup. The Bigsby pickup has a large wound coil in the center which the pickup screws go through. The coil has a large magnet on each side. It is potted with beeswax.

Potted with beeswax: a brief explanatory note here. Potting is when a finished pickup coil is dipped in a heated pot of melted beeswax. The wax flows into the pickup and when it cools the wax hardens, immobilizing the fine wires of the pickup coil. If this potting is not done, a high-pitched form of feedback could occur from the pickup wires themselves vibrating.

At first he didn't have a pickup switch. I think he hadn't decided how to do it. I'm sure he didn't want to cut another hole in the top of the guitar for it so he finally put it in the F hole. When Chet first hooked up both pickups he got them out of phase and did a few records that way. There's a big difference in the sound of pickups in or out of phase. When they are out of phase most of the bass or low frequencies are canceled so the tone is thin. Ray Butts told him he had them out of phase and he fixed the problem.

The switch Chet eventually used was a lever switch from a broadcast console mounted on a piece of metal. It was wired wrong and caused the guitar to go out-of-phase in the center position.

Chet didn't get a good sound on his records until he got the D'Angelico and Paul Bigsby built his pickup. Most of the time Chet used the P-90 or bridge pickup. There was no reverb. The studios in New York had limiters but that was it.

I think what Chet might have done on the D'Angelico was blend the pickups which lets you have more of the front pickup there for having more bass. Chet told me, and I found to be true, his D'Angelico had a great amount of sustain.

When Leo Fender started making a good amp Chet used a Fender Deluxe, which has about 15 watts, with the D'Angelico. The Bigsby pickups back then had low output so they matched pretty good. It was one of those things where everything matched up just right. Another factor was those tunes he did with that guitar and amp were recorded with a lot of limiting all of which made for a great sound. Nowadays we talk about what amp to use, what effect to buy etc. Back around 1951–53 there wasn't anything except tape echo and that was new.

An interesting thing about playing the D'Angelico standing up. Many photos show Chet playing the D'Angelico standing up and the guitar supported by the strap just looped over the cutaway. Mother Maybelle used her strap like that. I'm sure that's where Chet got the idea. It's simple: both ends of the strap attach to the peg at the bottom of the guitar. One part of the loop goes over the cutaway and over the back and up to your shoulder and back to the peg. Chet didn't want to put a second strap button on his D'Angelico.

The Life and Times of the D'Angelico

The Broken Neck and the Aftermath

At the Opry the dressing rooms were busy places and were on the small side. For whatever reason Chet had set his D'Angelico down for a moment. There are conflicting accounts of just how the guitar was positioned. It is said he leaned it or laid it on a chair. Other sources say it was on a cheap guitar stand. It doesn't matter because June Carter, wearing one of the country style "girl singer" dresses of the day, accidentally knocked the guitar over from where it had been propped with her flared skirt and the head of the guitar broke off when it hit the floor.

> I just broke Chester's D'Angelico guitar yesterday. He'll probably never speak to me again. I dreamed he beat me to death with the neck and what was left of the guitar. Both pieces still looked pretty good to me when I was still running.
> — June Carter Cash, "From the Heart"

June cried like a baby. A devastated Chet did what he could to comfort her.

> June told me later … that I was so personally attached to that guitar that she expected it to bleed when it broke.
> — Chet Atkins, "Me and My Guitars"

There was mention of an attempt to get the guitar repaired locally but that was unsuccessful. Finally it is known that Chet eventually sent the guitar back to John D'Angelico for a new neck and a new top some time after he signed on with Gretsch.

I've heard Chet tell about breaking the head off his D'Angelico. At the old Opry the dressing rooms were small and there were no guitar stands provided. You either had to hold your guitar or stand it up in the corner or lean it up against a chair. In 1953, he made a mistake and leaned it against a chair. June Carter caught her dress on the head of Chet's guitar and pulled it off the chair! It broke the head right behind the nut! Ruined one of the greatest sounding guitars ever made. It was never quite the same after that.

There was a grey period concerning the repair of the D'Angelico after it got broken. I know Chet tried to get it fixed locally. There was at that time a music store in Nashville by the name of Strobels. It was the best one in town. I heard Chet say once he had them try and fix his neck but it didn't work out. Back then I don't remember anyone in Nashville who could repair anything.

Over the years most references to the D'Angelico implied that the guitar stayed broken until Chet eventually sent it back to John D'Angelico to have the neck and top replaced but now it seems that was not the case.

In 2009, there was a discussion on a guitar forum (misterguitar.us, an online discussion chat site known as "The Chetboard") when one Barry Oliver, provided a couple of pictures taken in April 1954. Barry was in his teens attending a Chet Atkins Fan Club gathering in Nashville. The photos clearly show Chet playing the D'Angelico minus the toggle switch and showing no truss rod in the neck. This meant the guitar was working and had not yet been sent out for its new neck and top. The new neck that John D'Angelico put on much later had a truss rod installed. The truss rod plate can be seen in pictures of the re-necked and re-topped guitar. No truss rod cover is visible in Barry's photo. This would indicate a repair must have been done to it.

Things got a little awkward on this topic because Chet had never said anything to Paul about using the repaired D'Angelico after signing on with Gretsch in 1954. By the time Paul hired on as Chet's second the D'Angelico incident was ancient history and the guitar itself had been renecked and a new top put on it. Paul understandably had no reason to think the guitar had been repaired before it got returned to acoustic guitar status. Some tactful diplomacy allowed the topic to be discussed on the forum calmly. Nothing would be gained by bluntly saying a more or less accepted theory was wrong. Some research and Q and A came up with this logical sequence which explains what happened during that period...

As noted earlier, Chet had gotten his pickups out of phase when he first put them in. Ray Butts, who Chet didn't meet until 1954, noticed they were out of phase and "fixed it." This meant the guitar neck, broken in 1953, had to have been repaired and working in 1954.

At that time (1954) Chet was endorsing Gretsch. When I auditioned to Judge Hay, Chet loaned me his Gretsch 6121 solid body and amp, but the pictures taken in 1954, confirmed the D'Angelico was definitely usable at that time. The missing toggle switch in those pictures may be related to Ray Butts' involvement with the out of phase issue.

So what happened to the guitar itself? How did it get repaired?

Well, sometimes Chet would tell something and not tell every detail. The next time he would speak about the same subject he would add more details. Chet always told me that he "sent" or "had" D'Angelico fix his guitar. I always took this to mean when he had the new neck and top put on it. But it could have been to get just that broken neck fixed as it apparently

The D'Angelico as it looked after the neck was broken and repaired. Notice the absence of the Bigsby lever switch. Sources indicate it was left off at the recommendation of Ray Butts, who determined that Chet had the guitar improperly wired causing the pickups to be out of phase at the center switch setting. This would have produced a drop in volume and a thinner tone when both pickups were run together. *Photo courtesy of Barry Oliver*

was. He often went to New York to record. A repair like that, in competent hands, could be done in two or three days. He could have taken it with him and had John fix the neck on a New York trip.

Once again, Barry Oliver to the rescue, providing a copy of a fan club letter:

In a fan club letter dated April 6, 1953 (the year it got broken), Chet writes some odds and ends. Near the end he wrote:

Jerry Byrd and myself spent a week in New York a couple of weeks ago. We did some terrific records with Homer and Jethro, Lone Pine and Betty Cody and I did a few, I recorded some tunes for single release and an album which will be released some time this fall. Oh yes, I left my guitar up there to be repaired. So if I sound worse than usual to some of you, don't blame me. Blame this strange guitar that I am using …
— Chet Atkins
(quoted from fan club letter)

A little more research turned this up about the recording session Chet mentions:

> That would be the New York City recording sessions on March 18 and 20, 1953, featuring "Chet Atkins and his Galloping Guitar." Chet and Grady Martin on guitars, Jerry Byrd, steel guitar, C.R. Crean, bass, and Phil Kraus, drums, on the eighteenth, and Chet and Homer on guitars, Jethro, mandolin and C.R. Crean on bass on the twentieth.
>
> These songs were recorded: "Oh By Jingo," "Hello Ma Baby" and "The Bells of St. Mary's" on the eighteenth, and "Country Gentleman," "Memphis Blues," "Alice Blue Gown" and "Twelfth Street Rag" on the twentieth, some terrific records indeed. (Information from the CD collection *Chet Atkins: The Early Years 1952–1954*, JSP Records, 2007.)
> — Vidar Lund

It certainly looks like the guitar repair happened on that trip. Elsewhere Paul cites the D'Angelico as being the guitar used on "Bells of St. Mary's" and "Country Gentleman."

Eventually he did send it back, some say in the early 1960s, to John to be restored as a full acoustic. Seems to me, Chet would have been willing to let it go to John for a new top anytime after he got the original CGP. Just exactly when he sent it to John is really not important but I think it was around 1965.

John put a new top and a new neck on it. He used the original fretboard. The new neck wasn't as wide as the original. It is about like a Super 400. He used the original peg head front on the new neck. You can see where it had been broken.

Chet didn't like the pickguard John put on the re-topped guitar because it wasn't like the original. John didn't put the sound posts back in it either. He restored it as a regular arch top guitar. When Chet told John to replace the top I guess he thought he would never play it again as an electric.

Chet left it that way until the late 1990s when he decided to change it back to an electric.

When the Filter-Trons and original CGP happened I think Chet felt much more secure about using Gretsch as his main guitar. At that point he would have been making enough money that the expense of John's restoration would not be a problem. The restoration possibly came close to matching the price of the original guitar since the top carving and neck work is labor intensive. Chet was a frugal guy and would not have made the expenditure until he felt it was OK I think ... But that is just speculation. In the 1970s,

Chet had to have the binding replaced. As I remember the Gibson custom shop did it for him.

Full Circle

About 1995 or so, the phone rang and it was Chet. He said 'Paul, I want you to put my D'Angelico back the way I had it.' It thrilled me to no end but also I was afraid maybe I couldn't do it. I had to look at all the pictures of Chet playing it so I could get it right.

I went out to his house and started getting the parts together. Chet had most of the parts, but not all of them so I had to scrounge up some. For example, Chet gave me the old pickguard off of the D'Angelico. I had to have a new one made that was like the old one.

A fellow at Gibson made me a small saw blade, which I still have, to cut the holes for the pickups. I tell you when I made that first cut in the top I can't explain the feeling I had. I cut the hole for the front pickup first, then the back one. In the end it turned out great and it sounded great.

When Chet asked me to redo it I think I put the sound posts back in. As years go by I forget some things. When I finished it, it was as close to the way Chet had it as I could do it. Chet put wood dowels in it at first under the adjustment posts on the bridge as sound posts. I did the same thing when I redid it. I used ⅜-inch dowels. Chet never said what he'd used. I put the Rickenbacker Vib-Rola back on it too.

Chet had two old P-90s. I put one in but he didn't like the sound of it. I changed it to the other one he had. He said that one was the old original one he used. I wired it just like it was and used the same pickups. I don't think the neck and a new top would make that much difference because John D'Angelico did the work. I think it sounds like it used to. With the old gear and amp and Chet playing it ... that was a lot of the sound. I think Chet was thrilled to see it when I took it back to him finished. He said it was like seeing an old friend again. Chet didn't say if it sounded like it used to or not.

Chet used the D'Angelico after I restored it on the tune, "Big Foot," on the *Almost Alone* album. But I think he used his Standel when he recorded that song at that time. It didn't sound like the old tone he used to get out of the old Fender amp. One day when I went out to see Chet I played the D'Angelico through the Fender Deluxe Chet still had and it sounded great! It had that great old sound. That guitar had a great natural sustain. I wish I could have recorded with it but it didn't work out.

He always kept the D'Angelico in its case until I redid it. He then hung it on the wall in his basement studio. He'd hung two or three on the wall, the ones he used most often. Upstairs he had three or four guitars sitting around for him to play.

Redoing that D'Angelico was one of the most exciting things I have ever done. I'll always remember doing that. It was something that I'll never experience again. I think trying to get Chet's old sound is a waste of time. One thing I've learned is you can't go back. Everything has changed so much and Chet had something in the D'Angelico that no one ever had or has had since. Anyway my point is, if you are as great as he was on guitar you can do great things with what you have. His D'Angelico may have been the greatest sounding guitar ever recorded. That guitar has sustain almost like a Les Paul ... a one of a kind. That guitar is still really special ... it rings like a bell. The D'Angelico is down at the Country Music Hall of Fame now to stay forever.

I have all the wood that daddy cut out of Chet's D'Angelico when he put it back together, including the shavings. He saved every bit of it! He put it in a sandwich bag, wrote what it was on the bag and handed it to me saying, "You'll never see this again!"
— Micah Yandell

CHAPTER 10

A SPLIT PICKUP AND A SOLID TOP

"When Jimmie Webster first mentioned they should get someone like Chet Atkins to endorse their guitar Mr. Gretsch said, 'Why should I pay some hillbilly guitar player to use his name on our guitar?'"
— *Gretsch Book*, Bacon and Day, p.26

The Mid 1950s: A Period of Vast Innovation

The original prototype Gretsch stereo guitar was created for Chet Atkins in 1956 with the help of musician and electronics repairman from Cairo, Illinois, Ray Butts. Ray's ingenious split-dual-coil pickup was assembled on a prototype G6120 guitar with closed simulated "F-Hole" inlays on the body. Only one was ever produced.
— Joe Carducci
Gretsch Product Specialist

The second very important guitar in Chet's recording career was a certain 6120 "Chet Atkins" model that was specially modified.

The 6120 was the first signature hollow body guitar made for Chet when he signed on with Gretsch in 1954. The 6120 was based on the Gretsch Streamliner hollow body guitar. Chet added the idea of a metal nut (for sustain), smaller f-holes and the addition of the Bigsby True Vibrato and a simpler bridge than the elaborate Melita bridge that was on the Streamliner. The original 6120 was and still is available with an orange finish and a "G" brand on the lower bout. The 6120 was an immediate success for Gretsch (and Chet).

He used the guitar as per his endorsement contract but disliked the pickups Gretsch used. They were made by DeArmond. Today they are called "Dyna-Sonics." They were considered top of the line guitar pickups in the early fifties but Chet thought the magnets used in the pickups were too intense and kept experimenting with lessening their magnetic qualities. He once said Duane Eddy was the only person who could get a decent sound out of them.

The DeArmond pickups in those early signature Gretsch guitars had strong magnets. Chet said they were so strong they sucked the strings down. He took that back pickup out of one of the guitars seen in the color *Grand Ole Opry* videos for that reason. He also broke the magnets off under each string. Chet might have removed the bridge pickup to keep it from pulling

the strings. Chet told me he traded that guitar to a fellow in Chicago for that slot machine he had in his studio.

Chet asked the Gretsch Company to make one of his signature 6120 guitars with a closed, carved top instead of the usual press treated veneer wood. It had no f-holes. There were f-holes outlined in a light material but the top itself was sealed. In the interest of increasing sustain, Chet asked that they carve the top out of maple, a dense, heavy wood. Though still a hollow body, the top was very thick. This made the whole instrument extremely heavy but it increased the overall sustain. It was delivered to him, with stock DeArmond pickups, in 1956. When Paul refers to "the solid top guitar" it is usually this guitar he is referring to. This was only the beginning in innovations of that time. A LOT of things happened around that period of guitar history.

It was soon after receiving that special guitar when a certain amplifier builder and inventor from Cairo, Illinois, named Ray Butts, came up with an amplifier with a built in echo and brought it to Chet. Chet loved echo and would induce it in his recordings by using reel-to-reel tape decks. Now, Ray's new amplifier, the Echo-Sonic, meant he could take his echo on the road and have the effect when he was playing live. This amplifier will be discussed in more detail in a chapter dedicated to it.

Ever the tinkerer, always looking for ways to improve the sound of his instruments, he enjoyed his new friendship with Ray Butts and the two men would often meet to discuss guitars and amps and ways to make things better. One of the more important inventions their meetings caused Ray Butts to create a new pickup at Chet's request.

The guitar pickups of the day were what is called "single coil" meaning that the coil wire comprising the pickup is wound around a single bobbin. This coil is activated by a permanent magnet and the combination generates a signal when metal strings vibrate over it. This signal is amplified. That is how a pickup works. This "single coil" style of pickup tends to pick up a 60 Hz hum from any number of electrical influences in the area. Hum was always an issue when recording. Paul Bigsby, as we have seen, "potted" his pickups and shielded them heavily to try to deal with this issue. It helped but it did not eliminate the problem. Chet asked Ray Butts to see if he could come up with a solution. Ray did.

Using a technique familiar to builders of electronic transformers, Ray took two single coil pickups, wired them out of phase and the hum was gone. He made some sample variations on his single coil units small enough to fit into the popular DeArmond pickup casing and, *Voila*! Chester Atkins had access to the first operational anti-hum pickups to install on his guitar! About the same time Gibson came out with their similar but not identical "Humbucker" pickup. In one of the rare examples of corporate diplomacy and "play-nice" no lawsuit wars arose over the patent on the different but similar designs. Ray's design eventually became the famous Gretsch "Filter-Tron" pickup.

Ray and Chet then took it one step further. Chet noticed Ray had sketched out a method of splitting the pickup so three strings, bass and treble, could be separately controlled. Chet thought this was a dandy idea and had Ray make one of these pickups. He then had it installed in his new "secret weapon," the carved topped guitar in the bridge position.

The split pickup is what we would today call a "stereo" guitar but Chet never used it for stereo application.

The album *Finger-Style Guitar* used that guitar with the prototype Ray Butts pickups that eventually became Gretsch Filter-Trons. This guitar was the red/orange 6120 seen on the color *Grand Ole' Opry* style videos. It also had two separate output jacks. There is an extra switch on that guitar near the Bigsby that was used to A/B the wiring system from split to normal settings. Since that

The custom made carved top variation of 6120 made as an experimental version for Chet around 1956-57. This guitar was often referred to as the "red guitar" due to the way the Gretsch orange color would sometimes have a more reddish tint in some photographs. The Ray Butts prototype Filter Tron pickup can be clearly seen in this image. *Photo Source RCA Victor LPM-1383 Finger-Style Guitar*

pickup was in two sections, treble strings/bass strings he could put echo on the treble and leave the bass dry. He only used the split pickup mode in the studio where he could control the EQ on the board.

In 1957, I had a good friend named Jerry Smelker. He and his two brothers lived across state from where I was raised (Michigan). I would spend my summers at their home because the brothers were all musicians. I learned a lot about playing when I spent time with them. All of us were in awe of Chet.

The album *Finger-Style Guitar* came out in 1957 and the tone that album delivered really floored us. So much, in fact, that we wrote a letter to Chet asking him what he had done to his guitar to make it sound so good. Chet was good about answering fan mail. His answer? Nothing about a special guitar. Nothing about split pickups. What he said was, 'We equalized the echo a little.'

We accepted that as sufficiently high tech and "top secret" for us. Of course, we had no idea what "equalize" meant.
— Norm Van

After the Country Gentleman came out this guitar was given to Lowell Atkins, Chet's brother, who gave it back. Chet next gave it to his nephew Jimmy Atkins. (Lowell's son.) Finally it was sold at auction to a private collector.

I had an interesting talk with Jimmy Atkins in May of 2006 about that solid top 6120.

When Jimmy got married Chet gave it to him as a wedding gift. Jimmy said Chet was using that one when he was doing the Dave Garraway Show in New York when the neck got broken. Chet told me the neck got broken on the airplane so I guess baggage handlers haven't changed that much. Chet took it over to Gretsch and had a neck put on it. The new neck had the cowboy inlays replaced with plain ones. This is why different photos show that guitar with different inlays on the fingerboard.

Note: Gretsch had started eliminating the western motif on the fingerboard and the "G" brand in 1956–1957.

I never saw him use anything else on the Opry in that time period except one night he played the black 6120 with the gold sparkle inlays in the f-holes. I remember Chet playing that one on a Saturday night on the Opry. I was with the Louvin Brothers. I don't think he played it very much because that was the only time I saw it and I saw him about every Saturday night. I think that is

the guitar that Chet tried the automatic bass thing on. Ray Butts put a pickup slanted on the fingerboard as I remember. Chet gave that guitar to an engineer at RCA, Bill Porter, and as people do, it seems he sold it. It may be in the Smithsonian. Chet had the Ray Butts pickups in it in that video (playing "Dark Eyes") which is one of his greatest.

When playing on TV in those days he used stock models. My guess is the solid top wasn't on the market so Chet played other 6120s on TV to advertise and sell some guitars.

Jimmy said that guitar was so heavy that he took the pickups out once to see what made it weigh so much. He saw that the top was almost an inch thick. It was carved maple. I think if you look at the pictures of that guitar, the binding at the top is wider than the binding at the back, which tells you how thick the top was at the edges. I'm sure the top was a lot thicker in the middle. Jimmy said it weighed a ton. He didn't like to play it because of the weight factor.

About a year or so after he sold it, someone called Jimmy ... his wife thinks it was a music store somewhere ... wanting a letter about the guitar as if they were going to sell it. She thought it was a hoax and didn't tell them anything. So it looks like the guitar could be somewhere in the states.

I never got to play that sealed top red Gretsch. That is one regret I have. I never thought about it and I don't know why. Jimmy Atkins use to come to our show when we were in Atlanta while he owned it. I have talked to Jimmy many times about that guitar so I think I know almost everything about it without really playing it. I hope whoever has it is enjoying it. It would be nice to know who has it.

Chet played that solid top for many years and made many records with it. Chet's sound and the tone that he got back then was the greatest. He had the sound for about two or three years, then moved on to his '59. I think it was a combination of his guitar, the Standel amp plus the Neumann 47 mic he used. And of course, Chet himself. It's one of those things that will haunt us forever.

So What Happened to the Guitar?

According to Jimmy Atkins his uncle Chet gave his original solid top 6120 to his brother Lowell, Jimmy's father. However, Chet requested it back for some reason, kept it for awhile, and eventually gave it to Jimmy as a wedding gift.

Jimmy said Chet did that with another guitar he gave him. Chet would ask for it back, install a new device or modify it, then send it back for Jimmy to try out. At the time Jimmy was playing in various groups in Atlanta while giving lessons and working at several music stores in the area.

He said the Solid Top went back and forth between him and Chet several times. He added that Gretsch wanted Chet not to play the solid top 6120 in public because the carved solid top would cost too much to make as a production model and would be priced out of the range of most guitar players.

When the guitar got auctioned in 2002 it had been appraised at one hundred thousand dollars but went for significantly less than fifty thousand dollars.

— Ronnie Evans

CHAPTER 11

THE LEGENDARY '59

This chapter is essentially the biography of a guitar. It is about the inception, design, and creation of a certain guitar that Chet used for a long time. It was his most recorded instrument. A lot happened to it during its tenure as favored guitar.

Chet played that solid top 6120 with the prototype Butts pickups from 1956 until 1959 or thereabouts. I think what happened is that Gretsch saw he liked that model so the 6122 1958 Country Gentleman was made. It was just about the same guitar as the '59. It had a sealed top, short scale, and large peg head much like the orange solid top. He didn't care for it.

The '59: Concept

Starting roughly around 1955 and onward, Chet and Gretsch were working on expanding Chet's line of signature guitars. There was the 6120 in all its orange glory and the 6119, the "Tennessean," similar in body size to the 6120, which came out in 1958. Originally fitted with one pickup at the bridge, the Tennessean was offered as a less expensive model. It was, in fact, a stripped down 6120 minus the fingerboard pickup. It came in a cherry red finish and had a black pickguard. There was also the 6121, a smaller bodied instrument that resembled the Les Paul but had a chambered body and was not a true solid body. This instrument was also introduced in 1958 and discontinued in 1962.

Meanwhile, Gibson had released its beautiful black and gold Les Paul Custom in 1954. Jimmie Webster noticed this and thought Gretsch should offer a deluxe Chet Atkins guitar in response.

Chet was still looking to improve the sustain on his guitars. The maple top experiment sounded great but it was too heavy and building it would be too expensive to even consider as a production guitar. Instead of carving the top they could make an archtop using laminated wood like they were already doing on the 6120. Several models were tried and sent to Chet for approval and recommendations.

There were prototypes and earlier models but it was in 1959 where the 6122 Country Gentleman took its most well known single cutaway form. In the Russ Cochran book on Chet's guitars, there is a typo on page 89 where it says it's a '61. It is not. The serial number on that guitar is 31444.

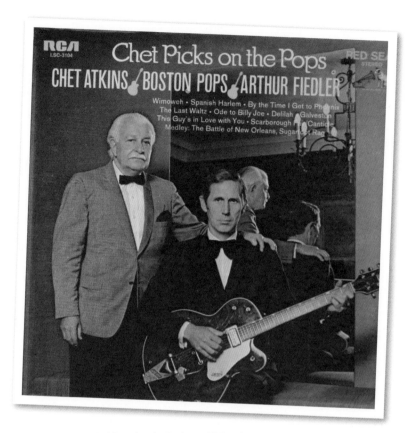

The '59. Although this guitar had a beautiful walnut wood grain finish, it often photographed very dark and featureless. Chet experimented with the switching on this guitar. Here the master volume has been replaced with a selector switch. *Photo source RCA Victor LSC-3104 Chet Atkins Picks on the Pops*

Note: Which put it squarely in the 1959 range. Serial number range: 30,000s to 34,000s = 1959.

The guitar is shown on that page is Chet's '59 in its final form. That is the guitar I used as a foundation for the Nashville Classic [*Author*: the Nashville Classic is described in detail later in chapter 20].

The Gretsch Country Gentleman doesn't have a block running down the inside of the top like Gibson has on some of their models. Chet always

wanted Gretsch to do that back then, but for some reason they didn't. When you get into using those solid blocks the guitars get heavy. The Country Gentleman has a brace under the bridge. It's about three inches across the top and bottom. I think you can get the same effect with sound posts underneath the bridge. Chet's old D'Angelico had a sound post under each side of the bridge that gave it the greatest sustain. It's hard, sometimes, to get the guitar makers to understand what works best. Most of the players who want sustain are rock and country players. I remember a lot of big people with Gretsch and Gibson were jazz players who weren't into sustain so Chet had to stay after Gretsch to change some things. I can tell you it happens with all the manufacturers. It takes someone like Les Paul, who won't stand for any bull, to get it done.

There are photos and videos available that show variations of design as they experimented with this sealed top concept in the mid-fifties. One version was a 6120 built in 1956, that appears to be very dark brown or black that has gold sparkle material cut into f-hole shape and inlaid into the top of the guitar. This is often referred to as the "Dark Eyes" guitar because it is used on a video of Chet playing that tune. Interestingly enough, according to Ed Ball, author of *Gretsch 6120: The History of a Legendary Guitar,* the actual prototype(s) for the Country Gentleman model were not walnut finished but were instead two-tone, with an ivory top and black back and sides. In 2013, Ed was able to inspect the actual guitar with the gold sparkle f-hole simulations (the "Dark Eyes" guitar) and he found that the top, while laminated, not carved, was a quarter inch thick.

As they got closer to the instrument we know as the Country Gentleman there were a few more changes applied to it. They started using what Gretsch called the "Neo-Classic" fingerboard. This used half moon shaped pearl inlays at the edge of the ebony fingerboard instead of block or dot inlays as used by other manufacturers. This was one of Jimmie Webster's better ideas.

They made the first Country Gentleman with the new fingerboard, dark walnut finish and installed black plastic inlays instead of open f-holes on the guitar. Eventually, these f-holes were painted on. They widened the body at the lower bout from sixteen to seventeen inches, added some binding on the peghead and finished it with a mahogany stain. They then topped it off with gold plated pickups and gold plated Grover "Stair Step" Super Imperial tuning keys that were the finest tuning keys available at that time. The Bigsby was not gold plated but even so the Country Gentleman was (and is) an elegant, distinguished looking guitar.

The first Country Gentleman came out in 1958 but I never saw a picture of Chet playing the '58. I don't think he cared for it. He gave the one he had to Jethro.

Actually, Chet's album *Chet Atkins in Hollywood* has a picture of that very model on the album cover. It also appears to be the guitar Chet was using in photos taken in the studio during the recording session of the *Chet Atkins in Hollywood* album.

The '59: The Zero Fret

Before the Country Gentleman came to be, Chet's signature guitars had a metal nut. Chet noticed that on Django Reinhardt's guitars, the Selmer/Maccaferri's, they inserted a fret at the spot on the fingerboard where the nut was usually placed and the normal nut was behind this extra fret. This fret became the nut and the familiar slotted nut behind that functioned strictly as a string spacing guide. Since this fret precedes the first fret this arrangement is called a "zero fret." Gretsch called it the "Action Flow Nut" in their ad copy.

The zero fret concept is a clever idea because fitting a nut can be labor intensive and tricky to do correctly, particularly on mass produced guitars. If they employ a zero fret it lessens the possibility of cutting the nut spacing slots too deep and they can also make the nut slots wide enough so the strings don't bind, a critical issue for instruments that use a Bigsby vibrato. This innovation occurred in the 1959 design.

I know it was Chet who suggested the zero fret because I heard him say so. His neck scale was changed to 25½. Gretsch made both scales the 25½ and the 24¾. Chet never liked the short scale on the original 6120. They thinned the body some, too. It may have been Jimmy Webster's idea to go to a thinner body or it might have been Chet's.

In 1959 all of the features described above fell into place, the zero fret, the bracing under the bridge, the thinner, wider body, the sealed top. Grover "Super Imperials," a top of the line brand of 16:1 fancy tuners, were added along with the new fingerboard design. Gretsch commissioned the folks at Bigsby to make a special version of their vibrato tailpiece. The basic unit normally had raised letters "Bigsby" in a black painted recess on the long part of the body/frame. That area was now polished aluminum. Instead of "Bigsby" on the unit it read "Gretsch by Bigsby" with "Bigsby" outlined in black. Near the top of the unit was a wedge shaped opening incorporated in the design which prompted guitarists to refer to the device as the "Vee cut" Bigsby.

The single cutaway Country Gentleman was complete. It became a popular, if expensive, guitar, selling for around $600 on release. It was the last version of the production Country Gentleman that included Chet's input. The later modifications such as mutes, double cutaways and such done to both the Country Gentleman and the 6120 starting in 1962 were not to his liking.

The '59: A Wide Fingerboard

Chet liked the final form of this guitar but had yet to focus on one particular instrument. This was to change. Chet had learned to like his fingerboards to be a little wider than what were put on guitars made at that time. His original D'Angelico neck had a wider than usual fingerboard on it. In the fifties he started playing a classical nylon strung guitar. Chet once remarked that the classical guitar had been featuring a wider neck for over 200 years so there had to be a reason for it.

There were a couple reasons, actually. A little more space between the strings allowed a guitarist, particularly one who used chord forms in their playing, to have cleaner fretting. They could hold their fretted notes with their left hand and their fingertips were less likely to interfere with the notes in the adjacent strings. At the right hand, the wider string spacing eased the picking of the strings by nails or fingertips that improved accuracy of execution. Chet asked Gretsch to send him a Country Gentleman with a wider neck. It is not known how many wider necked guitars he asked for and received prior to this but one day the Country Gentleman 6122, sn/31444, arrived.

Back in the 1950s I never heard anyone talk about a wide neck. No one was interested. I think Chet's '59 was probably the first mass produced model that made a wide neck available. Around 1959, as Chet was playing a classical guitar more and more, a short scale narrow neck guitar didn't quite make it anymore.

This instrument was to become legend as "The '59" as it is referred to by guitarists who obsess over such things today. It was one of the few Gretsch

The '59 RCA ad. Chester B. Atkins in his prime. The well-dressed guitarist and RCA executive in 1964 holding his most recorded guitar. *Photo source RCA ad copy*

guitars Chet actually held on to until he died. He was known for giving away guitars if for no other reason than to make room for more. He would modify this particular guitar extensively over the years, inside and out but this singular instrument was never out of his possession. Here Paul indicates what is probably the biggest reason Chet held on to this particular guitar.

He told me that he liked that one because the bass strings sustained all the way down the neck. He said it was hard to find a Gretsch that would do that.

A Note on Wide Necks

Chet had a few other Gretsch guitars with wider necks that I know of:

The double-cutaway Country Gentleman that he used around 1965–66. It had two SuperTron pickups. For a while he mounted a stationary bracket and chrome-plated Chet handle on the guitar, which was very obvious against the gold plating on the Bigsby and the rest of the guitar. There's a YouTube video of Chet playing "Yacketey Axe" on this guitar, on the Opry TV show.

There was an orange double-cut Nashville that he got about 1966. It also had two SuperTron pickups. It's pictured on the interior of the Yestergroovin LP. He later gave this guitar to Spider Rich, who wrote several tunes for Chet.

There is a brown double-cut Nashville that looks more like a Country Gentleman, from the late 1960s. Chet is holding this guitar on the cover of the Me and Jerry album. It was used for various experiments by Chet before being restored to (non-original) working condition by Paul Yandell. It's in the *Me and My Guitars* book, mislabeled as a Country Gent. (If you look closely, you can read the "Nashville" nameplate on the headstock.)

Chet's Super Chet had a very wide neck, about $1^{13}/_{16}$" or a tad more.
— Craig Dobbins

The '59 became his most recorded electric guitar. Over the years he would be photographed and seen on TV using different versions of his signature guitars largely to satisfy his contract obligations. Gretsch would send him the latest version of his instruments and he would use them or he would be photographed with them and very often just give those instruments away. But when he went into a studio to record, the '59 definitely was the instrument he used until he left Gretsch in 1980.

His favored '59 had a very nice walnut wood grain to it but photographs didn't always catch it. A lot of times in photographs or on television it had a uniform, really dark brown, sometimes almost black hue depending on how the lighting was when the photo was taken or the filters the photographer may have been using. In spite of that, the '59 was fairly easy to spot because of the double bar fingerboard pickup and the custom Bigsby handle. It just had a certain look about it.

The '59: The Pickups

The two bladed fingerboard pickup described here is now called a "Super Tron." It did not appear on production Gretsch guitars until 1964. It never appeared on single cutaway Country Gentlemans until Paul Yandell and Gretsch teamed up to create the 6122-59 debuting as the Nashville Classic in 2003.

On his '59 The front (fingerboard) pickup meters like the standard Gretsch FilterTron. The Filter-Tron pickup is 4k ohms which is the main reason it has the sound it has. It doesn't have a great amount of output compared to a Gibson humbucker. Ray Butts designed them that way. Ray was a musician and was concerned with how things sounded.

On the '59 Gretsch single cutaway Country Gentleman Chet favored for years, the fingerboard pickup is a two bladed affair instead of the standard twelve pole Filter-Tron. Ray Butts told me it was part of his original patent design. He made that one for Chet and he liked it. Chet said you got a fatter note, 'more note' with the pickup like that.

When Chet first started playing the '59 he used the front double bar pickup a lot. When I started working for him he was using both or sometimes the back pickup when he was playing live. As Chet always did, he changed down through the years.

However, the bridge pickup on the '59 is a little under 8k. Chet had Shot Jackson rewind it that way back in the 1960s. It gives a lot more output. I think the idea to have a Gretsch Filter-Tron pickup rewound to 8K came from the effect the higher output of the P-90 had on his D'Angelico.

When Chet used both pickups his guitar had more balls. He would blend the back pickup (turning it down a little). Most of the time he used both pickups. Remember, Chet always got a great tone out of anything he played so the pickups were only part of his sound.

Tone impact is impossible to accurately describe. Chet's tone on that guitar had to be heard in person to be believed. Replicating that tone was probably impossible. When Paul used that term he was describing a musical event pouring out of one man playing a special guitar. Whether it was intentional or not, a guitar will deliver more tone with the pickups wound that way even though they were not wound to read the same on a multimeter. The bridge pickup, due to its placement, tended to pick up more high overtones. This is why it was called a "treble" pickup. But it also generated less volume because the vibrating string did not traverse as much area as it did on the pickup closer to the fingerboard. The volume output of the bridge pickup was noticeably less than the fingerboard pickup. Putting a beefier pickup at the bridge boosted the signal there with the end result in both pickups having, if not equal, at least closer, audible output. Such volume imbalance would be easy to adjust usually by backing off on the bridge pickup a little.

From about 1958 onward, Gretsch dropped the tone knob and started using a two switch configuration in the upper bout of most of their electric guitars. One of the two switches in the upper bout is the pickup selector switch. The other is a tone switch. Often called the "mud switch by Gretsch fans," it was one of Jimmie Webster's ideas. He had Ray Butts design it and Gretsch incorporate in the wiring harness of most of the production Gretsch guitars. The idea behind the tone switch was to allow two shades of tone roll-off instead of using a tone control knob.

Chet could never get Gretsch to change that wiring format. Chet experimented with different things in switch applications and eventually eliminated the tone switch altogether on his '59, reinstalling a tone pot on the lower bout instead. He removed the old tone switch on his '59 and plugged the resulting hole.

The '59: Experimentation

For a long time he had a switch on the cutaway where the master volume knob usually is. I never thought to ask him about those switches in that configuration. At first I assumed the switch on the cutaway was a kill switch but I was never sure. Chet liked to experiment with things and try to get a better sound.

I finally talked to a fellow in 2004 who, back in the 1960s, had talked to Chet about his '59 Gentleman. He said Chet told him the switch he had

The '59. Another view with the selector switch in the master volume location (1964 release).
Photo source RCA Victor LPM/ LSP-2887 Best Of Chet Atkins

where the master volume goes was a pickup selector switch and that the two switches up top were tone switches for each pickup.

I think when Chet had that wiring setup the two controls down at the lower bout were: the front one was a master volume and the back one a volume control for the back pickup.

There are a couple of odd holes in the top of that guitar near the bridge. They don't seem to have any purpose and much discussion was made about what their purpose might have been. Finally, Paul explained their purpose:

Every now and then those inserts on Chet's '59 come up on the forums. At one time Dean Porter put a string pulling device on Chet's guitar. The inserts on his guitar top have threads so if Chet wanted to use the device he could put it back on his guitar. That's what the string pulling device connected to … used for mounting. When he did that Grady Martin had the same setup on his 355. Pete Wade had the same thing, too. Chet used the hand pedals on one tune, "Rhythm Guitar." He had to remove his vibrato to put them on. I have those hand pedals. They were made by Dean Porter. So that's the story of Chet and the hand pedals.

The '59: Final Touches

Chet had different Country Gentlemans. He gave away quite a few. He gave one to Jerry Reed and another to Jethro Burns. He gave away at least two more that I know of, so it's almost impossible to see a picture of Chet with a Country Gentleman and think that particular guitar was his. Maybe it is, maybe it isn't.

When he put out a new album he would often be photographed with a current model Gretsch to help the company sell guitars. When record companies did those album covers they might shoot it here in Nashville or New York or California. Gretsch would ship a guitar (a new one) for the cover.

He even used the Gretsch "Floating Sound" sustain device a couple of times when it first came out. The thing really worked but was a bitch to put strings through. I eventually put one on one of my guitars.

Still, Chet would settle on one guitar like he did the '59 Gretsch Country Gentleman he played for so many years. He recorded most of his records with that particular guitar. Later in life he wanted a phaser effect mounted in his guitar so he had me cut a hole in back of the tone and pickup volume knob, about 3" square. I put a plate over it. That was the only way to do it. He used the phaser on "Charade." There's a little micro switch between the two knobs on it. It was a phaser from an Electra guitar I had at the time. Back in the 1970s when I was with Jerry Reed I endorsed Electra guitars. They had modules that you could change out in the back of the guitar. One of those modules was a phaser. I took one of those and installed it in his '59.

He changed the brass knobs for aluminum to make the guitar lighter. Chet's '59 came to him with the standard Grover Super Imperial tuners but he didn't like them because they wouldn't stay tight. When the fat "kidney" knobs came along he change them out. The Imperials of the 1950s and 1960s did work loose as did most tuners. Later they started putting nylon washers on the shafts and that stopped that problem. I like the large buttons better because they are easier to turn.

Everyone who has a vintage Country Gentleman knows or remembers the way the bridges were fixed. The bar sat on two screws with the heads shaved and modified to have what looked like little rockers. They just balanced the bar. What that did was help keep the vibrato in tune by allowing the bridge to rock back and forth. If you didn't get them aligned properly the bridge could tip and cause problems.

When I first started with Chet I would, from time to time, do some work on his '59. Once, when I had it, I notice his bar bridge was setting on two screws with small steel balls instead of the screws with the heads shaved. That way you didn't have to be fussy about aligning them properly. I don't know when he had that done. I never did ask him about it. I do know his vibrato stayed in tune almost perfectly. He had the stock Gretsch bar bridge. He never changed it. I think he wanted to keep it original looking.

Note: About those "shaved" screws. It is likely that the screws were originally made with round heads on them like Chet had. Someone in the design department evidently thought having the balls ground flat on two sides producing the rocker look was better.

When I started working for him in 1975 he was still playing the '59 single cutaway Gretsch Country Gentleman. By then he had discarded the tone switch. He put a plug in place of the switch and put the master volume back in its original location. The other two knobs were a volume knob for the treble pickup and a tone pot. I guess we will never know all the facts about his guitars but it's for sure that his '59 Gentleman was and is one heck of a guitar which has thrilled us since he first got it.

A final note about the '59:

He played it for thirty years so what does that say? I don't think Chet liked any guitar 100%. He found them all wanting, but if anyone doesn't think his Gretsch guitars sounded better than the Gibsons just listen to his records and hear for yourself.

We never talked about it much but he knew that he had lost a lot of tone by switching guitar companies. That old '59 had the tone! I have a tape of him playing in Knoxville before I started with him. He was getting the same tone live as he got on his records. Chet could make that '59 sing!

Just because he eventually went with Gibson, I don't think Chet was sorry he endorsed Gretsch. He made money and it made him a bigger star. True, there were issues with some models but let's be honest... two of his best sounding guitars were the 55' solid top Gretsch and his '59 Country Gentleman.

I don't think anyone will ever find the tone Chet got back in the 1960s and 1970s using that '59. He created a sound that will never be again. Chet lost it when he started playing the Gibson Country Gentleman and changed his studio. One can tell most of that sound was in the way he recorded because when he played live he never quite got that same sound.

I think he knew but it was too late to do anything about it. Even later on, when Chet was recording the *Almost Alone* CD, I went out one day to play on the tune "Maybelle." We got to talking and he was upset with Gibson about something that day. He made the remark, "If they aren't careful I'll start playing my D'Angelico again." I don't think he would ever have done it and besides, I couldn't see him flying with that guitar but I was surprised to hear him say that. After he died I often thought 'Wouldn't it have been great if he had!'

I remember one time, after he went with Gibson, I said to him something about recording with the old Country Gentleman. He said he didn't want to. I think he felt it was dishonest to use it after going with Gibson. One day, years after he went with Gibson when I was playing a Gibson Country Gentleman too, I was over at his office and I said, "You know Chet that Gibson Country Gentleman doesn't have as good of tone as your old Gretsch Country Gentleman." He replied, "Well, don't tell anybody."

I used Chet's '59 on a session or two when I first started working with him. I sounded like Paul Yandell, not like Chet. Anyway it's fun to try and reach for it.

After I cleaned it in preparation for its display at the Hall of Fame I put a good coat of mini- wax on it.

The Country Gentleman is silent now. It stands in the showcase alongside Chet's Standel amp. They have done their work in Chet's hands and we are all the better for it.

CHAPTER 12

THREE ICONIC AMPLIFIERS

Amplifiers play a big part in a guitarist's tone. In his early radio days Chet and Paul both favored what would almost be considered "practice amps" by today's guitarists. Small, low wattage, Fender "Deluxe" amplifiers. They didn't need the big, loud amps favored by today's heavy metal and rock guitarists because they were on radio and the broadcast room was often small and cramped for space, sometimes only using a single microphone. Most of Chet's recordings with his D'Angelico involved a Fender Deluxe. It is uncertain exactly when it occurred but he stepped up to a Fender Pro amp probably about the same time he signed with Gretsch. Things changed a bit when he went with Gretsch in 1954. It was the mid fifties when two iconic amplifiers came into Chet's hands.

The Ray Butts "Echo-Sonic" Amplifier

The "Echo-Sonic" amplifiers were made one at a time by hand by Ray Butts in his repair shop in Cairo, Illinois. It was an amplifier that had a simple tape loop on a tray in the bottom of the cabinet. The tape continuously passed over a record and playback head so no rewinding was necessary. The preamp tubes and wiring were in the top. It had a Utah speaker.

This allowed the musician to have the distinctive sound of echo, heretofore only achievable in the studio, added to his notes onstage. Chet snapped up one of the first ones Ray built. Scotty Moore got one also and used it for the groundbreaking Sun sessions with Elvis. Chet had used this amp to record "Mister Sandman." "Sandman" got a lot of airplay and he was asked to demonstrate his playing and the unusual amplifier on Dave Garroway's popular *Today* television show in 1957. The portability of the amp allowed him to take the echo sound on the road.

It wasn't long before someone came up with a portable tape based "echo chamber" that would work with any amplifier. This allowed Chet to add echo to any amp he used on the road. In the studio he almost always used reel-to-reel tape decks for the echo effect in his increasingly elaborate home studio.

I know he used the Butts amp on some of his records back when he got it. "Mister Sandman" was one. Chet told me he didn't use it very much on records because he could hear the tape splice go by the head. It made a noisy "pop."

Chet with Echo Sonic amplifier. A fan
club meet and greet in the mid-1950s.
Since the lever switch is not in
evidence, 1954 would be correct. *Photo
courtesy of Barry Oliver*

**Generally, when you record you never used the amp reverb because
you can't do a punch in to fix a mistake so what you do is add reverb or
repeats when you mix the tune. I don't remember if you could vary the time
on the echo on the Butts amp. I think it was set at 200 ms.**

From Deke Dickerson's site:

It (the Ray Butts amp) had a built in tape echo (a tape loop built into
the bottom of the amp) with variable echo sensitivity, multiple repeats,
and footswitch. The only thing you couldn't change was the length of
the echo—it was fixed at one certain delay time.

**I bought an Echo Sonic amp from a friend who owned a music store in
Gallatin, Tennessee. I'm sorry I sold it now. When I had it I was trying to**

build my studio and I needed the money for that. Chet had one but it didn't work, so in the early 1990s, I suggested to Mark Pritcher that we get Ray Butts to reassemble Chet's amp and give it to him at the CAAS, which we did. All Ray did was put the tape machine back in it and tune it up.

Chet used it on some records but he said he could hear the tape splice and that bothered him. The week after Chet died Ray called me and ask if he could have the amp back. Chet's wife had me take it to him.

Interlude 6: The Echo Effect

The "EchoPlex" Paul refers to in this discussion was a portable unit that was first built and offered to the public in 1959. It used a tape cartridge that held about two minutes worth of tape. The tape splice could be heard as a *pop* sound as it passed over the playback head. It was a specially modified tape recorder that went between the guitar and the amplifier. The guitarist played his note that went straight through to the amp. The record head would record the note then play it back. How much time elapsed between the played note and the playback note depended on how far apart the record and playback heads were. This could be adjusted manually by having one head movable on a sliding rail. Then they could have their played back note fed into the record head again to get multiple repeats. There were balance controls that allowed adjustment of the volume between the primary note and repeated notes. It was a fun gadget, about the size of a small auto battery. Due to the noisy splice they were not often used in recording studios.

For echo ("Slap-back" is an old term that describes a tape echo effect, now it's called delay) Chet used different setups over the years. In the 1950s, Chet used a tape machine for adding echo on his recordings. On Chet's old tunes like "Chinatown" there was one repeat. They got the echo from another tape machine. It may have been one repeat was all they had.

By "tape machine" I mean a tape recorder, probably a three track. Back then he would change the speed on the capstan to vary the delay. Chet used an old Magnecord tape deck (You can see it on the cover of his *Chet Atkins At Home* album) for his echo effects. The advantage to Chet of this particular machine is that the playback and record heads could easily be moved around to make for a longer or shorter delay. He could also choose between a 7.5 and 3.75 ips tape speed. I'm sure it would have been possible, too, to vary the tape speed with a variable frequency oscillator feeding the capstan motor, as the Magnecords did have a hysteretic synchronous motor (IIRC).

He used a tape machine on really fancy echo effects like on "Snowbird" and "Unchained Melody." On the *Finger-Style* album, which is one of his best, Chet would have to have done the repeat echo with a tape machine because of the different tempo of the tunes. He recorded with the solid top 6120 on that album.

In the late 1950s, there were some tape machines sort of like an EchoPlex. I think they were called Echo-Fonic or something like that. Hank Garland had one, so did Harold Bradley. They were portable but they were about twice the size of an EchoPlex. Those machines weren't very good. Everybody kept having problems with them.

Note: Deke Dickerson has several of these units. They were called "Ecco-Fonic" and indeed they did not work well. According to Deke, they still don't.

On an up-tempo tune one repeat is best. A lot of Les Paul's tunes had one repeat. If you use more the chords will overlap and it's hard to play on the beat.

Chet used more repeats on slow tunes like "Sails." He always said a delay gives you more sustain. I remember once Chet and I went down to Florida to do the *Dinah Shore Show*. Chet decided to play "Blue Echo." We had his old grey EchoPlex and I was going to operate it. When he started playing the tune on the show he turned to me and said "Speed it up." Well, I made a mistake and slid the delay adjust the wrong way. Chet, being Chet, just slowed down and played it anyway.

Back in the 1970s, he used an EchoPlex. Then Lexicon came out with a delay unit. He started using a Lexicon PCM 42. That was about it for special effects that he carried onstage for a long time. Then I ran up on the Lexicon JamMan and he used it too.

I saw that JamMan in a music store and I bought it. I kept it for about a week then I took it over and gave it to Chet. He took it home and in a few days he had all that stuff worked out with it. I sold it to him and it became a part of the show. Chet was so good at things like that. He could see what you could do with something like that whereas I did not.

When I use that kind of effect I set the time where it repeats like an eight note (one AND) with the AND being the repeat. In later years on

tunes like "Sails" Chet would use four or five repeats up around 800 ms if I remember correctly. He would have the volume of the repeat very soft. For "Snowbird" he used a tape machine for the echo, not an EchoPlex or any kind of delay.

The analog (tape based) machines are rare today. Most effects pedal makers offer solid state devices that digitally replicate the tape machines pretty well. And they do it without the annoying *pop* of the splice passing over the heads. There are some holdouts, of course, who hang on to the old analog machines claiming a better more "authentic" sound. While still on the topic of echo units, here is a little side story on Chet's EchoPlex experience.

When I started working for Chet in 1975 he was using the first model EchoPlex, a grey one. They were so heavy! We hand carried it all of the time on the road. Then they came out with the black model with no tubes and it was pounds lighter.

At that time the company that was making them was running an ad stating Chet used an EchoPlex on his recording of "Snowbird" which he wasn't. Chet got a little upset about that and had his secretary write them a letter and inform them he felt that they owed him one of the new models; that he didn't use it on "Snowbird" and to stop running the ad! Which they did.

Chet didn't use an EchoPlex but very little in the studio. The only time I remember was on the *Chester and Lester* album and that was the grey one. I don't know where Chet's EchoPlex's went. When the Lexicon 41/42's came out he stopped using EchoPlex.

From discussion of Echo a segue back to discussion of amps and Chet's most defining amplifier.

The Standel

Bob Crooks, a designer and technician in Southern California, started making an unusually fine amplifier, the Standel, on special order in the early fifties. They were expensive amps for their day, costing quite a bit more than competing units but they were well known because they could be played loud but would not distort from being overdriven—a very clean sounding amp. They were one of the first amps to feature JBL D-130 15" speakers made by the Jim Lansing manufacturing company. These speakers delivered amazing clarity. The amps themselves were remarkably quiet running. They

Chet with his '59 Country Gentleman and Standel amplifier. The occasion is the recording of "Boo Boo Stick Beat" in Studio B. Here Chet tells his visiting fan club how he wants them to contribute to the recording by supplying the hand clapping chorus in the song. *Photo courtesy of Ron Vejvoda*

found particular favor with steel guitarists who required clear, well-defined notes with the ability to be heard in a band situation. Bob Crooks' Standel amps fit the bill.

Chet acquired one and it became his prized recording amplifier at home. In its day it was priced new at $295. Expensive for an amplifier in 1954.

Chet's Standel (25L15, #10200 built 4-24-54) was made for Jimmy Day, a steel player. Chet traded him a Fender Pro for it. It is stock ... still the same original JBL fifteen-inch speaker in it. He has used this amp on 98% of his records both for his electric and electric nylon string guitars.

Chet heard Jimmy Day using one of these and bought it from him. Chet couldn't buy it directly from Crooks because of his endorsement contract with Gretsch. He obtained the amp in 1954 and used it almost exclusively for recording in his home studio, seldom taking it out of the house.

But Did Chet Actually Get the Amp in 1954?

Jimmy Day ordered and bought the amp that eventually came into Chet's hands. According to Standel records it was indeed *built* in 1954. When Jimmy Day's amp was made Chet was enamored with the Ray Butts Echo-Sonic (also made in 1954). With that new acquisition he didn't "need" a Standel because he would have felt that he already had an amplifier and a fancy, almost one of a kind one to boot. When he wasn't using the Echo-Sonic he used a Fender Pro or a Fender Deluxe, both popular working amps of the period.

It stands to reason that Jimmy would have used the amp for a period of time after he purchased it and before Chet actually acquired it. Some research was done visiting various chat boards and here is a reasonable speculation of the circumstances of Chet acquiring the Standel.

According to steelers, Jimmy was still using the amp in 1956 when Ray Price recorded "Crazy Arms" with Jimmy Day on steel. From 1954 to 1956, the Gannaway Company made some color movies, now available on DVD, that had a very Grand Ole Opry feel to them. There are scenes in the movies showing Jimmy still using the amp. You had to look closely, but it's there. Chet could be seen using a Standel on some of the clips also.

Around the same time period Jimmy Day swapped his four neck Wright Custom pedal steel, (weighing in at ninety pounds with case) to Curley Chalker because he was tired of carrying the weight around. Maybe he felt the same way about the amp. After all, it weighs almost twice as much as the popular Fender Pro amp in use by Chet and others at the time. Based on this evidence, and since Jimmy was actively using the amp in the studio in 1956, the earliest Chet could have acquired the amp would have been 1956.

Everybody walked away happy and when the original 6122-59 came into Chet's hands the '59 combined with the Standel amp was a perfect match.

Chet's favorite amp was his Standel. Whenever I recorded at his house I used it too. Chet's Standel has a great sound. It sounded better than the ones I had. Chet used an RCA 44 ribbon mic on his Standel when he recorded. Those amps were a loud 25 watts. There were only around fifty of that model made. Chet told me many times how he thought his Standel was the best amp he ever had. They had some different amps at Studio A for people to use and people were always giving Chet an amp in hopes he would use them.

After Chet died Chet's wife Leona gave his Standel to me. I had Chet's amp for about two years and used it on my CDs. It was so quiet I had to turn the volume up full and put my head down in front of it to tell if it was on. It was one of the greatest. My own old Standel is the same way. I had to replace the filter cap in the power supply but it's the quietest amp I've ever had.

My Standel amp was made in 1955 and is #39. I bought it from a friend of mine, a steel player named Bobby Seymour. It was in terrible shape. I think it had been stored in a barn or at least it looked it. The covering

was in shreds. Micah, my son, suggested I recover it in blue which I did. It has had the audio transformer replaced. Whoever did it did a great job. I went through the power supply and replaced a lot of old wires that needed it. The speaker is a JBL D 130 and it is very quiet.

When I got it Chet and I knew Bob Crooks so I talked to him about once a month. One thing led to another. I asked Chet if I could send the preamp out of his Standel and mine to Bob Crooks to see if they were the same. Bob had told me he had made two versions back then, a steel guitar EQ and a lead guitar EQ. I sent them to him and he went though mine and made it just like Chet's. It may have been the same I don't remember.

Anyway, my amp is a sweet sounding amp. It's just what a Standel should sound like. I had two of those Standels. I gave one to my son Micah, and I sold mine to John Lewis a friend in North Carolina because I don't play much any more. I have too many amps sitting around. I had one of the newer Standels for a while and I think they are a better amp than the old ones ... beautiful tone.

I had the pleasure of recording on two albums with Hank Thompson. He was a fine gentleman. [Note: Hank at one time had purchased Standel amps for use of everyone in his band.] I asked Hank once what he did with all the Standel amps that he had owned. He said he had one or two of them out in the barn but he didn't remember what happened to the others.

The Standel amp isn't very durable for roadwork. The way it's made the power supply is in the bottom with the pre-amp in the top. If the airlines can destroy a suitcase, think what they could do to an old amp like that! When a person has an old piece of equipment you have to give it special care. Chet's amp has served him well all these years and is still going strong.

Chet's amp has the original JBL in it and he had it re-coned in the 1960s but I found out after I had the amp that the fellow who did it put the wrong basket in it and he also had put a paper cover on the center. I had Woody Woodall put the correct one (with the aluminum dome) in and it now sounds like it was suppose to. It has bottom end to it. I think Chet would have liked it, as it sounds like it did when he first got it. It's now in the Hall of Fame. It's where it belongs.

Speaking of the Hall of Fame display, one of his guitars had to go to make room for his amp. I thought all of his old guitars were too important to not stay and the nylon had to stay because that guitar was Chet in the last part of his playing life so that left the Gibson Country Gentleman. His Standel replaced it.

By the way, be careful about buying those Standel amps. The first ones were great but the later ones were bad amps; the transistor ones, in particular, were awful. Also nobody can work on them since some of them had the circuits epoxied, so beware.

Interlude 7: Another Kind of Sideman

Luther Perkins

The man to whom the words "Boom-Chick" truly applies. The sound Luther Perkins made wasn't new. Hank Williams used in the studio and onstage and in fact Chet often played the "boom-chick" on Hank's records. But it was Luther Perkins who mesmerized the musical world with it.

The sound is created by lightly muting the three lowest-pitched strings on the guitar with the edge of the palm of the right hand. Some called it "muting." Some called it "damping." Mose Rager called it "choking." The sound was played by alternating the two lowest strings of the chord on the downbeat and the third or fourth string on the up beat. Add melody and harmony notes to that pattern by using the first and second fingers it becomes what is called Travis Style … thumb-style … maybe finger-style.

When Johnny Cash was onstage and Luther played it, it was often called "boom-chick" because that describes how it sounded and was about all Luther played. Luther did not add melody or harmony to the steady four/four beat of the "boom-chick."

Would there be Johnny Cash if there hadn't been a Luther Perkins? Johnny Cash, at least the young Johnny Cash could be said to owe his career to the dry, spare twang of the "boom-chick" contrasting with the foundation-rattling low notes of his vocals. That said, there is no doubt whatsoever that the simplistic guitar style Luther played was groundbreaking in its day and had a far reaching effect in country music.

Luther was essentially a sideman … a rhythm player more than a lead player. It would be a stretch to call him a lead player although he made occasional forays there. There are no Luther Perkins solo albums in existence because he never made any. He is one of the few sidemen to fall into the category of "everybody copies him but no one sounds quite like him." Luther's playing is a great example of "it's in the hands" and "touch" that such a simple sounding guitar technique is so difficult to accurately mimic.

He is also one of the rare sidemen in that people actually sought to learn his name. He was comfortable playing with John. He had no desire to throw in with anyone else even when Cash went on some of his harrowing drug toots. Totally deadpan in delivery, urban legend claims learning a new song was sometimes taxing for Luther.

Interestingly, Luther took up knitting to pass the wearisome hours on the road going from one venue to the next. He got quite good at it, they say and Luther's hand knitted items were treasured. Another musician of whom it can be said "There's nobody quite like him."

Someone asked Micah Yandell if his daddy had ever said anything about Luther's playing. Micah replied, "No sir, I never heard him say much except that he admired him."

The Other Sideman ... the "Girl Singer"

Kitty Wells was not a "Girl Singer." Kitty Wells was a star and to many she was the "Queen of Country Music." At least it was so back in the fifties and early sixties. Jean Sheppard wasn't a girl singer either. Tammy Wynette wasn't a girl singer. Currently Shania Twain is not a girl singer. Certainly not Dolly Parton, although for a while she was the girl singer in the Porter Wagoner package. Reba McEntire, Carrie Underwood ... no, the ladies on this list, females though they be, are not girl singers.

They are bona-fide stars either as big bucks headliners or able to command decent billing on any musical advertisement. Some of them are country superstars in their own right.

The "girl singer" was someone a star or a touring show would hire the same way they hired a guitar player or a bass player. All that was required was that she be female, preferably pretty (but not too sexy) and be able to sing. And while she should be able to sing well, she should not be too much of a distraction from the star, the headliner on the bill.

There was a certain finger style guitarist, Bob Slater, in Canada who got a letter from Hal "Lone Pine" Breau, Lenny Breau's father, offering him a job. The letter is dated 1968, long after Lenny's parents had split up and Lenny had moved on to jazz full time.

In the letter, Lone Pine appeared to be finishing a few commitments apparently working as a duo with his then-wife Jeannie. Their agent wants a change in the lineup:

After that he wants us to go to four people. So we would like to go to four and hire you and a girl singer. Would you know of a girl singer, one that can do rock and roll and pop. A young girl. She doesn't have to play an instrument. Do you know of anyone that would be interested.

We will write to you when we get to the next job.

ps. The pay will be $110 a week and room for the girl. If she plays an instrument she'll get $125+ room.

The business end of this is that the more unknown the lass is, the better, because those starting out generally do what they're told and aren't as demanding or high maintenance as a more famous, well known vocalist might be.

It may be a little harder to find a girl singer than a good guitarist or bass player, however, like the unknown but talented guitarist or bass player, the more unknown she is, the less she needs to be paid. *Always* a factor when considering new hires.

CHAPTER 13

THEN CAME CHET: SECONDING TO MISTER GUITAR

Sometimes, after we came off of the stage and went into Chet's dressing room, I would say "You played great tonight Chet" He would answer, "Fooled them again."

It came about this way. As pointed out earlier in this writing, work with Jerry Reed started to drop off when Jerry went into making movies. Paul still did studio gigs having achieved "A" level status.

Chet and I stayed friends down through the years and when I was working with Jerry Reed, Chet produced Jerry's records. Sometimes I would record with Chet as a sideman.

But studio work could be spotty, "on call" work so he decided to ask Chet for a job. By this time Chet knew him really well having produced so many of Jerry Reed's sessions and seeing Paul in action. Jerry had no doubt praised Paul when he spoke to Chet. Paul told it short and sweet. A terse description of something that would have a major effect on his life.

I was working with Jerry Reed for about four years. Then Jerry started doing movies and had really cut back on the music end, working very little. It got so he really didn't need a band. I went over to Chet's office and asked him if he needed a guitar player. He said he might but he would need to ask Jerry if he minded him hiring me. He called Jerry and Jerry said "Not at all." So that's how I got the job with Chet.

Chet Atkins

An often told story about Chet Atkins:

> Chet had a new guitar and he was playing it in the studio. Folks kept approaching him to tell him how great that new guitar sounded. After a dozen people told him, "Man that guitar sounds great!" He stood up, walked over to a chair and set the guitar down in it. Then he asked everyone, "And how does it sound now?"

We will never see the like of his talent in one man. When you talked about who was the greatest guitar player, Chet's name was never mentioned, because you just took him and put him up there, and then you argued about the rest of them.
— Eddy Arnold
(speaking at Chet's funeral)

The legendary "Mister Guitar," was one of the architects of media-dubbed "Nashville Sound." Chet Atkins, as a producer and a musician, had an effect on Nashville and the recording industry that is still felt today. Chet was, after all, one of the finest if not the finest guitarists ever produced in the United States. The roster of talent on both sides of the microphone that he helped seems endless. He guided singers and musicians and trained recording engineers and producers in the nuance of musical craft. When he reached his pinnacle it was hard to imagine that he came from a childhood of harsh, grinding poverty.

Starting out as a teenage fiddler he soon became known as an innovative guitarist. A guitarist whose records would not sell and one who couldn't keep a job because his playing never quite fit in the music formats of the many radio stations he worked for.

Too country for some, too modern for others. In those days whether a guitarist like Chet stayed at a station depended on how much mail he got at the station. Guitar players who don't sing don't get a lot of mail. This is a fancy way of saying he got fired a lot.

Radio itself didn't pay well unless they were a really big name act. But radio was a way to get bookings for the road. Chet would sometimes get booked as part of a show but never as the star soloist he later became. It got so Chet was looking into doing side work as a piano tuner to be able to support his wife and child.

Enter the Carter Family

Daddy said he was going to be the best guitarist ever, and that we should hire him.
— June Carter
(talking about when the Carter Family hired Chet)

While working the Midday Merry Go Round at WNOX in Knoxville, Tennessee, he came to know the immensely popular Carter family. At the time they were Maybelle Carter and her three daughters, June, Anita, and Helen. Eck Carter, Maybelle's husband, was their manager and advisor. Eck listened to the young guitarist and saw something there. The Carters had a family meeting and prayer session and hired him.

Rather than just hire him as a sideman they cut him in as a full partner and from that day his star started to rise. He no longer had to struggle on *per diem* scale income in a package show or play for scale at a radio station.

The story of his rise from association with the Carters to association with Steve Sholes and RCA Victor and Nashville has been chronicled in book, TV special, and song for many years. His impact on the recording industry and guitaring will be felt for many years to come.

As his fame grew he achieved celebrity status and could book tours under his own name.

On the road Chet, like other acts, used sidemen, at least a bass player, sometimes a rhythm player. In later years, if the venue could afford it, he would hire a string ensemble, keyboard player, drummer, etc., again depending on what the venue required. He even did some tours with sax player Boots Randolph and pianist Floyd Cramer in an ensemble called The Festival Of Music around 1975, an association that ran for seven or eight years. Chet became famous. He could pretty well do what he wanted on the road.

After the Festival of Music finished its run Chet became more of a soloist—a guitarist who got bookings on the strength of his own name like top classical and flamenco guitarists did. He skirted the "star" presentation and effect. His shows were more subdued than the standard star tours with all the glitter and pyrotechnics. If they booked Chet they booked a guitar player. That's exactly what they got.

The musicians he hired to travel with him changed over the years. They were always top flight musicians but the number and makeup of his road band would change from time to time. Some of his public might even have noticed a slight change in his musical entourage starting in 1975.

The New Guy

In 1975, Chet had a new hire. Paul Yandell was to be his sideman, his guitar accompanist ... his second. This quiet, unassuming man became a fixture in Chet's stage performances. No matter what other musicians comprised the band in concerts or on TV Paul was always there. He would sit, seldom taking his eyes off his leader and mentor, never doing anything to attract attention to himself. He played the rhythms required, some of them hauntingly beautiful in their own right, and when he was not required to play, sat statue still so as not to detract from Chet's music. This calm, bespectacled guitarist was to become Chet's right-hand man and friend for over twenty-five years. Chet was fifty-one. Paul was forty.

> Chet changed things when he hired Paul. It was like he found a missing ingredient he'd been searching for. Before Paul, Chet never had a touring backup guitarist. He had guests from time to time, and once or twice

he would take a Nashville session guitarist with him to play rhythm, on special dates, but nobody permanent. Paul became an intrinsic part of the show. If you study Chet's stage shows before and after Paul, you'll see how different they were.

— Pat Kirtley

Life with Chet

Almost every other morning Chet would call me about 7:30 am and say, "What are you working on now?" Sometimes I would be doing something, sometimes not. I really miss those early morning calls. Repair and customization wasn't expected of me on Chet's part. I've always been a person who likes to fix things and I have always tried to think of ways to make things better. Chet was a lot like that too so we had that in common. Chet and I were always doing things to our amps or our guitars. We both were friends to Ray Butts. We used to go over to his house to talk about things. It was another part of Chet and me getting along and having fun.

When I first started working with Chet, coming from playing with Jerry Reed, it was completely different. I had to really be on the ball! Back then I had a quick memory. With Jerry, I had to play hard ... dig in and play with drive. With Chet it was just the opposite. Every now and then Chet would caution me to not rush or drag when we were playing. I made a great effort to learn not to do that. I practiced with a click track for many hours at different tempos. It helped me in the studio too. It's one thing to play a tune; it can be quite another thing to play it with a steady tempo.

When Chet and I played together I would listen to him and follow him. I tried to play in the groove ... play what he wanted and stay out of his way. I tried to play correct chords to what he was playing. Sometimes I would do harmony to what he was playing. It wasn't an easy job. It was always a challenge and I had to stay on my toes. You have to play to compliment Chet's playing so I really hold back when I play with him ... not that I can play all that much. He's doing so much that it's hard, sometimes, to find something that fits in.

He doesn't really need anybody when he's playing. In fact he probably sounds better by himself than he does in a group because then he can improvise, so I had to learn what he wanted me to do. I had to be real sensitive to how loud I'm playing because, after all, people come to hear him play, they don't come to hear Paul Yandell. When I work with other groups I blast out, but it's completely different with Chet.

When I'd go out with Chet he wouldn't want me to play like him because that would have been silly. He wanted something completely different. He wanted me to play something that sounded contemporary, you know, bluesy, string bending stuff. Chet's philosophy was he wanted little surprises on down through his records. He wanted contrast. If somebody else played on the record he wanted it to be completely different from what he was doing. That makes it interesting. That's why he cut records and if you keep that in mind you can see what he did. I wasn't foolish enough to try and play anything like him.

Chet was always looking for new stuff and trying to do something different. That's just the way he was. Every two or three weeks he'd come up with something new and want to do it onstage. He wanted to keep changing the show because he'd play a date somewhere and maybe play the same place again sometime. He might not come back there for a year but when he did come back, he wanted to be doing something new.

Chet Atkins no doubt had a pretty good idea what he was getting when he hired Paul. Chet lost no time getting him focused on the first show on his schedule—a date with a symphony no less.

At the time I got hired into his band Chet was playing a regular classical guitar on a microphone. I didn't have a classical to complement his guitar so Chet gave me an Alvarez Yairi Classic that the Mr. Yairi himself had made and sent to him. I still have it. It is one of the best recording classicals I've ever played. I used it later on "Mostly Mozart."

About a week after all this Chet had a date in Jackson, Mississippi, with the Jackson Symphony. I had never played with a symphony before! I had to learn all of Chet tunes he'd arranged with the symphony as well as the tunes that he and I would do in our regular show. I had about a week to do it! Chet and I rehearsed at his office two or three times the week before. I didn't have a tux either, so Chet rented me one. It was the first time I had ever worn one. We flew down to Jackson and had a rehearsal with the symphony. It was really thrilling to sit in front of them and listen to all those strings. The best I remember I did OK. I'm sure I was nervous and probably rushed the tempo some.

After the show they had a reception. I thought that night I had attained something that I had only dreamed about for years. It was a great thrill for me. The only thing equal to it was the first time I played the Grand Ole Opry.

As the years went by Chet played many great places and I was lucky enough to be with him. I never got over the thrill of going out on the stage with him. Working with Chet lasted for twenty-five years. We traveled all over the world. He was like a second father to me. He taught me many things about the guitar and about life. No one ever had a better job or worked for a nicer, more caring person, as Chet. He always treated me with respect and kindness. I know that I am a better musician and a better human being for working with him, Chet showed me that dreams do come true.

I can tell you, if I had it to do over again, I would do it exactly the same. Working for Chet was a once in a lifetime dream but I have to give credit to Jerry Reed too, because if I had not worked for Jerry and learned so much from him, I don't think I would have been qualified to work for Chet.

My philosophy playing with Chet was to just not get in his way. I stole everything I could from him. I think that's part of why he hired me because I played real close to his style so we sorta jelled together.

So that was the start of it. There was some shopping to do! Guitars to be bought!

I played a Fender for years when I was with Jerry Reed but when I started with Chet and got on stage with him the Fender didn't cut it. I had to have something that had some tone to it to compete with Chet. The Gibson Country Gentleman had come out so I started using that. Chet was using his '59 when I started working with him in 1975. His sound on stage was always the very best. I had that Peavey T-60 that I had rigged up. Chet sounded so much better than me that it really bothered me. When he switched to the Gibson Country Gentleman his tone was good but never what the Gretsch Country Gentleman was. I think Chet wanted the electric classical more than he cared about the electrics. He saw a greater future for it in his career.

No one can ever get the sound that Chet got on his records of the fifties, sixties and seventies. He had one of the greatest ears for sound. On the stage he always got a great sound. I use to stand and listen to him ... almost forget what I was doing. I think it was in his soul and when he

played it came forth ... there was never one like him and there will never be another.

It didn't take long for a close bond to form between Paul and Chet. Both men were avid guitar tinkerers looking for ways to get an edge, something different out of their instruments. Chet had ideas as to what a guitar should sound like. He was constantly tinkering and modifying guitars in his possession, looking for the instrument to produce that tone, the sounds he heard in his head. In that respect he and Paul were alike.

They would meet at Chet's house or his office and play guitars sometimes exchanging ideas or sometimes Chet would run a new song past Paul. That's what guitarists do, particularly if they're friends.

The times I enjoyed the most were when Chet and I sat on his back porch and played together. I could never get used to where I was at that moment. It was pretty good for a guy coming from a small farm in west Kentucky dreaming of a life in Nashville.

As I would sit quietly and listen to them play (sometimes practicing what they were going to perform, sometimes just jamming) they had amazing nonverbal communication. As they played, they gave each other knowing looks, they made facial expressions that seemed to say they were lifted to a new place by the music, and sometimes they would just smile as though the synergy of performing together gave them great joy. Once in awhile, Chet would look my way. He later explained that he was checking to see if I noticed a mistake, (of course I didn't). Paul would play right through it, or sometimes they both stopped, and without a word, they'd start playing again. No need to say where they were going to pick it up. They just started up again right on target. You see, there really is no way for me to describe that connection they had. They were just so comfortable, and familiar with what they were doing, and so close, that they seemed to know what the other was thinking. It was as if they could escape together into the music.
— Jan Hite

When Chet would write a new tune he would call me and have me come over to his office and play it for me. He said it meant something to play it for someone before he did it on stage. When it came to working out arrangements and new tunes as I remember it didn't take too long. Chet was really fast at working up a new tune. He always had trouble sleeping.

He would wake up sometimes at four a.m. and practice. Chet had such a command of his music and his instrument it didn't take long to work up new stuff. Whenever I would record with him he knew his part when we went to do it. When he was young, his energy made for arrangements that were the greatest. They are still being played over fifty years later.

"They are still being played over fifty years later." Aside from superb guitar playing, why does the music of Chet Atkins still command respect and dispense enjoyment? It is because Chet Atkins was a skilled arranger.

The American Federation of Musicians defines arranging as: "the art of preparing and adapting an already written composition for presentation in other than its original form. An arrangement may include reharmonization, paraphrasing, and/or development of a composition, so that it fully represents the melodic, harmonic, and rhythmic structure."

The process of arranging a musical piece is something that seldom crosses the mind of a consumer buying records or attending shows. When non-professional, even some professional guitarists post on YouTube or produce their own CDs it is the arranging that can make a piece memorable or makes it instantly forgettable. It is one of the most taken for granted factors in preparing music for selling to the public. Chet Atkins called it "Making my playing interesting for three minutes."

A mediocre ending, lackluster "reharmonization" or paraphrasing can doom a production or musical product. Chet released roughly eighty albums in his career so it could be fairly said that he was a good arranger according to the definition used here. The AFM calls arranging an art and in so doing they are correct. Another word might be "taste."

The Non-Mystery of whether or Not Chet Atkins Could Read Music

"Where's the melody?"
(a handwritten note Chet had taped over a Studio B recording console)

One of the most familiar Chet quotes known to country guitarists was when Chet was asked if he could read music. He would chuckle softly and say: "Just enough that it doesn't get in the way of my playing."

Musicians who play "by ear" are sometimes stubbornly proud of this ability and claim learning to read would erode this skill. Chet's remark could be used as defense, by some, against learning how to read music taking the implication "get in the way of my playing" to mean reading music has a negative effect on playing guitar. None of these arguments or defenses has any real merit. Reading music is like any other skill, you get out of it what you put into it.

Chet learned basic rudiments from his piano/voice teaching father when he lived with him for a few years in Georgia when he was about eleven years old. His dad had abandoned the family when Chet was six or seven but later took the boy in, hoping the change in climate would help his severe asthma. Chet's father, an itinerant music teacher, wanted his son to learn music and fussed at him when he seemed inattentive. His dad thought Chester should study violin or singing for he didn't hold guitar playing in very high esteem. He considered guitar as being too limited an instrument. It is very likely that young Chester learned the rudiments and the mechanics of reading notes during this period. As he expanded his playing, he expanded his grasp of written music even if he didn't actually depend on it for his living. He learned the spoken language of music, the use of chord substitutions and music theory by talking to other musicians … and untold hours of practice.

One of the West Coast's most successful "Wrecking Crew" guitarists, Glenn Campbell, couldn't read a note yet had first call status for recording gigs. It was well known that many of the Nashville session musicians couldn't read music. Some forms of music, particularly in the area of jazz, defy written scores since some jazz forms are purely from the heart. It requires more than a superficial knowledge of music and an experienced ear for jazz improvisation to work.

Chet was a strong melody man. When he worked out a tune he usually knew not only the exact melody, but also the words because the words are what the song is about. A song should reflect the mood of its title or lyrics. On his teaching DVD, *The Guitar of Chet Atkins,* he can clearly be heard singing the lyric to "The Lady Loves" as he sorts out the chording sequence for the lesson. He was unconsciously illustrating something that many "by ear" people gloss over. The more intimately and accurately you know the song, the better you can work it out. Most studio musicians could do quite well without written music. The recording industry of the day was staffed with musicians that could play for days without seeing any sheet music at all. But being able to read was definitely an asset.

Chet did most of his arranging by ear. Chet seldom worked from printed sheet music but he thoroughly understood the value of knowing how to read music.

> When we talked about music education, he expressed his view that all
> musicians should learn about reading, playing by ear and improvising.
> He asked me lots of questions about how I learned and how I taught.
> And I'll bet I'm not the only person he ever asked.
> — John Knowles

Getting back to the original question: Could Chet read music? Certainly he could! He could read well enough to check himself against a piece of music using traditional music reading skills. He, like so many others in town, was not dependent on written music but he was capable of taking a blank staff paper to write things out. Describing a certain recording session that also featured classical guitarist Liona Boyd, John Knowles said:

> The tune was "Leaves of Grass" and Liona's part was the tremolo solo at the end of the track. Chet knew that Liona played from music so he wrote out her part in classic guitar notation. It looked mighty good to me. And of course, Liona did a beautiful job on the recording so Chet must have written it out right. I'll bet that if Chet had planned to record that part himself, he wouldn't have gone to the trouble of writing it out.

Paul said this about reading:

I think it depends on what you want to do with your playing. If you have a desire to do studio work and play with symphonies then you need to read. If you are doing it for fun and your ear is good enough, you can get by without it.

I think learning chords is as important as learning to read music I have been around great classical players who didn't hardly know one chord from another because they learn everything by reading. I couldn't read a note until I started working with Jerry Reed and decided to try to get into sessions. I have been fortunate to have a pretty good ear so I can learn things without using tab. I read a little, mostly chords. All of the things I did with Chet and Jerry were by ear we just worked it up

Anyway that's the way it has been for me. Chet knew music and could read when he wanted to. I've heard Chet talk about going with his father when he went to give music lessons but his father left home when he was quite young so I don't know what all that did to form his musical tastes. I do know that when he started work at WKNOX in Knoxville, his first job on a radio station, the boss told him he wanted him to play a new tune every day. Chet said he listened to the records in the station library and learned the pop standards also he played with an orchestra and he learned to read charts doing that.

Jerry Reed also knows music. I've seen Jerry talk to conductors and explain what he wanted in a piece. It's like everything else in life the more you know the better off you are.

CHAPTER 14

RECORDING WITH CHET

In the mid seventies, Mike Poston was a maintenance and installation engineer and studio chief. He went from that to recording engineer and was quite proficient. He was hired by Chet to help him keep his climate controlled recording area current and in good repair. Chet's studio was air-conditioned. I have a memory of him turning off the fan while we were recording something.
— John Knowles

Chet met Mike soon after working with RCA. Mike describes Chet's well-known intent to focus on recording at home:

Chet had lived in this home since the early 1950s. Soon after moving into his house, Chet put up some studio walls, sound glass and wired the place. Before long, he had a studio/workshop where he could work on his recordings whenever he wanted to. Since Chet went to bed early, he got up sometimes in the early morning hours to work in the "magic of the moment." This was Chet's routine for many years.

Chet liked tape and knew how to use it to the utmost. He knew the best way to record his guitar and make his records. All you have to do is listen to what he did.

The first record I did with Chet was "Kentucky." I played my high string (a flattop guitar with the 3rd, 4th, 5th, and 6th string tuned up an octave) and did rolls behind him. "High String" was real popular back in the 1960s and 1970s. I don't remember the brand of guitar I used since I've strung different guitars that way over the years.

Chet always thought I was real good on rolls. I got that technique from Jerry but I also tried to work out some on my own. I tried to play rolls where you play melodies through them because that's what Chet liked me to do. I'd also add various harmonic things and play piano type rhythms, alternating the bass and pinching the inside strings. Things like that.

Chet's studio was in his basement of his house. There were two rooms, one smaller than the other. He changed it over the years. When he died, the control board was in the larger room which was about 12' by 24'. The small room had a piano, his workbench and a storage room. He did most

of the recording in the large room. Years ago he had the control board in the small room.

Someone close to the Atkins family described an aspect of Chet's home studio in this way.

> The studio part of the house was in the basement below the bedrooms, so when Chet was playing you could hear it come up through the air ducts in the floor. It was audio-insulated extremely well, well enough so no special effort had to be made to be quiet while recording was going on (which was ALL the time) not even for visiting grandchildren.
>
> Most recording studios have special "tech power" that is clean and free from spikes that happen ie: when an appliance kicks on. Kinda like how your lights dim in your house when the A/C comes on (at least mine does). Also most studios are free of ground loop/hums etc that are common in residential/old houses. This is probably the main offender in what Mark Knopfler described when he once commented hearing a spike when Leona's refrigerator turned on when he and Chet were recording. Needless to say, there was no tech power at the house. You have to be careful with all that stuff, or it will bite you when you go into a real studio to do the mix. You can hear it on big speakers.
>
> — Name withheld

There's not a lot of recording outtakes or errors around. Those two-inch tape machines eat up a lot of tape so when I recorded with Chet, if something wasn't right, he would rewind the tape and redo it. A roll of that tape wasn't cheap. Chet used Ampex tape which was about $125 a roll. You couldn't do very many tunes on a roll of tape at the speeds the recorders ran.

John Knowles had some experience recording with Chet and from his recollections Chet is seen as someone fully aware of the nuances of his home studio. We also get a sense of what the recording experience was like in that famous basement studio. For this home session the main control board is in the smaller room so the studio layout was a little different than what Paul's narrative has just described.

 At home Chet showed his famously gentle but firm "take charge" style. As John tells it here Chet is senior engineer and knows exactly how to delegate duties and either have a guest push the buttons or set things rolling himself.

> When we worked on the *Guitar Quartet* album, we did most of the tracks in his basement. He set things up so I could work the tape recorder.
> I recall one track where Chet, John Pell, and I were recording. Chet asked me to play his part on his guitar so he could set levels in the

control room where the recorder was. Then he started the tape, walked into the studio, sat down, and counted the tune off.

At the end of the take, he raised his index finger to his lips, waited a moment, and then went into the control room to stop the tape. It was all John Pell and I could do to keep from cracking up.
— John Knowles

If he did recording in Studio A in Nashville he would use an engineer but for work in the home studio he probably knew the system better than any "for hire" engineer he might use.

When we did the instructional video *Get Started On Guitar*, we pre-recorded the backing tracks in Chet's basement. Chet's parts were recorded live when we shot the video. The two student's vocals and guitar parts were pre-recorded. He then hired an engineer to mix the tracks.
— John Knowles

Mixing can be a whole 'nother thing and some studios send their product out to other studios that do mixing as part of their business. Sometimes, as John indicated, Chet did this probably to apply his time to other uses. But old habits die hard and sometimes the Chief would do his own mixing as John indicates here:

I recall mixing the "Brandenburg" track with Chet. I had done the arrangement, and knew the arrangement, so Chet and I rode the faders and track buttons live to get the mix.

Chet kept his basement studio current. He had a never-ending quest about making audio better or maybe finding some new ear-catching method to "keep things interesting."

Chet would hire Mike (Poston) to keep all of the gear in good working order. I recall him telling me that he set a couple of channels on Chet's mixing board to go direct to DAT. A lot of the basement sessions came from those DAT tapes.

Digital Audio Tape, or DAT, is a signal recording and playback medium developed by Sony and introduced in 1987. In appearance it is similar to a compact audio cassette, using 4 mm magnetic tape enclosed in a protective shell, but is roughly half the size at 73 mm x 54 mm x 10.5 mm.

As the name suggests, the recording is digital rather than analog. DAT has the ability to record at higher, equal, or lower sampling rates than a CD. That's a fancy way of saying a wider audio range can be recorded.

I had met Chet in the mid 1970s when I installed his first twenty-four-track machine while working for the audio supply company that provided a lot of his equipment in his studio. Because of my technical abilities, I also did most of the maintenance and wiring in Chet's home studio. For example, I set up a permanent direct input for Chet to use whenever he wanted. He could plug into it, raise that fader to "0," the preamp was preset, no EQ, and assign to the mix buss or to a multitrack input. I wanted to keep it simple so that the technical aspects wouldn't get in the way of the creative aspects. At any time, Chet could plug in and start recording to two-track or the multitrack.
— Mike Poston

Like his love of sharing music and guitaring, he also loved talking about his studio. It was a "feel good" place for him. John Knowles continues:

Chet and I talked a lot about the gear in his studio. He upgraded components from time to time. He showed me how it all worked. I realize he was teaching me things I could use later but at the time it felt more like a couple of guys talking about cars or fishing.

Some of my fondest memories of when I worked with Chet are when we recorded. People have asked me about what it was like recording with Chet. It wasn't easy! When you recorded with Chet there wasn't a lot of rehearsal. Sometimes he would play a tune a few times in concert before he recorded it.

He would tell me beforehand what I was going to do and I would only take the guitar I needed for the day. He had amps so I didn't have to take one. Chet didn't like to keep redoing a tune. If he and I were doing a tune, even though I had never heard it, he would play it through about twice and expect me to have it. He was ready to record it! If there was a part I didn't understand I would say "What is that part again, Chet?" and he would play it once more and that was it!

Chet wouldn't say a lot. When Chet ran down a tune he wouldn't tell you the chords or what he wanted you to do. It was up to you to learn them and figure out your part. He expected you to develop it. He's not one to show you every little nuance. Chet wouldn't have called you in to do it if he didn't trust in what you could do. I sort of knew what to play and if what I did didn't fit the tune, he would say something, or suggest something else. Chet always had what he wanted to record worked out. I had to work out my part.

If he didn't like it he would let you know. If Chet didn't say anything, he liked it. A lot of people who have worked with him have said, "I don't think he liked what I played! He didn't say anything." But if he liked it he never said anything.

With Jerry Reed, back when I was working with him, he used that Baldwin electric he had and he would plug straight into an amp. Most of the time they had an amp that stayed in the studio. I don't remember what make it was. Of course a microphone was on the amp. With Chet it depended on what guitar he was using. If it was a classical (non electric) he would just put a microphone in front of it. If it was an electric (Country Gentleman) he would plug into his Standel and use a microphone on the amp. After Scotty Moore gave him an RCA 44 ribbon microphone he used that microphone all the time.

I was talking to Paul one day and mentioned that someone told me that when Chet recorded "Amos Moses," he couldn't find anyone that could do the Jerry Reed licks right, so he had to call Jerry himself for the session.

Paul jumped on that one like a dog on a bone, and informed me that it was *him* that played the Reed licks. Jerry was nowhere around.

— Richard Hudson

Microphones and Studios

This history of Paul and Chet deals a lot with recording. Paul mentions six specific microphones he and Chet used. Few, if any of these microphones would be seen on stage. They tend to be fragile, less robust than the ones used in a live music venue of any size.

This section will explain some of the simple differences between the units Paul mentions. Microphones are interchangeably referred to as microphones or as "mics" (pronounced "mike"). If someone were to put a mic in front of an amp (as Chet and Paul often did) it will be said that the amplifier was miked, or they were miking the amp.

The chart is simple and basic. The term Frequency Response refers to a range of vibrations or cycles per second. Cycles per second are expressed in "Hz" (pronounced "hertz") named for a German audio physicist. Hz is not about loudness. Hz applies to the tonal or pitch range as in a musical tone/note. Every musical note has its own specific Hz. Concert Pitch A, the symphonic standard, is 440 cycles per second, or 440 Hz. The number 440 is how many times a string or tuning fork needs to vibrate per second to generate that particular A note.

Here, the normal frequency response ranges of the human ear and of the human voice are shown for reference. The mic list shown here is a list of all the mics Paul refers to. It shows how much frequency response the cited mic actually covers. All frequency response numbers are stated in Hz:

Brand	Model	Type	Frequency Response
Human ear			12-20,000
Human voice			80-1,100
Neumann	U 47	Condenser	40-16,000
Neumann	U 67	Condenser	40-16,000
Shure	5655	Dynamic	40-15,000
RCA	77-DX	Ribbon	50-15,000
Electrovoice	RE-15	Dynamic	80-15,000
RCA	44	Ribbon	30-20,000

Dynamic mics used a diaphragm to gather vibrations that were then amplified. They tended to be more flattering to the human voice and were popular with singers, media announcers and radio talk show hosts. This was because of proximity effect. As the voice gets closer to the mic the lower tones get more emphasis. This tended to make the human voice sound mellower and more pleasant.

Condenser mics used a modified condenser/transducer to convert sound into an electrical signal that was then amplified. The transducers required an external power supply to work. They were preferred for use on acoustic instruments or amplifiers because they do not have proximity effect. They could also have a much narrower pickup pattern, which was better suited for use as an instrument mic.

Ribbon mics used a metal ribbon to gather vibrations. The one Paul mentions most often, the RCA 44, was a fragile mic, however, it had an excellent range that explains why it was a very popular mic in its day. Working RCA 44 mics are still highly prized by recording engineers.

Many of the mics on this list are now collector items. Thanks to "progress" many of them are no longer made or used but the fact remains that Chet and others used these mics to record some of the finest music of the second half of the twentieth century.

A bit of trivia: the mic on David Letterman's desk was an RCA 77-DX.

Microphones are really important when you record acoustic guitars and electrics, too. It makes a big difference what mic you use on an amp when you record. One thing to keep in mind about Chet's electric guitar tone and sound on his records is the microphones he used with the Standel.

When Chet miked his amp in the studio he put the mic about 12 to 14 inches off center toward the speaker. Chet used an RCA 44 ribbon mic a

lot on his Standel when he recorded but he also used different mics over the years. Chet miked the DelVecchio using the RCA 44 ribbon mic, too. It gave it a big sound. Once I played his Del Vecchio on a track and he used that RCA 44 and it had the biggest sound you ever heard.

He used a Shure 5655 dynamic mic quite a bit. He used a Neumann 67, an RCA 77 DX, and an EV RE-15, and I'm sure others that I don't know about.

The Neumann 67 may be the best microphone ever made. There are many pictures of him using it during the 1960s. An EV RE-15 is an excellent mic also. They don't make them anymore but you can find them around in music stores and on eBay. RCA had a Neumann U47 at their studio. I know he used that on his classic and I'm sure he used it on the Del Vecchio.

Chet recorded direct sometimes but when he did he used a direct box and I would do the same. You get more presence going direct. Other times he used the Standel. The old Standels didn't have a direct out on them. Chet just miked his. Chet never recorded with those MusicMan amps but he liked them on the road.

Chet did most of his recordings at home, but back in the 1970s he recorded at Studio A at RCA. He recorded some sessions in New York, Chicago and Atlanta as well as Nashville. I recorded with Chet at different places, mostly at his house, but we sometimes recorded at the RCA studios. I did many sessions there. I always wondered, and I never thought to ask, (and I remember when they did it) was why did they shut down Studio B.? It was the best studio in town. It was my favorite studio to work in. Jerry Reed did about all of his recording there. When I was with Jerry Reed we recorded "Jerry's Breakdown" in Studio B. Lenny Breau did his first RCA album in B. I did an album with the Everly Brothers in B also.

Studio A is now under another name but when it was built in 1964 it was beautifully designed. There was a wall on rollers so they could make the studio large or small. They had every kind of keyboard that was available at that time and there were a couple of Fender amps around to use. They had Neumann mics, RCA ribbon mics ... top of the line stuff.

Chet would almost always do a rhythm track, then put his part down. To do this he would play the tune in the studio with the musicians, then, if he wanted to, he would redo his part at home. A lot of those credits you read where they list the RCA Studio as the recording site were really ones where Chet did the rhythm section at the studio and then did his part at home. The people writing those texts wouldn't have known that. I don't know why he would do one song or album at home and another at RCA. Maybe it was because his home studio wasn't all that big and he didn't have a drum booth. When you do a session where you have rhythm guitar, drums, piano and bass, it takes a lot of room because everything has to be isolated.

I remember when I would record with Chet I would use a tuner most times. I think on that Solo Flights album Chet tuned the guitar with the bass strings up above 440 because it's hard to get the bass strings to stand out. I've always had that trouble. If you aren't going to overdub a keyboard you can play above or below pitch however you feel like doing. Some people think if a person overdubs it's cheating. It is so expensive to make records nowadays that you can't waste time in a studio. If a musician plays a wrong note he or she punches it in and you move on instead of redoing the entire tune. I overdub on my CDs and I don't feel like I'm cheating.

Folks talk about subtle changes to Chet's guitar tone over the years. Well, different factors affect tone. I think when Chet quit playing his '59 he lost a lot of tone. That guitar had the greatest tone on the treble strings when he played up the neck.

Some of Chet's tunes were recorded at home and some at the RCA studio which made a big difference. Back when Chet was real busy producing artists, Bob Ferguson produced some of Chet's records, all these factors made the records sound different. I always thought Bill Porter used too much echo or reverb on some of Chet's records. Chet would update his home studio now and then. That changed the sound too.

Audio Evolution: They Can Look Back, but They Can't Go Back ...

In this excellent discussion of Chet's studio gear and the difficulty/impossibility of recapturing Chet's original sounds Bill Porter's name comes up. Paul wasn't exactly a fan of Bill's work but Bill Porter was something of a protégé of Chet's and engineered some of Chet's most popular albums.
Not many people are aware that Bill had a condition called "synesthesia" which means that the brain interprets a sense in a non-traditional way. In Bill's case, he heard sound as color which no doubt had an effect on his audio work.

The following discussion most likely centers on Studio B since Bill Porter is mentioned so much. Chet's home system is also discussed.

To try to capture the tone of Chet's early 1960s recordings is virtually impossible. First of all the chain of recording to get the sound would cost you thousands of dollars. Bill Porter, the engineer on Chet's records from that period explained what he did to get that sound and believe me, there is really no way you are going to put on a set of headphones and get that sound.

Bill distinctly remembers first of all the amp that Chet had, the Standel. He remembered the sound that it had was totally different than your standard fare Fender amp that virtually everybody used, even down to the not 6L6 outputs that the Standel had. I forget the outputs in the Standel, maybe 807s, whatever.

Anyway Porter also told me about the mic placement of usually a U47 or U67 Neumann Mic. That mic will set you back about $5-10K right now.

Now look at the console—a hand made RCA console with Telefunken mic preamps—cost is unthinkable! Next is the Pultec EQ used. You can see a pic of the big blue Pultec in the Chet guitar book by Russ Cochran on page 149. Next is the reverb itself that added an immense character to the sound of the guitar—a German made EMT plate reverb about 12+ feet long that weighed about 200 or 300 pounds.

Next in the chain is the tweaked out Ampex recorders that Bill Porter used, totally set up out of spec, to his secret biasing that even the RCA execs in New York did not know. The New York folks were always calling Chet and Bill up to ask how they were getting some tones and Porter says that they would not tell them. Lastly is the final step in the process that is the mastering through the Fairchild 667 compressors and the lathe cutter electronics.

Even his recording at home would have been done on the same recorder as the Ampex recorder at RCA. He had an Ampex 3 track machine that spun ½-inch tape. He could record the rhythm section at the studio and then come home and record one of several different ways. He could keep the rhythm section in stereo and record on the third track using the Ampex Sel Sync to be in sync with them or he could record in stereo and monitor the rhythm track in mono on the third track. I would say that most of the true stereo recordings of Chet Atkins during this time were done at the studio where the sound of the guitar could be set up to bleed into the other tracks and give a nice big stereo image.

The sound that Chet Atkins got in the 1960s is a result of the culmination of many years of experimentation at RCA with the tube equipment that they had. You would virtually NEVER be able to capture that tone. Even Atkins himself was never able to get that sound again. You can jump up and down and spin around until you turn blue if you don't agree with me, but Chet's guitar sound was never really improved over those years. In fact his sound in the 1970s and up was never really as good to me as the early tones. This is not his fault at all. With the advent of transistor technology and the use of isolation, the character of recording degraded across the board in the 1970s. Chet's later records on Columbia never really captured the vintage tone he got—maybe he wanted it that way. Make a clean cut with the past and try something new.

I never really liked the sound of the Gibson electric guitars he used. We have discussed that here before. They don't sound bad, just not the beautiful sound he got in the 1960s.

Last and not least is the real magic of Chet's sound is just the way that he attacked the strings with the flesh and nail, the action he used, the perfect left hand that seemed to never make any squeaks and such that other mortal guitar players make, the phrasing—on and on.

— Author unknown

I have so many memories of recording with Chet in his home studio. When visiting Leona (after Chet passed) I went downstairs to Chet's studio and a lot of his stuff was still lying around ... his capo ... For capos Chet and I used Shubb capos, they seem to work well ... and pencil ... there were notes he had written still on his mixing board ... it was like he was still there. It was tough folks.

The Making of "Solo Sessions"

These comments were posted over a period spanning a few months after Chet had passed.

Chet made tapes at home but I think he had been careful not to have any around where he didn't play well. If a tune didn't come off he would erase them. He didn't leave substandard stuff there. He told me a long time ago that any outtakes and recordings that weren't what he considered good he erased.

I know there are some unreleased tunes. A couple that we wrote years ago never made it out but I don't know if any of that stuff will ever be released. We will just have to wait and see. It will take many months to finish listening to them. I'm sure sometime in the future there will be new CDs released on Chet's music. When that happens I'll post it here. When you have a record deal with a company you just can't release any and everything.

Mike Poston, Chet's old engineer, Chet's grandson, Jonathon Russell, and myself have been going through Chet's tapes at his studio. There is hour after hour of music, many things unreleased. Some of the things I've heard so far are just wonderful. We almost didn't find them. I knew they were in his studio. The tunes were on two DAT tapes

Chet did the recordings in 1984. We were sitting at an airport one day and he said he was going to start recording some solos to a DAT so Leona would have something when he was gone. Most of the tunes were ones Chet had played over the years and had recorded some of them. A few were new tunes he had written. Most of the tunes were recorded direct with Chet playing his Gibson nylon. I remember when he was doing them. He probably did them over a few months. I don't remember all the tunes. There may be a couple Chet did in the 1960s on there. When we started looking and listening to the tapes in Chet's basement the first thing we found were the two DAT tapes. There wasn't any info or time sheets for them, just the tapes (that later became the *Solo Sessions* CD.)

I think Chet, just by himself recorded tune after tune. Some are old tunes with different arrangements. I can tell you it affects me deeply to listen to Chet playing. When we are downstairs in Chet's studio I expect him to walk in any minute. The night of the first day we did it I only slept about two hours. I feel honored to be a part of this great undertaking.

All the music has to be changed over to digital because most of the tapes are so old we are having to "bake" them which restores them to like new condition, however they can only be played two or three times after that. We have to change them to a digital format to preserve them.

Note: "Baking" old audio tapes is a risky procedure of applying 120-140 degree dry heat for a period of hours. It can have a temporary restorative effect on some tapes but is definitely something best left to experienced hands.

Please do not refer to them as "Lost Tapes" because they aren't lost. Chet had all his tapes there in his studio. He knew where everything was. This way anything that would be released will be the same way that Chet always did his records.

I went over to Mike Post's studio in Berry Hill and he made me a copy of the tapes for me to listen to because we had to decide which tunes to use. As I listen to the finished product, the DAT copy I have and the CD sound the same. Chet already had echo on the tunes so the only thing left to do was decide what order to put them in and master the finished product. There wasn't very much engineering to be done.

In any case, when people talk about the idea of doing a box set, well, think about this: If we were to do a box set there wouldn't be anything to look forward to in the future. I don't think that's a good idea. The estate wanted to do a two CD set. I advised a single CD release and then another one later but I got sick and had to have surgery and got out of the loop so I wasn't part of the project after that.

Everyone relax. It will be a long time before anything is released. Don't misunderstand ... it isn't just me that will decide what to release on Chet's unreleased tapes. I'm just helping out. There are a lot of things that have to be considered. It's not a simple thing. Other people will decide what is to be done so time will tell. We all will have some more great music from Chet.

In 2003, a two CD set called *Solo Sessions* was released

The Chet Atkins/George Benson Album

In 1985, guitarists George Benson and Chet Atkins did well on the smooth jazz charts with their collaboration "Sunrise," one of two songs they recorded that was released on Atkins' album *Stay Tuned.*

Producer Mike Poston states Benson and Atkins recorded an entire album's worth of music, but due to disagreements between lawyers for their record companies, the rest of the material has never been released.

This subject comes up every now and then but here are the facts: Chet got the idea for he and George to do an album. The tunes were recorded at Chet's house some months before Chet did the *Stay Tuned* album. They did two sessions at Chet's house. I forgot how many tunes they did ... I'd guess twelve. Sometimes after he did the tracks at RCA he would replace his guitar track. The mixing was done at different studios, sometimes at his house and sometimes downtown.

George's label, Warner Bros., wouldn't agree to the album being released. You can't release things without permission from the record companies. George's label and Chet's label never could get together on it. Later the *Stay Tuned* project came along and Chet decided to use two of the tracks on it. Chet used "Dream" on another CD. It has been many years since they were recorded. The remainder of the sessions and the tunes are at Chet's house but the tapes are in such bad condition they can't be played so I don't think anything will ever be done with them. What happens is, the tape goes bad and sticks together and becomes a big mess and is worthless.

Some Memorable Sessions

First, a little historical data:

Chet told me once that back in the 1950s he tuned his guitar to F and sometimes to F# instead of E. I asked him why and he said he liked the sound ... it made him sound different so that's the reason some of his records are in odd keys. He gets a great sound on "A Little Bit Of Blues" but for that he is tuned down a whole step. On "Somebody Stole My Gal" he used a 12 string electric. That recording came out about the same time as Jimmy Bryant's "Stratosphere Boogie" on which he used a 12 string. Also on the flip side of Chet's "Somebody Stole My Gal" was "Shine on Harvest Moon" done on the same guitar. I think he de tuned every other string. A normal 12 string has an octave string on the 3rd 4th 5th and 6th string.

What Chet did is have 2 6th 2 5ths 2 fourths and 2 3rds and 2 seconds and 2 firsts. He then detuned one each of the strings which gave it the out of tune effect. It gives a honky-tonk sound the same as the Crazy Otto piano stuff if you remember that.

I have done that on a session or two. Jerry Reed use to double track tunes by making the first track and then detune a little and playing the tune again. I think Chet used the Stratosphere guitar. I think Jimmy Bryant tuned it in 3rds. I think I'm right about how Chet did but then, maybe he double tracked it.

That guitar was a "Stratosphere" made in Springfield, MO. They had a six-string, a twelve-string and a twin-necked version with one six and one twelve string neck. The story around here was Chet used the twelve-string to record "Somebody Stole My Gal" and "Harvest Moon." It was noted on the record label as by "Chet Atkins and his Other' Guitar."

The company had developed a harmony tuning, where the string sets were in the same relation as the strings in a regular guitar tuning— you could play twin string leads, but you couldn't actually make a chord on it. However Chet evidently used a regular twelve-string tuning with some of the strings knocked down slightly to get a mandolin or player piano effect.

— Tom Galbraith

On "Fig Leaf Rag" he used his D'Angelico and just used his back pickup, which was a P-90, through that little Fender amp he had back then. I never liked his tone on that one but he played the fire out of it.

On "Gallopin' Guitar" he used the L-10 with the DeArmond pickup. "Main Street Breakdown" is the L-10 acoustically. His Gibson-L10 was a guitar his brother Jim got from Les Paul that he had given to Chet. Chet told me he just used his thumb pick on "Main Street Breakdown" but he later used his fingers.

A thing about that L-10: Les had Epiphone put that fingerboard with the first string extension on it because Django's guitar had a fretboard like that. Gibson made a reissue of that model but I don't think they will sell very many of those with no pickup on them. The reason Chet played his was that's all he had at the time. He had a DeArmond pickup on it, but as soon as he could afford another guitar he bought an L-12.

"Walk Don't Run" was recorded back in the early '60s. Chet is using a Gretsch with split pickups where he ran the bass direct and the treble into echo. On *Guitar Genius* Chet used a '58 Country Gentleman with some kind of split pickup that he put on the top between the regular pickups. It just sat on the top in front of the bridge pickup. There are some small pictures in the Russ Cochran book (page 170) down the side of one page where you can see part of the pickup and output wire.

There is very slight crosstalk between channels. I've checked it on my meters on my recorder but it's so slight you can't hear it. I have two stereo pickups that Ray Butts did for Chet and they have the same crosstalk so it's one of those things.

On "Bells of St. Mary" he used his D'Angelico through a tweed Fender Deluxe amp like the one in Russ Cochran's book. What makes that tune sound so special is he used a limiter on his guitar. He did the same on "Country Gentleman."

Limiters

In order to get hot enough on tape you have to use a limiter. When you record you record as much signal as possible to keep the noise down and without a limiter it's almost impossible to do it. A limiter is a piece of studio gear that keeps a guitar from having "hot notes" or in other words, loud notes ... a spike. It levels the sound, hence the name 'limiter.' Chet always used one and I have one that I use when I record. It's best to use a limiter at all times when recording. It keeps you from overdriving the recorder. I don't think limiters work too well live. There's not much point in using one in a live setting. They tend to take away a little presence so I wouldn't use one live myself.

Speaking of limiters, Chet nor I ever used any on the road. The only time we ever used any limiting was when we recorded. Chet used a LA2A limiter (by Teletronics) and I have one also. They are one of the best ones, I think. I found out, after many years, that part of Chet's sound was his use of a Teletronix limiter which has a unique sound. He used it from the early fifties. If you can find one used they are around $3000.

Chet often did a 'medley of his hits' as he called it. He did it with various tunes on every show and would change it every night. He almost always used "Country Gentleman" which is a very tough tune to do. You have to play thirds with your ring finger and your little finger. It's one of his greatest tunes and on the old record of it Chet gets one of his greatest sounds. It always amazed me. He could get all that out of a Fender Deluxe amp and his D'Angelico.

On the first *Stringing Along with Chet Atkins* album he was using his D'Angelico with a Fender amp. He redid the *Stringing Along* album where he played a Gretsch and used the back pickup and played the tunes slower.

On *A Session With Chet Atkins* Chet used his first 6120 and the Ray Butts EchoSonic amp. It was the same guitar he used in the video of "Mister Sandman." There is a picture of Chet with it on the front cover of the album.

Chet didn't like the pickups in those first 6120s, the Dyna Sonics, but he got a great sound out of them which proves Chet could sound great on about anything.

He used the front pickup on a lot of the tunes. Nobody, I mean, nobody has ever gotten Chet's sound. Some of us come close but it's just not there.

On the *Finger-Style Guitar* album he used the orange 6120 with the prototype Filter-Trons. I think he used the Ray Butts amp on that. I don't think Chet used the Butts amp all that much on recordings because he could hear the tape splice go by the head.

On Don Gibson's "Oh Lonesome Me" I think he used his thumb pick on the fast notes. Back then Chet was really quick with his pick. I've seen him play a real up tempo tune and play all down strokes with his pick. As to whether Chet used his thumb pick or fingers on a given tune, when Chet was using his fingers the finger notes would sound different than the picked notes and it would be easy to hear the difference.

Another thing about that song, the intro on that record wasn't played by Don Gibson but Velma Smith who Chet used a lot. She was a real good rhythm player.

The *Chester and Lester* and *Guitar Monsters* albums were done at RCA's Studio A. They did all those *Chester and Lester* cuts in two sessions, a 10:00 am and a 2:00 pm session.

I never saw Chet play better. It always seems to me that as they say, "When the chips are down," Chet played better between the two. Les played great too but Chet outplayed him at every turn.

Those are sessions I remember very well. I was either in the control room or out in the studio at the time and all the tunes in that album were done at those sessions. I played bass on one or two of them. Chet and Les would work out the intro and ending and then play the tune about once and then record it.

On the *Guitar Monsters* album I played rhythm. Chet played his old 59 Gretsch Country Gentleman and used a large Pignose amp that Paul Rivera had given us. Chet and I had a couple of those we used for about a year. It was about 100 watts and had a 12" EV speaker. They sounded great but had problems in the power supply so we eventually stopped using them. Chet was using his old gray EchoPlex on that session. Les was wilder than a March Hare. It was a contest and I really had a ball being there.

On "Avalon" I sat in front of Chet on the floor and adjusted the old EchoPlex that he used back then. You can hear him give me instructions. Les was playing a white Les Paul with low impedance pickups and all those switches on it.

If I remember correctly, Les went direct into the board and had a small Boss DD2 delay. It sounds to me like Les was trying to outdo Chet. I thought so, and so did Randy Goodrum, who was playing piano at the session. Chet was amazing on that session. I don't think he fixed anything later. Everything was off the top of his head. I think it was some of his finest playing ever and his tone was superb.

Chet didn't use that Super Chet pictured on that *Guitar Monsters* album.

He used his '59 Country Gentleman except on "Deed I Do." For that he used a Fender Telecaster with a B-bender that Shot Jackson built for him. I guess he thought the Super Chet would look better on the album cover.

Here's a little side story. When Chet and Les were talking about doing the Chester and Lester album Chet and I were in New York. Les came over to our hotel and he and Chet talked about the sessions. I had my Hascal Haile classical and Chet had his classical. Les took my guitar and he and Chet played for a little while and, maybe in about ten minutes, Les had put about a dozen scratches on the top of my guitar. I always pointed that out to people and told them that Les had done it.

The *Guitar Monsters* album wasn't quite as good in my opinion. Les had a bad cold and didn't feel like playing. I don't think the tunes were as good either.

When Chet and Les were doing that album I was playing rhythm. In between songs there was a lull, so I said to Les, "Say Les, play the intro to 'How High the Moon.'" Les replied "I only play that when I'm getting paid." I thought to myself, "Well, I guess he told me."

Chet always said Les made great records and he thought "How High the Moon" was the greatest record ever made. I would like to point out all of Les's big hits had Mary Ford singing on them. She was one of the greatest female singers ever and I don't think Les would have sold sixty million records without her because people buy very few instrumentals. She was the best thing that ever happened to Les.

When I talk about how great Chet played on those sessions I'll give you Les was older than Chet. I don't think that would make much difference. Les clowned around most of the time on those sessions.

I love Les's records. Some of the greatest were the ones he and Mary made, but on one to one, I don't think there was anyone around at that period that could outplay Chet. I'm not trying to cut Les, but there were other things that happened during those sessions I haven't told and don't intend to. It's just my opinion and everyone has one.

In 2007, they did a Les Paul special called *Chasing Sound* to honor his life as he reached ninety. I was interviewed for it and we talked about the Chester and Lester album. They released a DVD of the show with added footage and my part wasn't included. I was honest in my comments and told what happened during those sessions and afterward, but I guess they didn't want anything on there that would upset Les.

I saw a John Wayne movie around the time of the DVD release, *The Man Who Shot Liberty Valance* and they had a line in there "when legend becomes fact print the legend." I think this is another case of that.

The *Chet Atkins and Friends* video was made over at Vanderbilt University in a small auditorium they had there. Talk about talent in the band! There was David Hungate on bass, Clayton Ivy on keyboard, Larrie Londin on drums Terry McMillian on percussion and harp and myself. I remember I took the Tom Holmes guitar to the taping and then wanted my Fender Strat, so I went home and got it,

The lineup was good, too ... Waylon, Emmy Lou Harris, Mark Knopfler, Michael McDonald, the Everly Brothers, and probably others I can't remember at the moment. I remember the band had to learn about twenty tunes.

About an hour before we started Chet cut the end of one of his fingers on his left hand, right where the string goes, on his guitar case. Someone went and got him some "New Skin" and he put that on and played the show and never missed a lick.

Doing that show was a great experience for me playing with all those great people and being around them, another great Chet Atkins memory.

A Session Gone Wrong: Chet and Hank Snow

Back in the 1980s, Chet produced a session on Hank Snow. He called me to play rhythm and Hee-Haw's Bobby Thompson, the great rhythm and banjo player was the other rhythm player on that session.

About the second song, Hank was having trouble coming in after the intro. Chet pushed the talkback from the control room and said, "Hank you have to wait a couple of beats before you come in." Hank Snow was his own biggest fan and didn't like to be corrected. Hank replied something disrespectful to Chet.

Chet didn't say a word. He just gathered up his papers and walked out and went home. We had to finish the session with just the engineer in the control room. A day or two later I was over at Chet's office and he said Hank had written him a letter apologizing for what he had said. Chet said "I'll never produce him again." I have never forgotten that.

The industry has changed since Chet's era. Radio stations nowadays have playlists that come out of New York. Lately the only time I hear a guitar recording is on the WX channel. The money is in song hits and about the only people who care anything about guitar playing is other guitar players and that's a small market.

Chet had to record four albums a year. If you think that is easy to do while at the same time produce forty artists you are mistaken. I've worked for a lot of producers in my career but Chet was the best. He always knew what he wanted and how to get it.

CHAPTER 15

ON THE ROAD WITH CHET

To Paul, playing on the road was an unremarkable way of life. As he describes it here it is not the glamorous, exciting life the musical fan envisions. It was a matter of routine.

It's really difficult for Chet to get the same sound on the road that he got in the studio because in the studio they have hundreds of thousands of dollars worth of equipment, the best of everything, which is how they get a great sound. Chet came as close as anyone, but even he couldn't get the sound in person that he had on his records.

Chet was one of the few guitar soloists who could play and draw a large crowd. Chet was like all the other acts. He had a booking agent that got the play dates. Sometimes Chet would say he didn't want to work a certain place because we had been there a short time before.

We did the same thing every time we went out to play a date. Get on a plane, get off the plane, check in the hotel, go do a sound check, eat dinner. Go do the show, go to bed, and catch a plane back to Nashville ... mostly that was it. If we were out for say a week or so, we would fly in the day of the show and then the next morning either catch a plane for the next date or if it was close enough, we would drive.

Chet always hired good musicians so we all got along good. Nobody got in trouble or anything like that. Chet wouldn't have stood for anything that would have caused him a bad time. It was always great to travel with him. He was the greatest and had a great sense of humor.

If we were flying to a date, which we almost always did, we would arrive at the airport about forty-five minutes before flight time. Chet would drive his Mercedes or his SUV and have someone go park it for him. Then he would go to the gate.

Most of the time I would ask him which guitar he was taking when we went on the road. Chet didn't change guitars so much when he was with Gretsch. Sometimes he would take the Super Axe and play it but mostly he took the Country Gentleman on the road and used the Super Axe on TV. With the Gibsons it was different because he had different models to choose from

We checked all our gear except Chet's classical which Randy Houser carried on the plane and put in the overhead. His fiddle also went in the overhead. A Country Gentleman is too big to get in the overhang. I always carried my Gibson Country Gentleman in a gig bag on the plane. The last ten years or so I used a Reunion Blues gig bag and carried my guitar on the plane mainly because we had so much luggage to carry, about twelve pieces or so, and with a gig bag I could take my guitar to the hotel so I could practice. There wasn't any point in Chet using a gig bag.

Some people claim Chet paid for an additional passenger and put the guitar in the seat next to him. According to the story, he was tired of them being stolen. Well, he never did that while I was with him and I worked for him for twenty-four years. First of all, it cost too much and Chet doesn't like to waste money. Secondly there wasn't any need to because we had special travel cases made by a fellow here in Nashville. They are about eight inches thick and have heavy foam linings. They could handle the airlines.

Chet and I never loosened our strings on our guitars when we traveled. I really don't think that makes any difference. About the only thing that happens is that your guitar gets cold from flying so high. I guess we flew a million miles and I only had one incident. On the other hand our amps keep getting beat up all the time.

Chet always sat in First Class. He was always reading something, a new book or the newspaper. When we got to where we were going our road manager always had someone there to take Chet to the hotel we were staying at. Sometimes I would go with Chet to be sure he got checked in. The other guys came with the gear and the road manager and Randy went on to the gig to set up. About 3:30 Chet and the band would go to the gig to have a sound check which took about forty-five minutes. We then went back to the hotel. The shows were almost always at 8:00 pm we would get there about 7:15.

Chet didn't care about going through the house system like a lot of players do today. You have to rely on the monitors for your sound. If you use an amp your sound is right with you. Chet didn't like to play real loud. He always said if you want the audience to be quiet then you should play softer. Some players today blow people's ears out. If playing loud was where it was at Chet would never have amounted to anything. Chet and I played our amps louder than we would if we were sitting and playing at home. We'd set the amp mic about twelve inches away, pointed a little to the side, not at the center because you get a lot of highs if you point the mic at the center of the speaker. How an amp sounds when you're playing depends on where you are ... up close you get all the presence and away from it you hear the room.

Our last road setup was pretty simple compared to some. Chet had his MusicMan amp and his small effects rack which included a JamMan Delay and a Lexicon 42 Delay. I had a MusicMan amp, a volume pedal, a Boss delay and a Boss Tremolo. Chet had a tuner on a small board I made for him. It was connected to a switch box where he could turn the sound off going to his amp and still use his tuner.

For this tale I wasn't playing with Chet yet but it illustrates how things can go on the road ...

When I was working with Jerry Reed at one point Jerry still did the *Glenn Campbell Goodtime Hour*. We were in LA for about twelve weeks. Jerry rented a condo for myself, Larrie Londin and Steve Schaefer, over in Westwood.

We did the show at the CBS TV Studios over next to Farmer's Market. It was a great time.

On the Goodtime Hour there was a big name guest every week. One week Chet was guest. Now the way they did the show was you started rehearsal on Wednesday and did the show on Friday if I remember correctly.

When Chet went to rehearse he was standing on the stage of the set they had for him. It was about waist high and was lighted underneath in such a way that you really couldn't see where the edge of the stage ended. I was standing about six feet from the stage in front of Chet and Jerry was beside me. All at once, Chet stepped forward and stepped of the edge of the stage and went down on the floor! It was hard tile!

We all rushed up to help him get up. We found that even though he had his Gretsch Country Gentleman in his hands, somehow the fall didn't hurt his guitar. It did give him a twisted right knee, however. They called the doctor and we got Chet to his dressing room. The doctor put a bandage on his knee. Chet had to walk with a cane for about three weeks after that but he went ahead and did the show. After rehearsal I went with him back to his room and later we went down to Hollywood and ate dinner at the restaurant owned by Alan Hale Jr. the actor who played the captain on *Gilligan's Island*.

It really scared Jerry and I to death when he fell! Chet was a tough one all right.

Dealing with the impersonal rush and hustle of the backstage part of shows. Stage managers, TV producers and stagehands are not particularly impressed with celebrities. The Clock drives them and to them it is Business and little else really matters. Nothing matters except to make it all look smooth and streamlined in the broadcast that reaches the TV set.

When you do those big TV shows you have to set up your amp and turn it on and get everything ready to go in sixty seconds while they are doing a commercial.

Stagehands grab everything and throw it around and when they do they can hit the knobs, changing your amp settings. I had just enough time to turn everything on and set the time on Chet's delay, set my volume pedal and be sure everything was right before the host introduced Chet. Sometimes we just barely made it.

You have to be quick folks! I always marked the settings and I could tell at a glance if anything was off, and most of the time Chet would start a tune by himself so if something wasn't right I had time to change it.

Paul Yandell, Bandleader!

> I loved him for his brutal honesty. When no one else would tell you, Paul would!
> — Steve Wariner

The president's chief-of-staff tends to be a bit of a hard-nose. So does a gunnery sergeant in the army or a chief petty officer in the Navy. Their jobs do not depend on whether those in their charge like them. Their jobs depend on how well they deflect or deal with problems so their immediate superior doesn't have to.

"Band leader" is not a ceremonial job. When Chet made Paul bandleader it fell to Paul to make sure the band was ready to go when Chet Atkins took the stage. This meant delegation of equipment transport and setup/teardown. It fell to Paul to make sure accurate musical charts, specially written for Chet's performances, were distributed to any backup musicians, including symphony orchestras, as required. It fell to Paul to be sure that everything Chet touched during a concert worked because if it did not, the first person Chet would turn to requesting an answer would be Paul.

Chet didn't dump all this on Paul right from the start. Paul, along with being his sideman, sometimes became his driver to and from airports, but as time went on, after seeing how remarkably dedicated Paul was, Chet added responsibilities that eventually fell under the flexible title of "band leader."

Paul, while he has a great sense of humor and is respected by his peers, was not particularly outgoing. He tended to be quiet and reserved in his public demeanor. Some folks said he was cold. He was doing his job. A job he loved. He was second to the best and he knew it.

We had different musicians over the years. I was eventually the band leader. When I started working with Chet he didn't have a band. By that I mean he didn't have the same four people that went out all the time. After a while he told me I was the band leader and it became up to me to round up a band to go on the road.

When we changed someone in the band most of the time I would tell the person that Chet was going to make a change but sometimes he would do it.

He had a drummer (Randy Hauser) who was from Atlanta and he used different bass players. Sometimes we'd add a piano player. The last ten or so years we had the same band members except Chet stopped using a keyboard and hired guitarist Pat Bergeson. That was the best band we ever had.

As far as I know the artist's here in Nashville pay by the day (per diem) instead of signing a contract. Chet paid his musicians himself. He paid a certain amount per day. Every day we played a show we got paid and when we were off the road he would pay us a smaller amount to cover our expenses. Chet paid our hotel and transportation, airlines, or whatever. Sometimes the venue covered that. We paid for our food.

Randy Goodrum describes Paul as a bandleader:

I first met Paul Yandell on the day that I auditioned for the Jerry Reed band. He and I were musical opposites, at the time. I was a classically trained pianist who strongly identified myself as a Jazz Pianist. Actually the jazz part of my background is probably why I got the job with Jerry. Jerry (and later Chet) really liked improvisation, altered chords, unique scales, etc. In a word, Jazz, while Paul was a finger-style, country guitarist. I had moved to Nashville in 1973 to get work as a pianist, and to hopefully, eventually have some success as a songwriter.

Paul was the head of the band, just under Jerry, and, on the road, could be a harsh taskmaster to slackers and late-sleepers. The more time we spent together, the more we found a unique common ground. We both shared a common trait, or two. One of those traits was that we both were willing to change something if we found a better way of doing it, even if that involved changing our opinions about something.

An example of that would be: On the day of the audition for Jerry's band they were working up a song that Jerry had just recorded, "Lightning Rod," which was a blisteringly fast instrumental featuring Jerry's amazing finger-style playing. I was at home with that kind of song, as I had played loads of be-bop in my earlier development as a musician. I would play some of that when I was rehearsing and Paul said, "Son, you'll never get anywhere in this town playing free jazz." I wasn't offended, I just knew, by then, that Paul pretty much said what was in his head, unedited. So, that was Paul's attitude. Then, a day or two later, I asked Paul, who ran the demo studio in Jerry's office, if he would let me put a piano solo idea I had for "Lightning Rod" down. The record wasn't complete yet, as there was still an open section for a solo of some kind. Paul said, "Sure."

So, I recorded my idea, which was more of a counter melody than a jam session type solo. Surprisingly Paul loved it. I learned then that he wasn't bull headed, but simply honest. He heard something that was what he would have earlier said was free jazz, yet he loved it. As a matter of fact he suggested I play it for Jerry, or Chet. They were in the studio, so he called them up and told them about it. I dragged my Fender Rhodes over there to RCA Studio A, and plugged in.

They said, "Let's hear it, Son." I played it, they recorded it, they loved it, they kept it. On that day Paul and I had written our first chapter as friends and colleagues.

I worked with Paul for many years as a sideman, and fellow studio musician, with Jerry, Chet, and loads of others. Paul was always a bit self-deprecating about his musical abilities, but then again, so were Chet, and Jerry.

I went out of my way to try to hire Paul for guitar on any session I could. He would reluctantly say yes, thinking the music would be too complicated if I called him, but I told him that he would enjoy it and he always did. He always added his magic to every track he played on.

Paul was a true product of his cultural upbringing. I always sat on the edge of my seat to hear his homespun expressions. Bear in mind, I grew up in Arkansas and we had plenty of local expressions there, but Paul's southern Kentucky-isms used to crack me up. He'd say something like, "Yeah, he hung in there like a hair in a biscuit," or "Yeah, he was tighter than Dick's Hat Band," and the list goes on for miles.

I was lucky to know Paul because I left Nashville in the earlier 1980s to expand my career as a pop songwriter, to return in the late

1990s; however Paul and I managed to keep up with each other. I guess our unique common ground that we created, years back, was, in the end, true friendship.

Chet wanted to put Paul on a salary but Paul would not agree to it. Paul's earlier years with Chet were when he was doing a lot of recording/session work with others. He did not want to feel like he was getting paid by Chet while he was recording with, and getting paid by others.

By the time Paul hired on, Chet's backup musicians, bass, drums, keyboards and sometimes a harmonica player or percussionist, were top-drawer. When the fan sees a show that is on the road it looks smooth and spontaneous but the show is actually well planned and meticulously laid out in advance.

When there was a string ensemble (or even a full orchestra) Chet had musical scores, full arrangements, made that he had paid for. Some were made for his recordings, some for road use and all were carefully stored. They were Paul's responsibility.

Chet kept the written arrangements to all of his recordings. He had two large file cabinets filled with the music charts. Anything that a symphony played on needed to have the music for it and the conductor has to have a score for each tune.

It cost a lot of money to have those kind of charts made. Whoever the conductor or arranger (for the initial session) would be, they would have people who would write music charts for each musician. After the session, Chet would keep the charts for each tune. When he wanted to do one of the tunes on the road I would get the charts, put them in the music cases and we would do them for the show.

What was critical in a road band situation was to be sure everyone understood beginnings, endings, and where to come in if they soloed in the body of the song. According to Paul, little time was spent on full rehearsals with the road band but getting the beginnings and endings and entry cues would take up most of the rehearsal.

People ask if Chet and I rehearsed very much. Actually, the answer is, not all that much. If we were at home and he wrote a new one it didn't take too long to get it down. One of the first things he would do was play it for me, because it's always good to play a new tune for another musician. It helps to get over being nervous. Then, when we went to do a show, he would perform it on stage. After playing it for a month or two he would record it.

I remember when he would write a new tune or wanted to do something different on the show he would call me to come over to his office to hear it. He had a boom box on the back porch at his office or I would take my tape recorder and we would sometimes make a tape of something for me to learn from and work it out.

When we learned a new tune, most of the time it was out on the road when we didn't have anything to do. Chet would already know how he wanted to play a piece so then I would learn my part. When I got my part we would perform it on stage. Chet would play it differently but it would fit with what I was doing. He very seldom played a piece the same because he would think of something better to play.

If we were on the road, if we had a day off, we would get together in his room and play for maybe an hour or two then go eat.

I happened to watch a video of myself, Jerry and Chet at the Bottom Line and watching that video brings back memories. We rehearsed once on Chet's back porch about three or four days before we went to New York. When we actually did the show we just winged it. We did most of our rehearsing at the sound checks when we got to the date.

Any time you perform with a symphony you have a rehearsal in the afternoon before the show and do a sound check at the same time. Sometimes we went two weeks between concerts so we needed the refresher. Also it helped loosen our hands. We usually did three concerts a month. We performed with symphony orchestras or at colleges. We usually flew in a day ahead of time, rehearsed the performance that night and gave the concert the following night. We generally used the same act and same songs so rehearsals were easy. It was just a matter of coordinating the orchestra's music with ours.

Road Amps: A Quick Study on Amplifiers Used on the Road

When I first started working with Chet, in 1975 he was playing the Gretsch '59 Country Gentleman. A number of times when he or I would open his case at the gig the bridge would have fallen over. We would just push it back up and Chet would set the intonation by ear. Later we had those heavy cases made for them so the guitars rode well. Pinning the bridges helped immensely. We carried our own amps and we had special cases made for them but every time we would go to California the planes would bust a speaker or the transformer in Chet's amp would come loose. Many times I had to put his or my amps back together so we could do the show.

For a while we used Peavey Special 130 amps but we didn't use them for very long. They had a thick heavy tone that we didn't care for and Chet didn't like the way his nylon strings sounded through them. We started using them after we tried renting amps in the cities that we were playing instead of carrying them on the planes. After a while we stopped doing that. Chet and I each had a Fender Deluxe and a Princeton. Chet used his Deluxe on the road for about six months. We also used Peaveys and Pignose amps.

In the early eighties we went to the Chicago NAAM show and Chet talked to Forrest White with MusicMan. They sent him a RD model something or other that Chet didn't like. Then they sent him a RD-50 and he loved it. He played it for the rest of his career. Chet thought the MM RD-50 was the only amp he had found, other than his Standel, where his nylon electric sounded right. After he started using MusicMan he had me sell the others because he had too many amps sitting around.

For an electric steel string (Country Gentleman) a fifteen-inch speaker sounds better as it has a much bigger sound than a twelve-inch speaker. MusicMan offered two different speaker options in those, a stock speaker and an Electro Voice, which is a heavier one. Chet liked the stock one the best. Sometimes I used MusicMan RD-112, 50 watts. Sometimes Chet used them too. It was the road amp we used the last ten years or so.

People have asked me about Chet's amp settings but I only remember the settings on the MusicMan RD-50. He didn't use very much reverb. On the MusicMan amps the settings we used were: the clean channel on the left with the treble at 3 and the bass at about 8.

CHAPTER 16

SHOWTIME!

Some folks ask me how much notice Chet would give me as to what he was going to play next in a show. The answer is pretty easy. He didn't. He would start playing something and I would join in. Chet changed the music every now and then, adding new tunes to keep the show fresh. Sometimes Chet would do different tunes on every show. I never really knew what he was going to do until he announced it, so I had to be on my toes. Chet would do close to the same show all the time but it was never the same. He would just turn around and tell me what he wanted to do. I had most of his tunes in memory so it wasn't a problem. He did some songs in every show but he also did other tunes as he felt like it. Sometimes he would have requests. I just had to try to remember everything that he played. He was amazing. Chet played better off the top of his head than most people did rehearsing their part.

I never knew him to have an off night. When we would go to California with a two-hour time difference. It affected all of us because we would start the show about bedtime in Nashville. Or, when we went overseas, the jet lag would get us, but I never heard Chet play bad. It seemed that he came to life when he walked on stage.

Many times after flying all day or driving all day we would be tuckered out but after a shower and a good meal we were ready to go. I can't remember ever doing a show when I thought it wasn't a good one. Sometimes when we were on the road and I was tired and didn't feel like playing, I would remind myself how lucky I was to be working for Chet and it would get my spirits up. I can't begin to tell you what a great time I had all those years. Chet was the greatest to work for and I got a guitar lesson every night!

We did the same thing at every show: we would arrive about an hour before show time. Chet had in his contract that there was to be some soup, cheese, fruit, soft drinks and coffee back stage for us to have before and after the show. Chet would go into his dressing room to be by himself, to change, tune up and make out his program. About ten minutes before show time I would go to his dressing room and we would check our tuning and talk about this or that. Chet was very seldom nervous. I think in all the time I worked with him I saw him take a little coke-cola and J&B a time or two, but that was it. We never got nervous as I can remember. I never thought about it. We just went out and did it and had fun.

Chet never ever started a show late. I worked with Chet for twenty-five years and I never ever knew him to not start his show on time. Particularly when you perform with a symphony, because you have to start at a certain time and end at a certain time or you have to pay every musician more money.

When it got close to show time Chet's road manager would come to the door and get us. At about five minutes to show time the road manager would go out on stage and announce that no taping was allowed. We would walk out to stage right. At show time, the lights would go down and the spotlight would go up and Chet would walk out, plug in his guitar, check his delay and amp and start playing.

Chet always started the show by himself. He would do three or four tunes, then bring me out and we would do maybe four or five more. At that point, he brought the rest of the band out. We would do about forty-five minutes. After a thirty-minute intermission we would go back out and do about an hour.

After a show, most of the time, Chet rested a little while after he came off stage. As he got older he took more time before he saw anyone. Then he would give autographs. During that time the band would be loading up the gear. We would go back to the hotel and maybe go to the lounge, relax, and have a beer. The next morning we would go to the airport and go back home. That was the way we did it ninety-eight per-cent of the time.

I remember one time when things didn't go very well at all. We played with every major symphony in America. Chet enjoyed doing those and for the most part they were great. In the middle 1980s we played three days with the San Antonio Symphony. The symphony always did the first half, then there was a thirty minute intermission during which Chet's band set up for the show. As our part of the show started Chet turned to Tony Migliore, who was our conductor at the time, and said "The orchestra is out of tune" (meaning they weren't with us.). That's one thing Chet couldn't stand ... being out of tune.

Now, in an orchestra, the oboe player has a strobe and everybody tunes with that person. Tony stopped the show and told the orchestra they were out of tune and please tune up.

Well, that did it! They all got an attitude! They really turned against us. You could have cut it with a knife! This got Chet a little upset, so it was rough. I just wanted to get up and leave, but we did the show. They never did get in good tune. We had two more shows to do in towns close by but we never were comfortable with them. When we got home, Chet wrote the newspaper there and told them how he had been treated by the symphony. He let them have it! That was the worst time we had in all the years I was with Chet, I think.

Most of the musicians in those symphonies are snobs. The conductor has to be nice because he's getting paid to do it, but the string players and all the players except the horn players wouldn't even speak to you or make eye contact.

In the late 1970s, Steve Wariner was playing bass with us. We went to Europe and were in Hamburg Germany. We had a day off so Steve and I walked around the town sightseeing. We passed a jewelry store and in the window was a Seiko watch that played a tune by Mozart! We went in and I bought it. The tune was about thirty seconds long.

Chet thought it was great, so he asked conductor Tony Migliore, to write a string section part for it. After that, during the show, Chet would call me up to the mic and tell me to play my watch I would stick it in the mic and Tony would have the string section play along with it. You can't imagine how they enjoyed doing that.

Speaking of conductors, one of Chet's conductors, Albert Coleman, was a great man. We traveled many miles together. He had a great career. I've heard him tell about rooming with Danny Kaye when he was young and of his travels all over the world.

We played Carnegie Hall five times, once with the Boston Pops. Chet always liked playing with symphonies but I didn't. I really didn't enjoy working with them. I think, to Chet, it was Big Time. Like it was the epitome of performing. But to be honest with you, I didn't like it. Most of the orchestra players are snooty and they looked down on someone like Chet. I think they resent it because after all their training someone like Chet comes in and makes more money than they ever will. They are not very friendly.

Chet didn't let it be known and he probably wouldn't want me to say it but in his later years he really didn't want to be referred to as a country artist. He would get upset sometimes. Although that was his roots, he worked hard to get somewhere in the music business and he was more than that. If Chet had been out of New York it would have been different. But if you live in Nashville they think you go around in overalls, barefoot, swinging a jug.

Chet was always more interested in his music than in his fame. He honestly loved guitar playing, but not all the fanfare that surrounds it. He played with many guitarists and was always humble with them, always eager to learn anything they had to offer. By doing that he continued to grow in musical knowledge. Chet has been voted "Guitarist of the Year" by every major magazine from *Guitar Player* to *Playboy* and he consistently wins 'Instrumentalist of the Year' in radio polls and the CMA competition. When you've pleased that wide of an audience you've got to be the best. That's why it was such a thrill for me to be Chet's right hand man.

Note: Chet Atkins would rank as "Guitarist of the Year" so often in some publications and award giving organizations that some of the awards had to instill limits as to how many times a single artist could receive the award.

I never heard him ever brag on himself but I think he knew how great he was. He was too smart to brag. Chet didn't like arrogant musicians; he thought it was silly to be like that because no matter how good you are you still have a lot to learn. Chet just enjoyed playing guitar and being Chet Atkins.

What made Chet different than other guitar players was when he played it was like magic ... all that beautiful music just came pouring out of him. I recall many times standing beside Chet on the stage or TV and listening to him play and feeling like I didn't know anything and I was the worst guitar player in the world.

Then he would close the show with "Vincent." Everything would go quiet, all the stage lights were low and the spotlight would be just on him. I'd look at him, it would bring tears to my eyes because it was so beautiful. I would think, "Someday he will be gone." And I dreaded the thought of it. "Vincent" was one of his favorite songs. I also heard him say that the tune he was working on at present was his favorite, but in the years I worked with him I'd guess he played "Vincent" more than any other.

> Mom laid claim to "Vincent" as her tune.
> — Merle Atkins Russel
> (*Chet Atkins in Three Dimensions,* vol.1)

That "Mom laid claim to "Vincent" as her tune" seems to say it all. When Chet played "Vincent" he was playing for, and to, the love of his life, Leona.

Chet was playing great right up to the last date we did in Salt Lake City where we did three days, then in about a week he became ill. Once after Chet had gotten really sick, I went over to his office to have lunch with him. Chet didn't have all of his own albums. There were quite a few at his office. As we were driving to where we were having lunch, he said, "I was listening to some of my records today and they aren't half bad."

I told him he was the greatest ever and made some of the greatest records ever. But that shows how humble Chet was. He was a one of a kind and we will never see another like him.

I got to work for two of the greatest guitarists that ever lived. Chet and Jerry have done so much for me that I could never repay them. I never thought, as a boy in Kentucky trying to learn to play a Stella guitar, that it would turn out this way. God has blessed me more than I deserve.

Interlude 8: "It's in the Hands"

"It's in the hands," a phrase most often used when referring to musicians. Chet Atkins' hands were not outsized by any means. Chet was tall, topping out at a little over six feet. Chet's hands were proportional to his height. Chet was a "long and slender" man and his hands were too. His fingers were not unusually long except his little finger is nearly as long as his index finger. This gave him a little advantage in chord stretches. Chet's hands were a fascination to Paul, not their size or shape. It never occurred to him, for example, to compare hand spans with Chet. He was fixated on what happened to a guitar when Chet put his hands on it.

Initial setup for a show eventually got to be Paul's responsibility. In shows where they carried a full band the other musicians would set up their own gear. Paul would direct the placement of the other musicians. He would always personally set up and check his and Chet's equipment himself, tuning each guitar and playing them to be sure all was well. Every time he did this he got a re-education of the fact that each guitarist imparts his own touch to the instrument.

I remember sometimes when the band, would do a sound check for a concert. The band would go to the hall and set up. Chet would come a little later. I would set Chet's amp and delay and get his guitar, tune it and play it through the house system, then I would do the same to mine.

Then Chet would arrive and pick up his guitar. It always amazed me! Nothing had been changed except it was Chet playing his guitar! It had a completely different sound than when I had played it. Once Chet broke a string and he took my guitar and played it. Once again it was the same sound as his!

I always watched Chet play. I would watch his hands trying to discover how he got such a great sound. Seventy-five percent of it was in his hands, the rest in his guitar and amp. His sound was a combination of things. He used his nails and the ends of his fingers together when he picked the strings. He used a high action which let him get clear notes and sustain. Chet had really strong hands and his right hand was something else. His right hand was as fast as he wanted it to be. There has never been any player that had it together like Chet did. I used to stand by him to try to figure out what he did to be Chet Atkins when he played but I never did. It was because Chet had The Touch that made him what he was. It was his soul.

CHAPTER 17

THE CGP AWARD

It was my idea to start the CGP awards. The year Jerry Reed got it was (July 13) 1990. The idea came up about two months before a CAAS gathering. I suggested to Chet that they give Jerry an award and call it the CGP award. Chet had given me an obelisk of marble or jade he'd had sitting around in his office. We took that to Mark Pritcher and he had it engraved. Chet gave it to Jerry at the CAAS that year.

Note: Actually, the obelisk originally belonged to Marie.

A few years later I think Mark Pritcher got the idea to give one to John Knowles. He talked it over with Chet and they gave it to him on July 13, 1996.

After Chet did that CD with Tommy Emmanuel we all saw what a great player he was. I suggested to Chet that they give one to Tommy, which they did.

People ask me about it, but nobody suggested giving one to me. Over the years there have been quite a few discussions about Chet not giving me the CGP award. I always thought that, because it was my idea that it would be in bad taste and self-serving for me to get one. I don't care for awards. I got the best award of all I got to work for Chet for twenty-four years.

Chet did give me something very precious and dear to me on the night that Chet gave John Knowles his CGP at the CAAS. After Chet did John's presentation he turned to me and gave me a small book he had started in February 12, 1950. It contains a list of all the tunes that he knew down through the years from A to Z. The book is leather bound and worn ... frayed at the edges. Most of the tunes are as Chet typed them but many are in his handwriting. When he gave it to me on the stage he said, "and I can play every one of them!" So you see I would rather have this small book that Chet kept for over fifty years than have the CGP. I thought you all would like to know about it.

Chet gave out only four CGPs. Jerry Reed, Steve Wariner, John Knowles and Tommy Emmanuel. There are two or three people who claim Chet gave them one but that's bogus. There were and are only four.

Note: It would appear that Liona Boyd also got the privilege based on a TV clip:

> Chet: I just had a new album out called *Chet Atkins, CGP*.
>
> Liona: (pointing to a button he is wearing) I saw that on your braces (suspenders).
>
> Chet: That's my CGP. I always wanted a PhD. I never could get it 'cause I dropped out, so I gave myself.
>
> Liona: (inaudible … something about honorary doctorates)
>
> Chet: I gave myself an honorary doctorate. It's a Certified Guitar Player. I guess it's more like a CPA. But I figured as long as I've been playin', and tryin' to get it right, that I should be certified by now. So I gave myself a degree. I'll give you one if you'd like it. I'll give you this pin. (He removes pin hands it to her.) And you can pin it on your sweater there.
>
> Liona: Thank you. (the rest is inaudible).
>
> Chet: And, you can sign your name. When you sign autographs you can sign Liona Boyd, CGP.
>
> Liona: (pointing to the letters on the button) "Chet, the Great Player."

Paul got to where he didn't care to address this topic on the forum anymore because, as he put it, "we have talked this subject to death, folks." The pins mentioned in the Chet/Liona dialogue above might have been in connection with the release of Chet's album *CGP* (CBS Records 1988). In any case, Chet had no direct part in having the pins made up. They were souvenir pins.

Mark Pritchard, one year before the 1988 CAAS, made up a bunch of CGP pins. He gave them out when people checked in. I used to have a handful. Chet carried some around in his pocket. I guess you could say everybody who got a CGP pin is one.

Sometimes people talk about "carrying on the CGP awards" but Chet's wife Leona told me she didn't want anymore CGP awards given out because that whole CGP concept was something that Chet had done. It was his award to give and no one else's. He gave CGPs to four of his friends. Had he lived I'm sure there would have been more. Chet had a lot of friends. He couldn't give it to everyone. He probably would have but just didn't think about it. When he gave it to someone he made an occasion out of it.

In August of 2011 the Country Music Hall of Fame kicked off an eleven month special exhibit of Chet Atkins' life and times. On Saturday the thirteenth, at a ceremony at the Country Music Hall of Fame exhibit Merle Atkins Russell, Chet's daughter made a presentation and said, in part, "We had a wonderful time the other night when the event opened. It was really wonderful and everything and we saw a lot of people and a lot of friends. And I got home and I got a message 'from above' (if you know who I mean) and being the good daughter that I am, I am here to bestow a very special honor to our friend Paul" She read the inscription and presented Paul with the CGP Award. She then put a lock on the award saying that was it. No more were to be given out. Since the Atkins estate has a copyright on CGP that is it.

The inscription was as follows:

> Whereas, long a fixture as Chet's band leader and confidant, Paul Yandell was truly invaluable.
>
> Whereas, he is no stranger to accolades for his many contributions to country music, the Nashville recording community, and the guitar world in his own right.
>
> Whereas, observing that Paul Yandell was involved in the distribution of all the CGP honors as Chet's assistant, and being extremely humble and modest, rescued himself of that very honor.
>
> Be it resolved by the Atkins family that throughout the land Paul Yandell, thumbpicker supreme, be known as the last and final CGP, certified guitar player. Paul, you are truly the CGP's CGP.

Signed by Merle Atkins Russell, for the Chet Atkins Estate.

"Isn't that great? It's like winning the Academy Award!"

Paul receiving the CGP award from Merle Atkins Russell. *Photo credit of YFA*

He posted on a forum:

> It's was quite a week for Chet and myself. Merle Atkins-Russell, Chet's daughter, along with the Atkins family, gave me the biggest surprise of my life. I can't describe how I felt! I just want everyone to know I'm the same picker I have always been … just one of the guys.

The "CGP" is copyrighted. It can't be used without permission from Chet's estate. By the way, Grammy nominations really don't mean much. The way it works is, you fill out the proper forms and send in the right amount of CDs. Then you get ten of your friends to say they want to nominate your song or songs. The only thing that counts is if your song is in the top five tunes. Anybody can nominate any tune or song.

Addendum

> Paul always said people would try to rewrite history after he was gone when he would not be around to defend the record. He said, "If the CGP pin (or some other item) was not given to them in a ceremony setting in front of a crowd of people, then they were not made a designated CGP."
>
> Jerry Reed was the first person to receive the CGP designation from Chet. I had a jade green obelisk that Paul took to Chet to use. Chet gave it to Mark Pritcher to have engraved for Jerry.
> — Marie Yandell

After years of seeing this topic endlessly bandied about on various chat boards Here are a few observations by the author:

> 1. Chet used to say 'anyone who plays guitar is a friend of mine.' He even signed some of his photos that way. I think he would have considered all guitarists to be "CGP." That's the way Chet was.

> 2. The whole "CGP" concept was, to him, a little on the tongue-in-cheek thing. It's a made up title that he could bestow with some ceremony on friends of his. I doubt he had any idea it would be so heatedly argued after he passed on. It is unknown if anyone asked Chet if there was a difference between the fully ceremonial trophy- plus-certificate presentation or the quick use of a souvenir pin presentation. Or which one would have had more "value." People lose track of the original idea. It was to bestow a made-up musical degree on people he thought deserved an extra pat on the back.

3. It almost seems, given the opportunity, he would have happily passed out one of those pins to people and bestowed "CGP" on them out of love for the guitar and the fun of passing out silly little souvenir pins and making people smile. But as Marie, Paul, and Merle indicated the ceremony and trophy object plus the written certificate/decree is what makes the true CGP Award.

Anyone is free to think "person X" should be or is a CGP but the fact remains there were only five CGP Awards given in public ceremony.

This horse is about beat to death now, one would think.

Interlude 9: Lenny Breau

Lenny Breau was a truly remarkable guitarist. His skill is really difficult to describe, and must be heard to be believed. He made several albums, three produced by Chet Atkins, the first two being *Guitar Sounds of Lenny Breau*, and *Velvet Touch of Lenny Breau.*

Lenny had unfortunately acquired a taste for drugs, most notoriously, heroin. The last album Chet produced for Lenny took well over a year to make. When Lenny was in Nashville he would stop in to see Chet. Sometimes he was fine. He had periods where he would do rehab and get off the hard drugs. When this happened, Chet would hustle Lenny to his home studio and try to get some good tracks made. If Lenny showed signs of being "strung out" or on heavy drugs Chet felt it was pointless to try for a recording. At this rate it took a long time to accumulate enough songs to make an LP.

Lenny had an almost childlike quality in many ways. Constantly needing others to help him, sort of everybody's kid brother … with issues. But anyone who heard him play knew they were hearing a truly phenomenal guitarist. One of those who would practice ten, twelve hours a day as he constantly expanded new horizons on the instrument. Unfortunately, he was one of those musicians who took bad advice and tried too many drugs for too long. It was a sad business. An American tragedy

I was working with Kitty Wells when I met Lenny Breau. We did a lot of tours in Canada. Lenny was in Winnipeg where he had a network TV show on CBC. We played Winnipeg one night then after our show Lenny came over to Odell Martin's and my room and played for awhile. After that, every time we were in the area, Odell and I would try to see him. He would come to our room after his show to sit up and play with us for half the night. We thought he was the greatest thing that ever was. And he was! One time he brought me a tape made from his TV show and said 'Would you mind taking this to Nashville to see if I can get a record deal?'

Chet knew Lenny's parents (Hal, "Lone Pine" Breau and Betty Cody) because he had recorded with them on RCA years before. I took the tape to Chet one morning but he wasn't in. I left it on his desk. He called me the same afternoon. "Who is this guy? Do you have a phone number on him?" He called Lenny and in two or three weeks had him come to Nashville where he signed him to do his first album for RCA. Jerry Reed and Lenny knew each other but I don't think they ever played together. I showed Lenny "The Claw" but of course after he learned it he changed it to play it his way.

Lenny stayed at my house for about two weeks so I got to know Lenny very well. When he stayed at our house he was pretty much straight. I think he did pot but not the hard stuff.

Marie, who never was around any people who used marijuana, reflects on those two weeks:

Lenny smoked pot in the bedroom he was occupying and in the bathroom when he was in it. I was so naive I didn't know what marijuana smelled like and had no idea he was smoking pot. I said something to Paul about Lenny's hygiene and his odor. I thought maybe the odor was in his clothes or maybe he needed a bath. Paul knew what it was but wouldn't tell me. Paul knew I wouldn't want him in the house if he was smoking pot. The odor was so strong that I raised windows to try to get the smell out of the house. Sometime later after Lenny was no longer staying with us, Paul finally told me what it was.

Paul and Chet tried to help him when he came to Nashville. Lenny couldn't drive so Paul helped him to find a one-bedroom apartment on Music Row. I gathered up some of our linens and kitchenware for him to use in the apartment.

Paul and Chet helped him to get a guitar and amp as well as a gig at Ireland's Restaurant (near Music Row) so that he could make some money to live on but that didn't last long. He ended up hocking the guitar at a pawnshop so that he could buy drugs. Paul found out about it and went to the pawnshop and paid to get the equipment out of pawn. Paul would go by the apartment to check on Lenny. Lenny had people who appeared to be drug dealers in the apartment with him. It was a sad situation. Lenny was so addicted to hard drugs. Add to that, he had no common sense. He didn't know how to do anything for himself.

One problem Lenny had was that he didn't drive. He had to rely on others to get him around. I asked him once why he didn't move to Nashville. He said he was afraid he would get drafted. You really can't blame him. Lenny wouldn't have fit in the army.

Down through the years we spent a lot of time together. I never saw anyone, other than Chet, so dedicated to the guitar. Lenny did things on guitar that no on else has ever done. He was in a class by himself. Lenny was one of the greatest guitar players that ever lived. I've heard Chet say Lenny was the greatest. I, of course, think Chet was the greatest but Lenny was just unbelievable! He could play anything! He had great hands. He had the strongest little finger on his left hand that you ever saw.

Here's a funny story about Lenny. Once, Odell Martin took Lenny up to Mose Rager's so he could play for Mose. I think it was on a Sunday afternoon. Mose and his family were church people. There were a number of people there and Mrs. Rager went around asking each one what they wanted to drink. Most of them wanted ice tea but when she came to Lenny he said 'Like man I'll have a beer!'

That's Lenny for you.

Lenny had a lot of demons and they finally got the best of him. He was a free soul; all he wanted to do was play. He told me when he was married he practiced so much it drove his wife nuts so she divorced him. Lenny was a one of a kind person like Chet, Jerry Reed and Elvis. Those type people come into this world to leave their mark for the rest of us to marvel at. There will never be another like him and I say that without reservation

It was really sad that his life ended the way it did. He deserved better.

CHAPTER 18

RESEARCH AND DEVELOPMENT

Guitars are imperfect things. I've had at lest fifty guitars in my life but I never had a perfect one and Chet didn't either.

Paul Yandell was very much a "hands on" guitar player when it came to maintaining instruments. In the early days of his career finding a repairman was not like it is today. We, as a musical nation, are spoiled being surrounded by guitar makers who do repairs on the side or dedicated shops that focus on repairing and modifying all kinds of instruments.

As far as working on guitars, I've always been one to work on my own instruments. Back in the 1960s I hung around the Old Time Pickin' Parlor here in Nashville and I asked a lot of questions. I would rather work on mine than have someone else do it. I've always tried to come up with ideas about guitars, something different, that is worthwhile to make a guitar play better and sound better.

Conceptualizing a Guitar … Yandell Style

Chet always was trying to improve his sound and his guitars. Manufacturers are slow about change and that includes Gibson. You can't do a sudden change in a guitar line. I've been lucky in dealing with the modern day Gretsch Company. They are open to new ideas and my ideas are listened to. They might not agree but at least they hear what I have to say.

Gretsch

The Release of the Fender/Gretsch G6122-1959 Nashville Classic in 2003

I know a lot of players don't like guitars made in Japan with good reason because there are a lot of bad guitars out there. But there are some that are good, well made guitars, too … Yamaha, D'Angelico and Gretsch for example.
I wanted to do the '59 Country Gentleman, serial number 31444 (Chet's guitar), for three reasons. First to remember Chet, second, because he cut most of his records with his old one, third, I thought a lot of players (including myself) would like to have one of those if it were available.

Gretsch Nashville Classic. Paul was instrumental in getting this guitar into production making it as close to Chet's original '59 as possible. It is now listed as the 6122-59 Country Gentleman. *Photo courtesy of Derek Rhodes*

It's not a perfect guitar. Some won't like it. Being made in the USA doesn't mean a great guitar either. I've seen some Gibson Country Gentlemans in music stores that were pretty bad ... it just happens.

I think when the Nashville Classic gets on the market and everyone plays it they will see it for what it is, a pretty good guitar that has a great sound. After all, how a guitar sounds and plays is what really counts. As far as I know they will be made in Japan, but that doesn't bother me because if they are as good as the one I have, it will be a great guitar.

I got the idea for the Nashville Classic one day while having a cup of coffee. I called Fred Gretsch and asked him if he was interested in doing it. He said he thought it was a great idea.

I knew a fellow who worked at the Country Music Hall of Fame who he let me go down to take all the measurements off Chet's actual guitar. I'd had the '59 at my house many times so I knew the guitar pretty well anyway. I made three trips at different times to double check things. I had several conversations with TV Jones about the wiring and pickups.

When I got it all together, I sent everything down to Fred. He had three prototypes made. It took about three months to do it. I came up with the name "Nashville Classic" to make the guitar stand out from the other ones in the Gretsch line.

I didn't have anything to do with the internal bracing. That's the way the prototypes were made. Later on we changed the tuner buttons to the fat ones because Chet liked them. Gretsch had to have Grover remake them. When I played mine I knew it was a special guitar. We had a winner!

The following is Paul's forum posting about the release of the Nashville Classic in 2003:

Now that the NAMM Show is over and they have shown the guitar I can comment on it.

Fred Gretsch had asked me at different times in the past two years to come in with Gretsch as an advisor so about a year ago I suggested to him they reissue the Country Gentleman but do it just like Chet's favorite. Fred told me to go ahead.

I went down to the Hall Of Fame three or four times to take measurements of Chet's guitar and we built it. I have had the prototype for about two months. After I got it and got it set it up I put my Gibson Country Gentleman in the case because I can truthfully say the Nashville Classic is the best guitar I have ever had.

The prototype I have sounds like a Gretsch. I suggested they go to the old bar bridge that worked on two height adjusting screws ... maybe they will do that. As for getting Chet's sound I never heard anybody get Chet's sound because most of that was in his hands. But having said that, I think you can get close to it. Sound depends, too, on the amp. Chet always used his Standel which had a unique sound.

Because we made it like Chet's it's not like the standard 1959 issue. The new model has Chet's preferred wide neck and it has a SuperTron pickup in the neck position. Chet didn't like that stock tone switch because it didn't work right. The new guitar is wired like Chet's ... no volume control for the front pickup ... it has master volume, volume for the back pickup and a tone control. You don't need a front pickup volume control with a master volume control when you are using both pickups because you always turn the back pickup down when you blend them.

The pickups are wound just like Chet's and are by TV Jones. The front pickup is 4k like the standard Gretsch SuperTron, the back pickup is a little under 8k which is what Chet's was. He'd had Shot Jackson rewind it that way back in the '60s. It gives a lot more output. When Chet used both pickups his guitar had more balls. He would blend the back pickup (turned down a little). Most of the time he used both pickups.

This new one doesn't have a block running down the inside of the top like Gibson has on some of their models. When you get into using those solid blocks the guitars get heavy like the first Gibson Country Gentleman. It had a block of maple down the center and weighed a ton. It has a brace under the bridge in between the top and back. It's about three inches across the top and bottom. I think you can get the same effect with sound posts underneath the bridge. Chet's old D'Angelico had the greatest sustain and he had a sound post under each side of the bridge. The guitar has good sustain down the neck on the bass and treble strings.

Chet's neck at the nut is 44.16 mm or 1.7585 inches. At the 5th fret it's 48.00mm or 1.89 inches and at the 12th fret it's 52.75mm or 2.0765. The new one is right on these specs. The height of Chet's frets on his '59 Gretsch Country Gentleman is 0.50 or 1.29mm.

It comes standard with the Chet handle and bracket. I know the fixed handle is a problem for some owners. Finally, in February of 2004, because of all the trouble that almost everyone was having with the fixed handle, I saw I probably made a mistake putting it on the Nashville Classic. I thought everyone who bought the guitar would want one because Chet had one but I now see I was wrong. I have asked Mike Lewis to change the fixed handle to a flat swing around one. Maybe that will be better for everyone. They are going to make some kind of arrangement so people can have an option.

The Nashville Classic is a fine guitar, so those of you who have it and can't deal with the fixed handle, order the flat kind and sell the bracket and handle. It will be easy to sell the on Ebay or by posting in a forum because those brackets are getting hard to find since Gretsch uses them on the Nashville Classic.

It was my decision to go with the gold plating even though Chet's wasn't gold plated. The '59 Country Gentleman isn't gold plated so you can see how much better the gold plating looks. For the price of the guitars today I thought it should be gold. I felt that Chet would have wanted gold plating.

I appreciate all the nice comments regarding the Nashville Classic and I am gratified by the sales figures. The idea was keep Chet's memory alive and have a great guitar for everyone to own. Every time I pick mine up I think about Chet and how I used to tune his '59 for him ... those were really "the good old days."

I'd had a 1961 Country Gentleman I bought new but this guitar is a better guitar. I hope you-all get to play one.

On New Year's Day in 2007 the Gretsch company announced the return of the Chet Atkins name to the 6100 line of signature guitars. The Nashville Classic became the 6122-59 and was called the Country Gentleman as were all the other variants. This was an idea motivated by the Atkins estate.

The newly renamed Nashville Classic is the same guitar; it just becomes more like Chet's with the name Country Gentleman on the name plate with Chet's name on it. I've retired most of my other guitars and I play my Gretsch Country Gentleman every day. Things are back like they should be. Gretsch is more than Chet. They build models to appeal to young kids which is a larger market, but Gretsch promotes Chet much better than Gibson ever did. His models sell very well so I'm happy that Chet is back home. Gretsch builds great Chet Atkins models. I'm sure Chet would like the girl they use, too. (Model Kim Falcon) She looks a lot like Bettie Paige.

The first issue models of the Nashville Classics were not the shape of the original '59 models. Mike Lewis of Gretsch bought a vintage Country Club which has the same body shape as the '59 Country Gentleman and they redid the body shape to what the old ones were using that as a template.

The Nashville Classic has a brace underneath the bridge that is shaped like an H. It's about a half inch thick so it doesn't add much weight. The old Gretsch guitars were made with three-ply wood. The Nashville Classic is five ply or four ply, I forget which. The vibrato and the pickups add quite a bit of weight. The maple neck adds a whole lot, plus the tuners. The Nashville Classic, being a large guitar, is what some people call heavy.

A few more thoughts on the Nashville Classic and what might have been ...

Would Gretsch have made this guitar if Chet had stayed with them? I don't know. After Baldwin moved the factory to Arkansas everything sort of fell apart. None of the people who worked at the factory in New York had moved down there so the quality suffered. Chet never made any secret about how he had his pickups wound. If he had stayed and the quality had come back I think Gretsch would have reintroduced the '59 single cutaway Country Gentleman and the pickups would have been like Chet's, but who knows?

Note: "… never made any secret about how he had his pickups wound." Prior to the release of the Nashville Classic there is little, if any, reference to Chet having a specially wound bridge pickup on his personal guitar. Chet's '59 was his personally modified recording instrument, his "secret weapon" as it were, and it would be speculative whether he would have wanted that guitar made available when he was actively recording.

In 2008, when Chet's name was back on the Gretsch guitars, someone asked me if the new 6122-59 Country Gentleman was as good as or better than the Brooklyn era Gretsch's.

I said they were better made but one has to remember Chet was playing his own guitar and no one ever got the tone he did. The 6122-59 Country Gentleman is like I wanted it. I wish it was a little lighter but it's hard to make a large guitar with a vibrato and good bracing without it being somewhat heavy. I think it is all around a better guitar than the Gibson Country Gentleman which was a great guitar, but I never liked the tone of it. I think the number of players who are playing the 6122-59 Country Gentleman answers that question of whether the new version of the '59 is a better guitar.

The Gretsch "Chet Atkins 6120 CGP" Guitar

"The original prototype Gretsch STEREO guitar was created for Chet Atkins in 1956 with the help of musician and electronics repairman from Cairo, Illinois, Ray Butts. Ray's ingenious split-dual-coil pickup was assembled on a prototype G6120 guitar with closed simulated "F-Hole" inlays on the body, Only ONE was ever produced."
—Joe Carducci
Gretsch Product Specialist

It gives me great pleasure to announce the forthcoming new Gretsch "Chet Atkins 6120 CGP" a reissue of Chet's "Red" solid top one-of–a-kind 6120/55 heard most notably on A Session with Chet Atkins and Finger-Style Guitar albums. (It was actually Gretsch orange like on the regular 6120's but in some photos the guitar was more of a reddish orange.)

The CGP Guitar. This guitar was created at Paul's request and direction. A close replica of the famous "Finger-Style" album guitar, complete with split pickup but without the carved top. This Bigsby has a special tuner described in the text. This model was to become his favorite "player." *Photo courtesy of Derek Rhodes*

This has been a two-year project with myself, TV Jones and the Gretsch Guitar Company. Gretsch is really nice to work with. They listen to my ideas when I have some. TV Jones has done an outstanding job on the pickup and wiring requirements on this guitar. We have made an effort to make it as close to Chet's guitar as possible. It has the same pickup setup as Chet's original guitar.

Chet's guitar had one stereo pickup (splitting the treble and bass strings) and it was the neck pickup. The CGP has two output jacks so you can use two amps or record two different tracks with effects on either track. This is what Chet did in the studio sometimes. He only used the split pickup mode in the studio where he could control the EQ on the board. You can, of course, use the CGP mono like a normal guitar.

Note: The word "pot" as used here, is short for "potentiometer." The pot is the actual volume or tone control inside the instrument or device, out of sight except for the shaft. This shaft is what the control knob is attached to. Paul was using "control" and "pot" interchangeably.

This is how it works. In mono mode it's like the 6122-59 Gentleman, in that the pot next to the vibrato handle is for the back pickup and only one cable/output jack is required to use the guitar. You then have your master volume and a volume pot for each pickup. There is no tone control at all as Chet didn't have one on that guitar.

There is a black switch (often called an a/b switch) that cuts the guitar from mono to stereo. When it comes into play the use of the controls changes considerably. When the guitar is in stereo, only the front pickup is working and two output jacks are used. When both output jacks are used (in the split pickup or "stereo" mode) the pot nearer the edge of the guitar controls the three treble strings and the master volume pot controls the three bass strings. The pot by the Bigsby is muted in the stereo mode as well as the pickup selector switch. In other words, only two pots work in the stereo mode: the master volume, which is the volume for the bass strings and the bottom volume pot for the treble.

Here's a little back-story on the design effort reported by "Proteus" (Tim Harmon, creator of Tru-Arc bridges). Proteus was at the CAAS 2008 in July when it was first unveiled to the public:

They made the pickups and the wiring harness TV Jones' problem. Since no one involved had physical access to the original guitar—nor had ever played it – development depended on Paul's research with Chet's relatives who had owned and played the guitar. TV designed and wound both pickups – the split/stereo Classic at the neck in its DynaSonic case and the mono Classic at the bridge. Then it just had to be wired.

Over a period of many months and countless phone calls, he determined how the controls behaved—and relayed that to TV. At first, Tom said that electronically it couldn't work that way, but Paul insisted it had. Tom stuck to it, worked over the period of a month—and when he was done, it DID work just as Paul had described.

The development team did not, however, replicate the ultra-thick solid top of the Prototype. No one wanted a beastly heavy 6120. Instead, Paul worked with Gretsch and Terada over a series of prototypes to develop a top and bracing which would respond as they all sensed the original plank must have.

In the judgment of all involved, they came as close as humanly possible to "productionizing" what had never been anything BUT a prototype, and making the stereo 6120 a reality.
— Tim Harman
(Proteus)

As for the guitar itself, the neck is the same at the nut as the 6122-59 Gretsch Country Gentleman. The taper is the same as the Gibson Country Gentleman. It has a rosewood fingerboard like the original guitar had. It has an aluminum nut like Chet had at the time and will be shipped with both fixed or swing away Bigsby handle brackets and the Chet handle.

Chet's original guitar had a carved top that was thick in the middle and thinned out to the sides. We couldn't do a carved top because of the cost. The factory in Japan isn't able to do it. Very few people would be able to afford it if they could do it and not many would like the weight of it. Chet's original instrument was as heavy as a Les Paul or heavier.

Jimmy Atkins, who owned the original, told me it was so heavy that he never played it. The CGP has a one piece maple top that is more than 1/8 inch thick and has the inlaid F holes. When you do these guitars for production you have to have trade offs. Other than that I think we nailed it pretty good.

It is 24½ scale like all 6120s. The prototype I have has great sustain all the way up the neck. As for the short scale, that's what Chet's was at the time. If I'd had them make it with the long scale the purists would say, "Why didn't you make it like Chet's? His had the short scale!"

There are some folks who don't like the orange color or the G brand styling Gretsch used at that time but I wanted the guitar to look like Chet's. We could have used more knobs and made a tone control and such but Chet's didn't have a tone control so we left it off. It's the same body size as the old 6120 which means, at sixteen inches, it is narrower than the Country Gentleman and the body is a little thicker.

The pickups are spaced about like Chet's was on his old guitar. The CGP has its own sound compared to the Country Gentleman. They are different guitars in size, body thickness and pickups so it's going to sound different than the Country Gentleman as it should. Remember Gretsch only made one of those so I'm sure they weren't easy to make back then.

Here's a little side story about the pickups on that guitar:

Ray Butts received a patent for the Filter-Tron pickup and the stereo pickup at the same time in 1956. I remember when Ray invented those pickups that Chet had on that guitar. Odell Martin had Ray make him a set for his 6120. I think Ray charged $125 each for them. I didn't have the money to get some but that's show business.

Does the CGP sound like Chet's original? I can't really answer that, for two reasons. First, Chet's nephew Jimmy Atkins had the guitar for about twenty years and he told me all about it. We talked about it many times so I feel like I know the guitar as well as I could without having played it but I never got to play it. Still, I think it sounds more like Chet's guitar of the mid 1950s

The second reason is that Chet was Chet. He did it his way. Nobody has ever gotten the sound he got and no one ever will. The sound he got back then was a number of things starting with the guitar he was playing and how he recorded it. That's the best answer I can give you. I tried to make this guitar as close to his guitar as I could. I'm satisfied with the guitar. I wouldn't want to put anything on the market that wasn't right and I think this would be a guitar anybody would be proud to own.

Gretsch hasn't given me a price as of yet (January 2008.) Joe Carducci Gretsch Marketing Manager intends to have a CGP at the CAAS. They will be available later in the year. I know everyone will be as excited about this guitar as I am. I wanted to bring the CGP out because it was one of Chet's great guitars and means so much to so many.

While the CGP was released in 2008 most of them were actually built in 2007. The serial numbers bear that out. The way it works is you design the model. Then it takes time to get the circuit right. While all of that is being made right the factory is making all the other models. Then the CGP has to get in the production pipeline. Meanwhile, Gretsch decided how many to make and when to release it. All of this takes time. The CGP wasn't the only model they were concerned with. Finally it was on the market and everything worked as it was supposed to. As things stand now Gretsch intended to make seventy-five a year.

Some people nit-pick the CGP. I'm always amused when someone runs down something they have never seen. So it's got a big G on it! I don't think that had any effect on how the guitar sounded. Some of Chet's greatest records were made with that guitar. I really don't think the thickness of the top was that critical in the sound. True, it would have something to do with sustain, but that's about it.

I'm proud of the CGP, big G and all. It will be on the market in September then everyone can judge it for themselves

I think Chet liked the original "CGP." He played it for many years and recorded many records with it. The solid top idea morphed into the silk screened f-holes on the 58' Country Gentleman which had most of the features of the "CGP."

From 1955 until Dec 1958 almost every Saturday night I worked the Grand Ole Opry with the Louvin Brothers. Chet was on the Opry almost every Saturday night too and I saw what guitar he was playing at the time. Sometimes he would stop and talk to me. There is a picture of Chet, myself, Merle Travis and the Louvins on my web site. It was taken in the spring of 1956. Chet is holding the solid top 6120.

I never saw him with anything else on the Opry in that time period except one night he played the black 6120 with the gold inlays. When playing on TV in those days my guess is the solid top wasn't on the market so Chet played other 6120s on TV to advertise it and sell some guitars.

A footnote ... He only used the split pickup mode in the studio where he could control the eq on the board.

Since I have had the modern prototype of the CGP I have played it almost exclusively. I really like it. I always wanted a short scale guitar with a good neck and the CGP is that. It won't replace the 61252.-59 but it will be a good partner to it.

Thoughts on the Super Chet

The Super Chet was a beautiful guitar but it wasn't what the '59 was. I had a Super Chet and I could never get it going right. For some reason I just didn't enjoying playing it. I never thought it was all that great. I have played others but they never had the sound the '59 Country Gentleman and the CGP had.

Chet didn't play his Super Chet all that much. I think he was photographed with it on the *Guitar Monsters* album to give it some advertising for it. He would play it on TV for the same reason.

That Super Chet (photographed on the *Guitar Monsters* album) had extra switches on it. Ray Butts put those switches on there when he first got that guitar. They were phase switches and coil taps on each of the pickups. I don't think Chet ever used them. I never saw Chet use them because I think they thinned out his tone. I believe that particular guitar was left to one of his secretaries.

He didn't play the Super Chet too much because it didn't have a vibrato on it. The pitch on the necks on most of them isn't steep enough to use a vibrato. You don't have enough down pressure on the bridge. Still, Chet always said he thought the Super Chet was the prettiest guitar Gretsch ever made. If someone has a Super Chet they might keep it as an investment.

And finally:

Gretsch had many quality problems back in the seventies which was one reason Chet left them. They were great looking, but had things that needed correcting. The frets wear off sometimes, and they always had internal vibrations.

Here is piece on Gretsch's bad quality control during the time they were owned by Baldwin written by a man who was a Gretsch employee in the seventies:

> I met Chet on numerous occasions in Nashville during the "DJ Week."
> I actually played (bass) with him, Roy Clark & Buck Trent at an impromptu session which was a real treat. I had no business being on the same stage ... but I was ... so I enjoyed the moment.
> During my tenure, Quality Control (at the Booneville plant) became an issue. There was virtually no R&D and new product development, because that department wasn't funded by Baldwin.
> Fender Stratocasters and Gibson Les Paul's were selling at the rate of 2,000 a month, but Gretsch was relying on the Country Rock and other outdated designs to reap the rewards of the burgeoning rock'n'roll industry.
> The wealth on the Baldwin side of Gilbert Ave. didn't care whether Gretsch succeeded or not, a fact that was manifested by a lack of proactive management, unregimented, off-site manufacturing (in backwoods Booneville), and ZERO financial support for basic business staples. Baldwin was only across the street but they might have well been in another hemisphere because they didn't acknowledge the value, history, or heritage of Gretsch, and that underscored its demise.
> Chet, among other things, was an American cultural icon and a well-respected businessman, a former VP of RCA, and needed to be associated with "winners."
> Gibson & Fender may have changed parents over the years, too, but their durability was never in question. I think (psychologically, certainly not financially) Chet needed to have his name on a major manufacturer's headstock, and when he heard the rumors and rumblings about Gretsch's bleak future he chose to jump ship.
> — Ed Preman

Paul had issues with the changes in design of the Chet Atkins model guitars. Although this started before Baldwin entered the picture he clearly thought the changes took away from the instruments he respected.

I always thought the double cutaways were not as good. They where hard to hold (out of balance). This is because with the double cutaways, you have less weight in the forward part of the guitar. The necks were real small too. Chet told me once they (Gretsch) were always putting gimmicks on his guitars without asking him about it. They often changed the design on his signature guitars without asking him. The older Gretsch guitars were made of three ply sides and top and back. The new ones are five ply. That's just the way they do it now.

A Trick or Three ...

By the way, I have been working on my personal Nashville Classic trying to improve the returning to pitch factor when I used the Bigsby. I think any guitar with a zero fret is harder to stay in tune with a Bigsby because the nut is not quite right. I think I have found one solution: I put a lubricated nut on my Nashville Classic. It was an old one I had used years ago. It improved the return to pitch 100%. You can use a bone nut which has natural oils or a graphite nut which works well. Anyway, I thought I would share this with you-all because staying in tune is a headache we all face.

Another 'tinker' I like is that I have put many master volumes in guitars that didn't originally have them. What I do is put the master volume in place of the front pickup volume control. You don't need one for the front pickup if you have a master volume. A master volume is the only way to go I think. They might knock a small amount of highs off your tone but I think most guitars have too many highs anyway. One way to avoid that roll-off is to put a small capacitor across the in and out post of the control.

Sometimes, to cut down on the string noise, I took 600 grit sandpaper and sanded the wound strings. You can do that and have a semi- flat wound string. Chet, when he played and recorded, would get body oil on his fingers. He would go behind his left ear and alongside his nose with his fingers. There is always some body oil there. I've seen him do it many times so I picked it up too. That's part of being Chet ... Like everything else, he had the answer.

For those who have trouble with their pick sliding around on their thumb: Just wet your thumb and your pick will stick like glue. I got that tip from a friend up in Kentucky, Gene Francis.

The Gibsons

The Gibson Country Gentleman

Chet and I were in on much of Gibson's designs of his signature instruments. I remember when Chet and I went up to Kalamazoo Michigan to meet with Jim Hutchins, Bruce Bolin and Tim Shaw about designing Chet a guitar. Some people ask me how much was I involved in the design of those guitars. Well, I didn't have anything to do with the neck sizes on any of Chet's guitars. Gibson would do them, take them to Chet and he would approve them. There wasn't any talk of Gretsch guitars. It was my idea to do the Orange color on the Gibson Gentlemans which Gibson originally didn't want to do as some of them thought the guitar wouldn't look right. I borrowed a beautiful Gretsch 6120 from a friend of mine to use as a sample to use to get the color. The orange color has changed over the years. They never seemed to get it right. As it turned out it was their best selling color.

Gibson Country Gentleman. This is a later version as attested by fingerboard inlays. Paul has a Ray Butts pickup at the fingerboard. The dark strip is a piece of velcro or tape on the pickup designed to lessen "pick click" noise. This also has a hand rest near the bridge pickup and fine tuners in the harp section behind the bridge. *Photo courtesy of Derek Rhodes*

They made the first one, then in a few months made another one with low impedance pickups. Les Paul uses low impedance pickups but I don't care for them. They sound thin to me. Chet played it a few times but didn't care for it. He gave it to his brother in Indiana. Bob Foster, who was a friend of Chet and his brother, has it now.

The Gibson Country Gentleman guitar just came out the way it did and they never changed. I remember Chet wanted the neck pickup as far forward as possible so his pick wouldn't be hitting it. They made the neck one fret shorter to do this. Chet always wanted the frets to come over to the edge of the fretboard like classical guitars do. Most of Gibson's guitars don't do that. When you have binding on the neck you have those nibs and the strings fall off when you do pull-offs.

If you don't have binding down the neck it doesn't look right to have it on the peg head. Chet never really cared one way or the other about that. Another thing is, it takes too much time when they make the guitar to fret them over the binding and would add unnecessarily to the cost. Personally, I don't think a guitar looks better with binding

The Gibson Country Gentlemans have armrests on them. An armrest helps keep sweat off the top of the guitar, plus they look good. The story about the armrest is this:

Back in the '50s, Merle Travis had one on his Super 400. I got the idea one day about making one for my guitar. I took Merle's album cover out to Gibson, showed it to a fellow who at that time drew the plans for their guitars who drew it out for me. I got the material from Jim Hutchins and made me one. I showed it to Chet and he wanted me to make him one so after that, Chet requested that they be put on the Country Gentleman. So that's the rest of the story.

I started turning the back pickup around to get a little fatter sound out of it. Chet liked it so he did it too. I put some TV Jones Nashville Classic pickups in one of my Gibson Country Gentleman's out of curiosity. It didn't sound anything like the Nashville Classic. Probably, I think, because the guitars are made differently. The block on the inside and the difference in the guitar tops affect it.

Chet played the first Country Gentleman that Gibson made for him longer than any of that series, but the first ones weigh a ton. Chet got tired of playing that first model because it was so heavy. For a time his neck bothered him so he asked Jim Hutchins to build a lighter one which resulted in the compressed balsa being used.

The first model Gibson Country Gents had the switch down by the controls. Chet was always looking for it when he was going to switch pickups. The fixed bracket didn't have enough room to work right, it seemed. I suggested they move the switch up top because it was in the way of the fixed handle bracket.

At the same time Chet told Hutch to make the F-holes the size of D'Angelico's F-holes. They did a second model and at that time made all of the changes at the same time. After that, Chet would play this one or that one. He had about six or seven of them. I have the very first Gibson Country Gentleman, a Christmas present from Chet.

After he got the second model he never played the first one that I know of. I think the first model sounds better. It has more sustain, but as far as I know he recorded with the same one he used on the road. Of course I wasn't around him all of the time so he might have used others, too. At one point Chet asked me to start going out to Gibson to, you might say, keep and eye on the quality of his guitars.

I also have one of the Gibson Gentlemans with the balsa block that I used for about ten years playing with Chet. When I got it, I dug the balsa wood out from under the bridge and put sound posts in it. I did it this way: I went in through the bridge pickup cutout. I made a tool that had a curve in it and I took a small hammer and sort of chiseled the balsa out. I then cut two pieces of maple and put them real tight under each side of the bridge. I dropped a little wood glue around the base of the posts and that was it! It made it sound more like the first model (that had the maple block) and the sustain was much better. I used it on many of the tunes on my CDs.

I suggested to Ray Butts at one time that he build some Gibson size pickups that had the old Gretsch sound which he did. He showed them to Henry J. (Henry Juszkiewicz) at Gibson but Henry didn't want to pay what Ray wanted for them so it never happened. Chet and I liked them.

It's sort of hard to describe tone but the Butt's pickups have more output and a little more highs. I don't think they sound like the Gretsch pickups but I think they sound great. I have used them for years. I just use one in the neck position and keep the Gibson in the rear position, that's about it. Chet didn't use them because he didn't think it was right for him not to use the stock Gibson pickups as he was a Gibson artist.

With Chet's touch he always sounded about the same on any guitar. However the Gretsch '59 Country Gentleman he played had a great tone to it, much better than the Gibson Country Gentleman I think. When Chet left Gretsch and went with Gibson, he won and lost. He won on the CEC nylon electric and lost on the Gibson Country Gentleman. The Gibson Country Gentleman was a beautiful high quality guitar but it never came close to having the tone of Chet's old '59.

Chet gave me the first Gibson Country Gentleman about ten years ago. He played it until the orange ones came out. It's the guitar he uses on that first teaching video with those kids (*Getting Started With Chet Atkins*). It is really a good one, slightly different than the production ones that were made. It's just like it was when he used it. He had an unplated handle on it. It didn't have any position markers on the neck. He took some red print tape and used that to put position markers on the fret board and that's how the red fret markers came to be. Gibson Country Gentlemans are fine guitars but they have that heavy Gibson sound that I never did like. Gibson never made a guitar that sounded as good as Chet's old '59.

The Gibson Tennessean

The Gibson Tennessean was my idea. I felt like Chet's fans needed a lower price guitar than the Country Gentleman. Because of the cost of designing a new model from scratch, Jim Hutchins suggested just making a single cutaway 335. We took a 335 and made it into a single cutaway. It costs about $10,000 in tooling to come out with a completely new model so we had to do it that way.

The B-6 Bigsby wouldn't work on it because of the pitch of the neck and Chet didn't like the Bigsby's with the tension bar, so we went with the stop tailpiece. Chet didn't want the square red position markers on it so he suggested the pearl dots. I suggested a wider neck. Gibson probably made a few of them before the final design was arrived at because there are a few prototypes out there.

I think it is a really good guitar. It has a different sound than the Gibson Country Gentleman. It is a long scale. I wanted to do a short scale but it didn't work out. If you put a Bigsby on it you got a great guitar. The neck is a little fatter than the Country Gentleman but it plays really well. It's a great guitar to put the two bass strings on like Chet and I use to do for the "Octabass" sound.

Later Chet got the idea to have the pickguard in the shape of the State of Tennessee, I made one and put it on the Tennessean that Chet had. Henry J.

didn't like it so they didn't use it. As it worked out, Gibson kept raising the price which defeated the original idea of a lower price guitar.

Gibson Super 4000

Gibson's Jim Hutchins and myself designed the Gibson 4000. Gibson wanted the most expensive guitar they sold to be a Chet model. Hutch and I tried to do something different.

If you had the 4000 and the Super 400 side by side, you would see a lot of difference. The color is different and the 4000 has wider binding. The pickguard is bigger with no screws in the top. They were going to make twenty five of them but I don't know if that is cast in concrete. As for price, Gibson charges what ever the market will bear. A week after it was brought out the price of the carved top guitars doubled, so I think will be mostly doctors and lawyers and rich people, rather than pickers, who buy those kinds of guitars for investments. Maybe if Chet had gotten to play it more on TV the 4000 would have been a big seller. I believe he only played it twice on TV before he got sick. I think the 4000 is the best looking guitar Gibson makes.

The Electric Classic Series

The biggest reason Chet left Gretsch was because of their refusal to build the CE (Classic Electric) classical which he was playing at the time. He was playing the prototype made by Kirk Sand but he couldn't get Gretsch interested in it. He knew it was a great idea so between the quality control issues Gretsch was having at the time, plus their reluctance to develop the CE series, Chet was moved to go to Gibson.

The idea first germinated after a relationship with guitar builder, Hascal Haile. Mr. Haile was a great person, always telling stories about his childhood and people he had known. He was a master builder. Before he started making guitars he made staircases for rich people's houses. He made beautiful mantles and grandfather's clocks. I don't know what gave him the idea to start making guitars but he made one and brought it down to let Chet see it. Chet gave him some advice, he kept making them so his guitars got better and better. After a while he made one Chet liked. Chet played a number of them and had two or three of them. I owned two of them. They are a great sounding classic.

Chet had two or three Hascal Haile classical guitars. The first one Mr. Haile made for Chet was placed in the Smithsonian when Chet died. He had two more, one with the inlaid pearl on the fretboard and the plain classical which he played and used to record with.

I was with Chet several times when he visited Mr. Haile. Chet and I used to drive up to his house in Kentucky. Chet and Hascal had a special arrangement that made for a different spin on the words 'Chet owned.'

Mr. Haile would build a guitar and give it to Chet. In a few months we would go up to Mr. Haille's house or he and his wife would come down to see Chet. He would have a new guitar with him and if Chet liked it, they would just swap them. So this way Chet would have played different ones and traded them back to Mr. Haile. Those guitars would, of course get sold.

Note: It is said that Andres Segovia, one of the greatest of the classical players, had a similar arrangement with guitar maker Jose Ramirez. Once a year, Segovia would personally choose a new guitar to use and leave the instrument he had used the year before with Ramirez to keep or sell at his own discretion.

Chet liked the idea of a solid body electric classical guitar. He liked playing a classical guitar, but to play a classical guitar in public you either had to be super conscious about mic placement or you would have to install one of the pickups of the day which, frankly, were not up to the task.

On one of his visits to Hascal Haile's house Chet saw a fingerboard on a plank and asked Hascal to expand on the idea. Make him a solid body classical. Mister Haile built two of those prototype electric classicals for Chet. I went with Chet up to Mr. Haile's while he was building them.

The body was solid and they had a bolt on neck. They weighed a ton!! They had the Prismatone pickup on them. Chet took the idea to a different luthier, Kirk Sand, to work out a better prototype. Kirk made a demo model and Chet asked Gretsch to pick up on the idea. They didn't want to do it. This was right around the time Chet left Gretsch.

As I remember it, Kirk Sand came to the CAAS one year and showed his prototype guitars to Chet. Everyone had a fit about his guitars. Chet asked Gibson to build something like Kirk's. I think Mike Voltz got together with Kirk and Gibson paid Kirk a royalty for each guitar they made. This was the birth of the CE (Classical Electric) models.

Gibson did their own version of Kirk's guitar. Chet didn't care for the controls being on the top (face). He liked them better on the side (on the upper bout edge). While Gibson was building the Studio Classic Chet played one of Kirk's with the Gibson logo on the peg head. As I remember, Chet didn't like the preamp at first so he asked Ray Butts to build a better one.

After the Studio Classic came out, Gibson made the fancy version with the Fleur de Leis ("marijuana leaf") design. Chet didn't like that. It was Henry J, the owner's idea. Still, Chet liked to play that guitar over the others for various reasons so he played it until he got sick.

Gibson has always had problems with the pickups on the CE model. When they would make a batch, about 30% would be bad. On Gibson's redesigning of the Chet Atkins Studio CE/CEC that came out in 2004 it looks like they just decided to do away with the old pickup along with redesigning sound hole placement. I think they were just dumbing the guitar down. They more than likely will discontinue the old model and say their new one is better.

I haven't ever seen a non-adjustable piezzio system that was balanced. Chet requested they build an adjustable pickup when Gibson first started making the CE. Tim Shaw developed the CEC pickup with each string having a volume pot.

Ovation had a pickup that was almost the same so they sued Gibson over it. Tim changed the look of it for a solid top. It took a long time to get the pickup where it would work right. They finally got it right but when they made them a lot of them were bad.

The Gibson CEC and CE, Studio guitars aren't shielded very well. When you try to record with them you get a low frequency hum. Guitars with piezzio pickups have a lot of gain so they have to be shielded or you get hum, radio stations, other kinds of interference. Different things can be used to shield an electronic circuit. Those CE-CEC pickups are shielded around the preamp and the cables to the controls are shielded but it isn't enough. One time I had a CE with the Gibson pickup that hummed so bad I couldn't record with it. I painted the top of the pickup with conductive paint and that stopped it.

One thing I learned from Chet. He used to take a wire and connect it to his guitar, then clip the other end to his watch. It grounds out the hum. I have a wire with a clip on both ends so I can do that when I record.

Gibson gave up trying to make their own pickup and wound up in the 1980s using the German pickup, "The Shadow."

The Studio Classic was a great guitar Chet really like them. They were just about everything he wanted in an electric nylon string. The CE and CEC were great, but when Kirk Sand built his it was a different ballgame. Chet was concerned about how a guitar looks and the Studio Classic he played was a beautiful guitar.

Gibson, possibly to avoid paying Kirk Sand a royalty, redesigned the electric classicals to have a hole in the back on other changes. That redesigned Studio Classic was everything Chet didn't like in a guitar. The electronics were bad and it looked cheap. Chet only played his through his amp or direct, so having a hole in the back so you could hear yourself doesn't make much sense if the rest of the guitar doesn't make it.

Different Guitars for Different Tone

Chet's DelVecchio guitars

The DelVecchio's are a resonator guitar similar to the National resonator guitar but not nearly as loud or as robust as their American made cousin. They were built in Brazil, usually of beautifully grained rosewood, with a light aluminum resonator that supported a puck-like bridge. They were flimsy, the necks tended to warp to a back bow easily in northern climates and the fret boards were notoriously inaccurate. But they were the only ones that had their distinctive tone.

They were first popularly heard on the Los Indios Tabaharas song "Maria Elena" played by Natalicio Lima and his brother, Antenor. The guitar, for all of its flaws, was a very sweet, clear sounding instrument, Chet Atkins had great affection for their tone. The instruments he acquired usually had the necks reworked and a truss rod installed. Paul says here that Nato Lima "gave" him his first one. In fact, Chet paid Nato over $350 for the instrument according to an interview given to Russ Cochran for his very excellent book *Me and My Guitars*.

All I ever heard Chet say was that Nato Lima gave him the first one he got. It was the one Nato used on "Maria Elena." He had a second one but I never heard him say where he got it. He gave the second one to Earl Klugh. He had truss rods installed in both of them. The third one he has come from

Doyle Dykes. It is a good sounding one. It is in the Hall of Fame display at present. But as far as I know the one he recorded with all the time is the first one that Nato gave him. When people ask what Chet's favorite guitar was I usually tell them Chet's favorite was his DelVecchio. After that it was his Gibson nylon electric. When Chet really wanted to play something pretty he used that guitar. A lot of the times when he recorded with another guitarist he would use it also for contrast.

Chet used silk and steel strings on the Del Vecchio but even so it was like most guitars with steel strings ... they eat up your nails. I would say about 50% of the time he just used his thumb pick and played down strokes.

The Peaver

"The Peaver" was a guitar I built for Chet to record with. I had made myself one and he liked it. He had a Peavey T-60 so I took that body and put a wide type Strat neck on it. I then put two EMG pickups in it. He used it quite a bit. "Sunrise" was one tune, "Laughing at Life" was another. It wasn't very pretty as guitars go, but sounded great.

When I started working with Chet I was playing Peavey guitars but I never heard Chet say anything about going with Peavey. When Chet did the album Stay Tuned he used the Peaver guitar I made for him. When the CD was released he played the Peaver in person with George Benson and others who were on the album.

Gibson didn't think much of that, so Jim Hutchins built the Phaser for Chet. He used it a few times but really didn't care for it. Someone gave him a Roland transducer and he put it on the guitar and fooled around with it some, but it didn't track very well. Besides, who wants a

Chuck Schwickerath's Peaver guitar purchased from Paul Yandell. Paul built at least two of these guitars. *Photo courtesy of Chuck Schwickerath*

guitar that sounds like a keyboard? Gibson couldn't settle on a name for it. I think I named it Phaser because of the Strat sound. They only built two, I think. Chet had one and I had the other. Gibson asked me to return it and I did. They weren't interested in going into production on it so it died.

A Funny Thing Happened on the Way to the Peaver ...

People trade, sell and swap guitars all the time. It's like any other item or artifact people place value upon. Some folks got 'em, some folks want 'em. So a transaction of some sort is arranged.

Paul would often lament how the sale of a special guitar was such a sad, regrettable thing. But Paul (and Chet) were at a level where their "guitar room" was usually overflowing. This meant that, from time to time, it was necessary to "thin the herd" either by giving surplus instruments away (as Chet often did) or selling them (as Paul and Jerry Reed sometimes did.).

The Peaver was an instrument Paul made—put together for Chet. After Chet died it was one of the guitars Liona wanted Paul to have. Paul kept it for a while then sold it to Russ Cochran, author of the excellent *Me and My Guitars* biography of Chet Atkins.

Russ had some unfortunate medical expenses and decided to thin his herd of guitars. He sold The Peaver to one Chuck Schwickerath. Chuck is an excellent thumb style player and guitar trader, who for years wanted to have "a guitar that belonged to Chet."

Chuck was thrilled with his purchase and decided to write a brief article about the instrument to share via the *Mister Guitar* CAAS magazine. He tells Paul he wants to do this. Chuck and Paul had a nice relationship of mutual assistance and trust having helped each other over the years on various projects so Chuck gets more details about the guitar and wrote the article. He sent it to Paul for approval. Oddly, Paul wanted the sale of the guitar to Russ to be left out. Chuck is puzzled but agreed. Edits were made and approval was granted. Chuck went to the editors of *Mister Guitar* magazine and things started rolling.

Now, Paul is really sensitive about Chet and Chet's family. The one thing he did not want to do was hurt Leona's feelings and he suddenly got worried that Leona might be offended that Paul sold The Peaver, one of Chet's guitars that she had given to him.

While Paul certainly had guitars he liked better than others, he also had to curb sentimentality in the face of an overstocked guitar room. In the grand scheme of things, guitars were tools. The Peaver, since it was something Paul had made himself out of what were very nearly odds and ends, may have had no real sentimental value to him. To him it might not have been viewed as "one of Chet's guitars" but more like an item he just cobbled together for Chet to use when he felt like it, which seemed to be the case. Gibson never picked up on the idea of replicating it when Paul and Chet discussed it with them so … get rid of it.

But Paul suddenly worried that Leona might take offense and started to regret having sold the guitar in the first place. He sends this email essentially okaying the article but also requesting some editing: "Hi Chuck, that sounds ok. I just don't want people to know I sold it, and I don't want Leona to know. I shouldn't have done it. Thanks, Paul."

Corrections were made and the magazine patrons were treated to a well written, in depth, discussion of how The Peaver was made and used. They were totally unaware of the two men taking care not to cause any hurt to Chet's widow.

It also could be seen as a parable about how haste and impulse can cause problems further down the road.

The Octabass

With the supply of guitars Chet had it was easy to do experimental projects. One of Chet's favorites was an "Octabass" guitar. This was a guitar that had the low E and A strings substituted with thicker strings so they could be tuned down a full octave and deliver a sound like the electric bass guitar. Chet and Paul used a guitar set up this way for smaller venues they played or even on some of the larger ones. The setup extended the range of the guitar and gave a little variety when played by a thumb-style guitarist.

Converting a regular electric guitar to this purpose was not a simple task as outlined here:

A Quick Study on the Octabass Guitar
(like Chet used on the *Solo Flights* album.)

I've always been a person who likes to fix things and Chet was a lot like that too. We had that in common. We always had fun tinkering guitars. It was this, curiosity and love of tinkering that brings about things like the "Octabass" guitar.

When I starting working with Chet he had a Super Chet strung up that way.

It was converted with bass guitar strings on the low 6th and 5th to use on Drive-In. On Drive-In Chet tuned up to the key of F so the bass strings would have more tension.

It's not easy doing that conversion to a guitar. It's quite an undertaking and if you aren't going to use it very much it's not worth all the time to do it.

It takes a wider neck. You have to have a bridge that you can hook the bass string to as they are a lot larger than a guitar string. You have to use D'Addario short scale bass strings, 080 for the 5th and 0.100 for the 6th.

You have to file out large notches in the saddles for the strings and also enlarge the notches in the nut. Next, you need to drill out the holes in the tuning keys posts so the bass strings will go through. Then you have to raise the action pretty high on the bass side for it to work. It's not easy to set the intonation on the two bass strings ... they always note sharp.

When Chet went with Gibson, we got a Tennessean and a Country Gentleman which I converted to Octabass. The Country Gentleman had the Schaller "finger" tailpiece and the other guitar was a Tennessean with a stop tailpiece. Chet had me put the Super Chet back to the regular way since it was the prototype.

One other thing: That guitar in the picture (on the *Solo Flights* back cover) doesn't have bass strings on it if you look close you can tell this by the size of the 5th and 6th strings. Chet only used the guitar with bass strings on about half that album I think he overdubbed that at home. Most of the rest of the tunes he was playing that classical with the Prismatone pickup.

Picks

Chet said he couldn't keep good thumb picks because Jerry Reed would steal them if he liked them.

Over the years Chet used different thumb picks. When I started working with him he was using a small narrow pick, the same kind Lenny Breau used. Jerry Reed told him his thumb wasn't loud enough so he changed to something a bit heavier. He also used that blue nylon pick that's still being made. I have some of those. Then Herco came out with a pick that looks like a straight pick. He and I used it for a while.

Finally, a fellow by the name of Jason Lambert, who used to own a music store in North Carolina gave Chet and I some of those old great picks that were made in the 1970s. Chet used them from then on. Jerry Reed used them too. They mostly were white but I have some that are different colors. Sometimes they weren't formed correctly and I couldn't use them. I heard the place burned where they were made.

What Chet would do with his picks was round the tips off to where they weren't so pointed; a more oval shape. He got a bigger note and could play single notes that way. They were the normal thickness.

I first met Paul about 1980, when he and Chet played a Christmas concert at our local community college. I introduced myself, and told him how much I loved his playing. When I mentioned the Louvins and Jerry Reed, his expression changed. He said something like "Awww, I can't listen to those old records. My playing was pretty bad." I told him I thought it was great. I asked if we could trade thumb picks. He seemed hesitant, but reached into his pocket and fished out a well-worn pick. "This one's about had it, so you can have it," he said as he handed it to me. I gave him one of mine.

He looked it over and said, "Nah, I don't like those," and gave it back.

I still have the one he gave me.

— Craig Dobbins

The Chet Handle

Gretsch reissued the so-called "Chet Handle" based on Chet's personal handmade unit. Paul is a stickler for perfection and when they first came out they weren't quite right. Paul told people how to properly bend the handles to make them more like Chet's.

Speaking of those handles, if you get one for yourself you might need to bend it to suit your own hand and style because for some reason they aren't bending the handles far enough. What happened was when Gretsch bought Bigsby some of the operations were moved to Korea and they started bending them wrong right from the start. I wasn't connected with Gretsch at that time and I guess no one else noticed the error. The handle is bent the same as the old ones except the knob end. It's not parallel to the first string. I've worked to get that changed since the Nashville Classic came into being. They finally got it right in early 2005.

One thing about the new handles I like better than the old ones is that the knob unscrews so I could bend the end up a little which is the way I preferred. What I use is an old ratchet wrench I have that has a hole in the end of the handle. The hole just fits that quarter-inch rod to allow some leverage so I could bend the metal. If you have to bend the handle at the

knobbed tip remember that the knob unscrews. Take the tip off so's not to break it at the threads. Bend the end around straight and bend it up a little... then bend the handle back where the first bend is. You can make it higher or lower according to your needs.

Another thing you can use is a piece of oak plank cut about 2" wide and 7" or 8" long. It needs to be about one inch thick. Drill a hole in one end a little bigger than the handle and you can bend it with that. Bend in small increments. A little goes a long way. You might want to warm the handle up some by holding it under your arm so it's easier on the gold plating. If the metal is too cold the plating could flake. Of course you have to take the handle off the guitar to do all this.

CHAPTER 19

PSSST ... WANT SOME ACTION?

I have heard Paul talk on that subject so many times, and sometimes he would say (when he was aggravated with the question), "Just put a #2 lead pencil under the strings and raise them until it rolls around under there, then you've got the action as high as Chet's.
— Gayle Moseley

"Action" is a word used to describe how a guitar is set up. Action defines the guitar's playability to the individual. It refers to amount of muscle energy needed to press a guitar string to the fingerboard. Action is a combination of bridge height and the gauge (thickness) of the strings on a guitar. There is no "standard" action. What constitutes a good action is extremely subjective. This means that a good action for one person may not be a good action for another. The debate on the pros and cons of the differences between high vs low action is a never ending talking point on most guitar chat boards and gatherings of guitarists the world over. Briefly it goes like this:

Low action is the best because it allows a player to play faster with less fatigue. Low action, if too low, can promote string rattle and buzz.
High action is best because it allows the player to play more forcefully (Louder). The high action tends to prevent string/fingerboard rattles and buzz but requires more hand strength and callusing.

In the days prior to the electric pickup, the instruments needed to be played more firmly to even be heard, particularly in orchestral situations. High action combined with heavy strings played very firmly was a requirement for the guitar, which was originally strictly a rhythm instrument in orchestras, to be heard in a big band context. Gibson's design genius, Lloyd Loar, came up with the idea of the carved arch top that was based on violin shaping methods. The idea of carving a guitar top similar to the way a violin top was shaped changed guitar making from the 1920s onward. Gibson had several models based on the Loar concept: the L-5, L-7, L-10, Super 400 and others. Other guitar makers were quick to use the innovation. John D'Angelico's superb instruments were based on Gibson's L-5 model. The other feature of this design was the incorporation of the so-called "floating bridge." The bridges were movable and the height could be easily adjusted by turning two elevation wheels. Using this bridge allowed the guitarist to easily change the action on their instruments.

Chet Atkins, Merle Travis, and other guitarists who were young performers during the 1930s and 1940s sometimes only had one microphone, often shared with others, in the radio station or stage situations they played. When they played shows booked through their radio contacts, sometimes the public address situation was so primitive as to be almost nonexistent, which required guitarists to exert more physical effort to be heard. This tended to force players to work with a higher action.

Electric amplification made the requirement of high action and forceful playing history. Action was now a matter of choice. For some, like Chet and Merle, the high action was a direct contribution to their overall tone. They were used to playing firmly and were reluctant to change. However, not all guitar stars liked a high action. Jerry Reed and Lenny Breau, both legendary guitarists in their own right, preferred a very low action. Chet Atkins, according to Paul Yandell and others, had an extremely high action, steeply canted at the bridge to be high on the bass string side.

Chet always used a high action. That's one of the reasons Chet got such a great sound. He told me he started using high action when he first started playing to keep the strings from fretting out as hard as he played. He said he discovered early on that you got a much better tone that way. Chet always ran his bass side of his bridge up higher than his treble. He did that on all his guitars.

I use what I consider a high action and his was higher than mine. I would say his action would be uncomfortable for most people. Take my word for it. When Chet was playing the '59 it was too high for me. I borrowed it for a session once. I had to work to play it! Chet had real strong hands.

With higher action, when you pick the string, the string is above the frets high enough that you get more sustain and a cleaner note. Low action results in buzzes, fretting out down the neck and all sorts of problems. Its best to have your action as high as you can play comfortably.

I once measured the distance on Chet's old Country Gentleman, the '59, from the top of the bars on the bass side to the bottom of the 6th string and found it to be 0.2170 inches or 5.52 mm, the same on the treble side, I didn't measure the back pickup but he had the screws up some. Over the years, in interviews, Chet would say that he favored a low action on his guitars. I don't know why he said that because when I started with him in 1975 he used high action on every guitar he played. On his classical, if anything, it was higher. On the nylons he would shim them up. I just know what I saw.

One year for Christmas Chet gave me the first Gibson Country Gentleman, serial number 001. I had never played it ... just kept it in its case ... it still

has the same strings on it that Chet played on. I took it out one day to look at it and I measured the action. On the bass side at the 12th fret from the top of the 12th fret to the bottom of the 6th string was 1/8 inch. It was the same on the treble side.

I'm sure he used higher action on different guitars, but that's what he used on that particular one. When Gibson would send him a new guitar the first thing he did was run the bridge up. Still, some people like a lower action. Jerry Reed, for example, likes his action low on his nylon guitars.

I worked with Chet for twenty-five years and I never once heard him say he had a fret buzz or that there was anything wrong with his guitar. After I started working for him he had larger frets installed in his '59 but that was it, nothing else.

I get emails sometimes about the current (Gibson) Country Gentleman having fret buzzes and harmonics behind the bridge or the bridge not being made right on and on. I think a lot of the fret buzzes happen when a player gets his new guitar and runs the action down.

I've played Chet's guitars on several occasions thanks to my long friendship with Paul and to me Chet's action is in 'nose-bleed' territory! I couldn't play the Wildwood Flower on the darn things. Paul used to tell me that the first thing Chet did when he got another guitar from Gibson was open the case and start ramping up the bridge thumbscrews before he even picked the guitar up out of the case!

As an example I was with friends after one of Chet's shows Saturday afternoon at the downtown Sheraton in Nashville, at a CAAS, Chet let us play on his first Gibson Country Gentleman (that wine colored one) right after he finished his concert. The guitar was high enough to be very uncomfortable to hold the strings down. It would hurt your fingers after a very few minutes! Paul walked over to the group and said what a great guitar that was going to be for Gibson and all us Chet players were not to worry about how rough it played because, "it was Chet's and that's the way he liked it!"
— Gayle Moseley

Closely related to action is the gauge (thickness) of the guitar strings used.

Nowadays people can build their own guitar string set by selecting their own gauge preference. Chet had his strings pre-packaged as a sales item, "Chet Atkins Strings," so he didn't need to make special trips to buy strings …

Chet and I used the same strings, Gibson 10-12-16-28-38-48. In his earlier days he used a bigger bass. Chet, in an interview with *Guitar Player* magazine in October 1979, said at one time he was using Gretsch "Chet Atkins Country Style Strings."

He gave the gauges as .010, .012, .020 wound, .028, .038, .048 or .050. Chet also remarked that he especially liked the Gretsch Country Style strings because they had good magnetic qualities. "They have a lot of steel" he said. I used those Chet Atkins strings back when I bought my first Gretsch 6120 in 1955. That's the only string I ever used for a long time. I still have a couple of sets of the old Chet strings. I would like to use them but then they would be gone. Chet used his Gretsch strings for years. When he passed away he still had a few sets in his cabinet where he kept his strings. Leona, his wife, gave me all of Chet's strings and it was a bunch, friends! Most of them were Gretsch strings of different gauges so I'm pretty sure he used Gretsch strings.

Chet didn't like flatwounds. He said they are dead as a doornail ... no sustain. He hated the sound those jazz players got and they used flatwounds. Chet once said that Johnny Smith was the greatest musician he had ever met. Johnny got a better tone than most of the jazz guys who, for the most part, sound like they had a quilt over their amp.

Chet used different gauges but I know sometimes when he recorded he used a wound third. I don't think he would go to a smaller string than the 10-48 set because they are harder to play in tune and have a thinner sound. Sometimes Chet would play harder. That would cause the string to "ping," something he did a lot.

For nylon strings Chet and I both used D'Addario Pro-Art, although both of us at times have used LaBella 500p Professional concert & recording strings.

He used Silk and Steel strings on his DelVecchio. On his "Octabass" guitars he used D'Addario XL-170S short scale bass strings using the third

Gretsch "Chet Atkins" string label. Sold in a round plastic box with an extra first and second string, these strings were very popular but were discontinued. The company that made them went out of business. *Photo courtesy of Gretsch/used by permission*

for the guitar fifth which is an .080 with the bass forth for the guitar's sixth which is a .100.

Chet changed strings when they had been on for a while. He was always afraid the first or second would break during a show. Chet used to change his strings on his nylon string guitars pretty often. It seemed like he changed them before we would go out to play a date. If left on too long I think the bass strings become dull in tone. Sometimes the first and second will start noting flat. I have always played on my strings until they become somewhat dead. I liked the sound of strings after they have been played a little. I used different guitars on sessions but I would change the strings on my main electrics about every three or four weeks depending on how much I played. Chet changed his about the same and sometimes he would ask me to change the treble strings before a show.

There are some folks who will always want to argue about the advantages or disadvantages of a high or low action. Not surprisingly, most of the arguments will favor the action used by whoever is doing the arguing. As previously noted, there is no standard action and a good action for one person may not be a good action for another.

The other thing is the nattering that goes on about Chet's action. He set his action the way he thought it should be to make the guitar give him what he wanted. It's a matter of personal taste. Those who obsess on having everything "just like Chet's" might look at it this way.

Setting up a guitar is a lot like setting up their car. When they first get into a vehicle that will be their permanent auto, there is a certain adjustment period: seats, mirrors, that sort of thing. These adjustments can take a couple of days before they feel they are just right and the car is truly theirs. Needless to say, if someone else uses this car, unless the user's body size is the same, some adjustment is needed to make the auto safely drivable...it's like that. Guitar action is equally personal.

Submitted for consideration is this—a scan of a Gretsch catalog cover showing Chet and his '59 (with the Bigsby handle temporarily removed—most likely at the photographer's request) taken probably in the late sixties or early seventies. Clearly visible is the extremely steep slope of his bridge adjustment.

By examining photos of Chet's action and close observation of his videos, particularly those made in the fifties and sixties with some diligence, it can be seen that Chet had a very high action on his bass strings side. There is a black and white video of Chet playing "Alabama Jubilee" that can usually be found on YouTube. Watching it closely, a gap can be seen between his sixth (lowest string) and the fingerboard. It is clearly visible that the string has a goodly distance to go when Chet chooses to fret the string in the middle of the song.

Paul, over the years, maintained that Chet's action was high. While he certainly has his own opinions, Paul does not seem prone to exaggeration about guitar setup and construction particularly when it comes to things related to Chet.

The pro/con argument about high or low action will continue as long as guitars are played because there is no right or wrong. It is ultimately a matter of personal choice.

Gretsch 2007 catalog showing steep bridge angle on Chet's 59. *Photo courtesy of Gretsch 2007 catalog. Used by permission*

CHAPTER 20

PAUL'S WORKSHOP

Daddy was always searching for the musical answers. Whether is was in musical ideals, pickups, the Bigsby, he was always searching.
— Micah Yandell

Chet and I were always doing things to our amps or our guitars. Almost every other morning Chet would call me about 7:30 am about something he was working on or a new idea. He would say 'What are you working on now?

Refining the SuperTron Pickup

Paul and Chet were long-time friends of Ray Butts, the man who originally designed and made the Super Tron and Filter-Tron pickups so famously used by Gretsch. He and Chet visited with Ray frequently. When Ray passed on Ray's son asked Paul to come by to help him sort out his dad's workshop. Not surprisingly he found some "historical treasures" there one of which is indirectly connected with this chapter on pickups.

The first picture is the prototype of the first humbucker. The second is the stereo pickup.

The Genius of Ray Butts

If there was a genius ever in Nashville, Ray Butts was one of them. Some years ago I had him build a pickup that I still have, that has the bass strings out of phase and the treble strings normal. It sounded a lot like the tone of Chet's D'Angelico. All you had to do was give Ray an idea and he would build it.

I remember at the time I started working for Chet, Ray Butts was working for RCA. He had a small room in Studio B with a workbench. Ray built the first cue system in Nashville. By that I mean each player had headphones and control box so everyone could hear each other. He also ran the tape machines at sessions.

I used to drop by and spend time with Ray. I learned so much from him about pickups and amps.

Ray and I had lunch one day and I suggested he make a Gibson size pickup that had the sound of the Filter-Tron to use on the Gibson Country

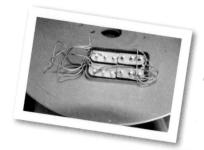

Butts pickup #1. An example of a partially split pickup assembly. *Photo courtesy of Paul Yandell*

Butts pickup #2. An example of a three strings only pickup assembly. *Photo courtesy of Paul Yandell*

Gentleman. He started making some out of some dud Gibson pickups that I had. Chet liked the sound of them and suggested he show them to Gibson. Some of the players at Gibson tried them out but didn't care for them. They mostly played rock and roll.

Ray wanted too much to produce them so they never made a deal. I have always used them. I think they sound better than the Gibson pickups. Most of my CDs are me using Butts pickups. If you want tone Ray's Filter-Tron has it. If you want output the Gibson has it.

Note: "They mostly played rock and roll." As a rule, Ray tended to keep his pickups around 4K on the meters, whereas Gibson Humbuckers meter out closer to 9K. The stronger pickups are easier to overdrive, a tonal effect rockers seem to prefer.

Ray Butt's son Randy and I went through Ray's things in his work shop sometime after Ray died. We found the very first Gretsch humbucking pickup and the first stereo pickup like the ones he made for Chet. It was a big thrill for me. I think Paul Bigsby and Ray thought about doing something together. We found a box of Bigsby's pickup castings that Ray apparently never did anything with.

Ray's son Randy is working with a friend of his who lives in Gallatin, Tennessee. They are building some new EchoSonic amps. I think Randy is planning on having a couple at CAAS. I played through one and it sounded great so there's always something new to look forward to.

Ray liked to keep his pickups right around 4K. They weren't as hot as some other manufacturers but they also made for a very identifiable tone. Chet had his bridge pickup rewound to reflect around 7.5K and TV Jones made one accordingly to use on the 6122/59. Years ago, when I was having lunch with Ray Butts, I asked him about the bar pickup he built for Chet's '59. He told me how he built it and what he used in it. When the Nashville Classic came along I asked TV Jones to build it the same way which he did.

Paul considered Ray Butts a genius and said he could make a pickup to get any sound Chet wanted. He said Ray never would throw anything away and Ray's home was like a maze inside with stuff stacked to the ceiling. You had to walk a trail from one room to the next.

Paul said Ray had an old Lincoln Continental that he never drove over thirty miles an hour. He said you held your breath as Ray drove down a ramp to get on the Interstate at thirty miles an hour and continued driving at thirty miles an hour.

Chet would play Ray like a violin. Chet bought a camera and something broke inside it. Chet knew Ray could probably fix it, but he also knew Ray wouldn't fix it until he wanted to. Chet called Ray to come over to his office for something and just had the camera lying on his desk. Ray arrived and Chet talked to him about something else. Ray noticed the camera and asked Chet about it. Chet told him it didn't work and nobody could repair it and that he was going to throw it away. Ray said, "Hell, I can!" Ray picked up Chet's camera and walked out. Ray returned the next day with Chet's camera repaired with Chet and Paul holding straight faces.

— Gary Cochran

Modernize That Bigsby ... and Other Drills!

The Bigsby vibrato string bar, a round piece of steel, is held in the frame/chassis of the device by means of a removable "O" ring on one end. The bar is slipped through bearings in the frame. The other end of the string bar fits into the handle assembly and is held in place by an Allen screw.

The bar has six holes drilled in it and steel pins are inserted through those holes in such a manner that they protrude on one side of the bar by about ⅛ of an inch. The little round grommet at the end of most guitar strings has a hole in it that slips over this pin. When strung and tuned, the tension of the strings keeps the handle assembly pressing onto the spring and the Bigsby is ready to be used.

When a guitarist has to restring a guitar with a Bigsby on it there is some extra work involved. A fresh string taken out of its wrapper tends to be straight. The string's grommet will not stay on the little pins without some extra persuasion.

Some musicians say that all is required is that the guitarist "take some needle-nose pliers and bend a curve in the end of the string." Others say the little grommet will behave if something like a wedge shaped eraser is wedged between the pin and the top of the guitar trapping the grommet onto the pin. There are other methods, too complicated to envision, involving capos or having a patient wife or friend holding the grommet on the pin long enough for the guitar owner to snake the other end of the string through the tuning peg hole and tighten it. Once the string has tension the grommet usually behaves, staying on the pin.

Wouldn't it be much simpler if the pins were left out and the holes drilled to allow the string to pass directly through the string mounting bar? It certainly has been tried to good effect by the bold and fearless but it was never explained why Bigsby didn't go to the simpler way and make them pinless except a vague "They've always done it that way."

Perhaps the better question might be why did Paul Bigsby make the things that way to begin with? It adds labor to the manufacturer to have to deal with drilling the string bar and fixing those steel pins in it.

Here is a plausible theory. When Bigsby first made his vibrato, music stores did not sell strings by the individual string by gauge as they do now. If a guitarist of the day wanted a lighter first and second string he usually would buy banjo strings for this purpose.

Banjo strings have loop ends instead of grommets. If Bigsby had initially offered the unit without pins it would have been difficult to use loop end strings on his device back in the day. Bigsby most likely had these guys in mind when he designed the unit. He had steel pins installed in the string bar so banjo string loops or guitar string grommets could attach to equally. When the single strings were commonly offered in all music stores starting in the sixties, for some reason the Bigsby management never thought to simplify the unit. In 1966, Bigsby was sold to former Gibson executive, Ted McCarty, and after that it was bought by the Gretsch company which now owns Bigsby manufacturing. They didn't drop the pins in favor of holes either.

In 2005, I tried a modification on the Bigsby. I pulled those little string mounting pins and had the shaft drilled so all I had to do was run the strings straight through making the whole string changing process easier. I changed it on my Nashville Classic and it works great, maybe even better than the pins. I sent the idea to Gretsch but I haven't heard anything from Fred so I guess he's not interested in doing it.

You can do it yourself. Just pull the pins out (get a good set of hefty pliers. Be careful not to break them off, then take the O ring off. You

can buy a special tool for that at Lowes or Home Depot. Slide the bar out and have a machinist drill the holes all the way through, then put it back together.

After some time passed, Paul took up the topic on the chat boards and via email again:

I decided to make one of those bars to be sure everything worked ok. I changed the angle of the string holes, also this one is a little longer than normal. I'm going to talk to the Gretsch tech next week about it.

I have a small workshop underneath our house. I have a friend who is a machinist. He did the retaining ring groove for me. It turned out great. By accident mine is a little longer so the spring is straight.

Sure enough, he posted a picture. This is one of his first modifications. Notice how the string ends stick out a bit.

Then later:

I talked to Fred Gretsch over the weekend by email. He asked me to draw a blueprint of the pinless bar which I did. I suggested a kit this morning. He said they will start working to put the kit into production.

After a week or so here came another picture. The holes are countersunk a bit.

Here are a couple of pictures of the pinless string bar I had Fred Gretsch make for me. I'm trying to talk him into changing the vibratos.

Notice how much nicer the ball ends seat in the holes. Having a machinist friend is a blessing.

Paul's "straight through" Bigsby string bar. *Photo courtesy of Paul Yandell*

Chamfered (recessed) string bar made for Paul by Gretsch. "Champfering" is when the holes are slightly countersunk. *Photo courtesy of Paul Yandell*

Notice how the string ball ends seat deeper into the string bar when the holes are chamfered. (recessed) *Photo courtesy of Paul Yandell*

This is something Fred Gretsch made special for me. I would hate for everyone to think Gretsch is going make a change.

As of now Gretsch has not made the change. Paul offered instruction on how to remove the pins on the more modern string bar. Until about 1964 the pins unscrewed from the string bar because the pins were threaded Allen screws. Later the company just attached the steel pins by machine but those did not unscrew.

It takes a little work to change the bar out on the newer bars. You have to break the pins off, then file them down even with the bar so you can pull it out. Then you take it to a machinist and have them drill it out. Put a little grease on each end, slide the new bar into the frame and put the O ring back. I'm not sure everyone could do it. But by the same token, this isn't the space program.

It really doesn't make any difference to the vibrato operation if it has pins or goes through the shaft. I've had two guitars fixed this way for about two years. I drilled them out myself. It's just an idea. I'm just trying to help others and move things along. It's just hard to get things changed that have been in place for years. I'm not sure what the Gretsch people used but the ones I drilled I used a 1/16 drill bit. You have to be careful and not let your bit get real hot or it will freeze up. I guess you know that.

Note: In 2016, Gretsch issued a Bigsby unit they called the "String-Through," that is exactly like the one they made for Paul. They are featured on the new "Player's Edition" models of their guitars. A Portent? Certainly hope so.

As far as I know Bigsby sells a short spring and a long spring. One way to soften (reduce tension) a spring is to heat it. If you have a heat shrink gun, put the spring in a pair of vise grips and compress it a little and heat it and let it cool. That will take some of the tightness out of it.

Daddy spent a lot of time working with the Bigsby bushings. These are the two needle bearings in the main frame of the unit that the string mount bar goes through. A lot of times the bushings aren't seated correctly and would be set in at a slight angle causing the unit to bind. If he couldn't take his fingers and rotate the bushing with ease then that meant the Bigsby would be stiff. I've seen him hammer on a bushing until it was properly set. Sometimes the bushings would just be damaged. Sometimes he could remove them and repair them but that didn't happen often. Needle bearings can be hard to work with.

He always used the 7/8" short spring. He would bend the handle so it fit his hand properly. Everyone's hand lays differently so there isn't really a recipe for this, just what feels comfortable to the player. All the stuff about placing the little finger on the pickguard just wasn't factual. With Chet and daddy, they just made it comfortable for themselves.
— Micah Yandell

Another thing Chet and I did to our guitars was to anchor the spring cup on the Bigsby. We drilled a small hole through the cup and put a screw through it into the top of the guitar. Chet said it helped the guitar stay in tune better because it stopped the vibrato from shifting.

The way Chet and I did it was to put a strip of masking tape on each side of the vibrato to mark it, then took it off and drilled a hole in the center of the spring cup.

If you do it be sure you drill the right size hole for the screw you are going to use. Put the vibrato back on and line it up. Drill the hole in the top for the screw, then screw it down tight and string up the guitar. I think Bigsby put the play in the hinge so a person could align the vibrato up on different guitars.

In January of 2004, I decided to make myself a vibrato handle for my fixed bracket. I went over and got some quarter-inch welding rod. I already had some half-inch brass rod so I cut a seven and a half inch long piece. I

drilled a hole in my desktop which is over an inch think and bent the handle. I then took the handle and a piece of the half-inch brass rod over to a machinist friend of mine and had him put the knob on it. It's great! I sent it to the platers and had it chrome plated. I could have had it gold plated but I like the chrome better.

Any of you can do the same thing and make them as long or as short as you want. I just thought I would pass it along.

Pinning the Bridge

Chet and I flew almost everywhere we went. When we got to a date and opened our guitar cases the bridges would be everywhere. When Chet was playing his Gretsch Country Gentleman the airlines would knock the bridge completely off the guitar. Many times I've seen him put it back on and set the intonation by ear so we could rehearse. We pinned them down and that stopped that.

Bridge pinning is a somewhat controversial subject among guitarists but I think you should do it or have it done. Chet and I have done it for years. It keeps the bridge from shifting around.

The way I do it is this: I use what they call brads, a small nail that has a small head. My friend, Sonny Thomas, uses a screw like the ones that hold the pickup frames. In either case, you do it the same way. I set the intonation and then take masking tape and tape each end of the base of the bridge, then loosen the strings so I can take off the top of the bridge leaving the base taped down. I drill a small hole for each of the brads (or screws) on the inside of the adjustment screws on each side of the base. I put a small drop of super glue on the brads head to hold them in, being careful not to get any glue on the guitar. Then I put the top of the bridge back on, tune up the strings and remove the tape and that's it. You'll never have any more trouble if you do this. One more thing. I think it's a mistake to put anything soft underneath the bridge. It should sit solidly on the top otherwise it will affect the sustain. When you set the intonation on the Gibsons you put the first string saddle in the middle of the adjustment slot (on the Schaller bridge that Gibson uses there is almost ½-inch travel). Not many people will change up to much greater size string I have gone to a .050 on the 6th and a .048 on the 5th without any more adjustment on my guitar.

Bridges and Hand Rests

I thought you would like to see my '62 Country Gentleman. It has a Tru-Arc bridge. It is a great guitar. It has trestle bracing. You can see a small hand rest near the bridge pickup. I have that on almost all of my guitars. I just like it.

The "Tru-Arc" bridge is an innovation by Tim Harman, a journalist who posted at gretschpages.com as "Proteus." He and his machinist brother developed a variant of the standard "bar bridge" that offered a variety of metals and, more importantly, were radiused to the curve of the user's guitar fingerboard. The two customizations of metal and curve improved the fingerboard action and increased sustain to a degree that impressed Paul and other Gretsch professionals enough to buy and install them.

Gretsch with hand rest near bridge pickup. Paul liked to use hand rests and made several. *Photo courtesy of Paul Yandell*

I put a copper model Tru-Arc on my CGP. I think it is a little more mellow. The pickups in the CGP have quite a bit of highs. I put the aluminum one on my 1958 Country Gentleman. It sounds great too. If you get brass it will sound about the same as what you have but your guitar will play easier I think because of the radius match.

That bit of grey near the Bigsby on Paul's guitar is a piece of foam. The harp section between the bridge and the Bigsby can generate overtones that don't show up on the pickups but people with sensitive hearing can hear these high tones. The foam is there to eliminate those overtones. The foam and the wrist pad illustrate how Paul, like many professionals, saw a guitar as a tool of trade.

Many non-professionals obsess about keeping a guitar "original" and refuse to alter their personal guitars at all. However, Paul, like many pros, felt if he thought adding or subtracting something to the guitar would improve his playing or make it more comfortable, well, he'd just do it.

The Tuning Fork Bridge

Jimmie Webster was a spokesman for Gretsch guitars for many years. He was a pioneer of the "Touch System" of guitar playing more recently popularized by Eddie Van Halen. He also was responsible for some of the design features of Gretsch guitars, some good, some, well … maybe not so good. It was Jimmie who pushed for the double cutaway and the padded backs that came out on some models. Another of his ideas was the mechanical string mutes used on some Gretsch guitars. He also designed a thing called a "Tone Twister" that was supposed to be a poor man's vibrato but it didn't work all that well. It broke a lot of guitar strings.

One of his ideas was the "Floating Sound Unit." This device, a machined piece of brass, required a new hole made in the top of the guitar in the area the bridge would normally be located. When the guitar was strung they were passed through the device that now became the bridge. It was aligned above the hole and held in place by string tension. The purpose of the new hole in the guitar top was to accommodate a tuning fork. The idea was to increase sustain in the guitar.

In December of 2009, I got the urge to try one of those "Floating Sound Units" that came out in the sixties. They were a Jimmie Webster idea that used a brass assembly that had a tuning fork attached to it that went into a hole made in the top of the guitar. It was used on some White Falcons and the Gretsch Viking guitar. Chet had one installed on one of his double cut Gentleman's. I remember he said they worked pretty good. I got my mind set on trying it out so I finally called Fred Gretsch. He was kind enough to send me one and I tried it out.

The tuning fork bridge is an interesting idea. Fred Gretsch introduced me to a fellow who knows everything about the thing, He was a big help to me understanding how it is suppose to work. The tuning fork itself is about four inches long. It screwed into the top part that the strings are threaded through. The fork goes inside the guitar. It doesn't touch anything. When you play it, it vibrates therefore making the sound sustain. The top of the unit becomes the bridge instead of the bar bridge which is still on the guitar to keep the string spacing correct.

It was just something I'd wanted to do to see how it worked. I didn't record with the guitar right off but the sustain was great. When I played the guitar through my board it was like everything else; there is an upside and a downside. You have great sustain, but if you don't have the bass strings dampened, they want to sound also. I didn't notice any bass roll-off but the guitar is more microphonic. A lot of things can cause the tuning fork to vibrate. It didn't seem to change the tone. I'm glad I installed it and I'm going to leave it on the guitar. The guitar I used was an Epiphone I had that uses a Bigsby/P-90 pickup combination like Chet's D'Angelico had. It was fun dealing with it.

Here's a picture of it. I had a bit of trouble getting the mounting hole right so I covered it (for now) with a piece of Velcro. Somebody asked me what I thought about it after I'd had it on my guitar a few months. It works ok. It has more sustain, like I said, but putting strings on it is sort of a chore. Since it replaces the normal bridge you have to get the intonation correct. I wouldn't mind having one on a guitar I play more.

"Sort of a chore." If the guitarist had to string a Bigsby as well as one of these units as Chet and Paul did on theirs it is likely the instrument would spend a lot of time in its case. Needless to say, the device never caught on.

Pickups Again

Chet had different sets of pickups wired different ways. Leona gave me all of Chet's pickups after he died and there was a variety of them. Chet had a coil winder that he eventually gave to me so he had the ability to do his own windings. I have a set of Filter-Trons that are split that Chet did himself.

Tuning Fork Bridge. Notice lever switch and P-90 pickup. This was done on an Epiphone guitar.
Photo courtesy of Paul Yandell

Hybrid Bar/Screw Pole pickup in a Dyna-Sonic casing. Paul made this. *Note*: Around 2014–15, pickup guru TV Jones made a commercial version of this pickup called the "Paul Yandell Duo-Tron." *Photo courtesy of Paul Yandell*

Chet did all kinds of things back in the '50s with his recordings. Les Paul gets a lot of credit for things he did, but Chet did a lot of things too that hadn't been done before too.

I'm always trying to think of something different. This pickup is mono. Chet always said the bars (on his Super Tron prototype) gave him a bigger note.

It's balanced really well and the treble strings have a slight edge like the pickup on the Country Gentleman. It's something I have been thinking about building for some time. I made these myself out of other pickups. I like the sound. It's a little different than the regular pickups.

Here's the same idea in the more familiar Gretsch pickup housing.

Tuning Gadgetry

> Daddy's ear was awesome! When it came to tuning, he could hear beyond the normal range. That's why he put the little piece of wire at the nut on the third string on some of his guitars. Playing the "E" cord at the first and second fret ran him nuts for being out of tune. He worked as much at being in tune as he did his tone.
> — Micah Yandell

Toward the end of his career Chet started using fine tuning adjusters like violinists use. These affix to the string itself and use a thumbwheel to make fine tuning adjustments. It is not clear if this was an issue with Gibson guitars or just a change in the men's hearing as time went on.

Chet and I used (on the Gibsons) and (I still use) violin tuners which work very well

Paul used these also and later on came across an invention by a fellow that used the thumbwheel arrangement built into a single unit that kept all the wheels aligned to make it easier to use.

Here is a picture of the first new model of the "Sta-Tuned" Tuner. It works great! The inventor is Reynald Chaput

There are also several versions of string locking attachment that installs at the nut.

I thought I would show you something I did on one of my guitars. I've figured out that the B and G strings are the ones that always go out of tune when you use a vibrato so I locked the two together behind the nut with this clamp affair. I use fiddle fine tuners down by the bridge to tune them. It solved a big problem for me.

Hybrid Bar/Screw Pole pickup in Filter-Tron casing. Another "made by Paul" experimental. *Photo courtesy of Paul Yandell*

Fine tuners on Bigsby harp section. Originally designed for violin family of instruments. These devices allowed for extremely fine adjustment in tuning. *Photo courtesy of Derek Rhodes*

Chaput fine tuning device. The dark material is padding to quiet string harp overtones behind the bridge. *Photo courtesy of Paul Yandell*

Due to the nature of fret spacing it is impossible to tune a guitar perfectly. Guitarists learn to "temper" their tuning by adjusting the tuning to sort of an average/close enough tolerance. Even so, a guitar that sounds in tune when an E chord is played will sound out of tune, to a sensitive ear, when a C chord is played. There is a remedy of sorts. The remedy Paul describes was also done by Chet on his '59.

You will notice an odd thing underneath the third string at the nut. I have always tried to solve tuning problems with guitars that I have owned. Here's a neat trick. It's pretty simple. It's a tuning mod on the third string I use based on an old idea from back in the 1970s.

You get a one-sixteenth brass rod at the hardware store and file one end of it where you have a flat side then cut about ¼-inch off of it. Put it under the third string up against the zero fret. Note the third string at the second fret to see how much distance you have between the string and the first fret. You keep filing until the string is almost touching the fret then put a small drop of super glue between the zero fret and the brass rod to hold it into place.

Intonate the string and there you have it. I can tune my guitar in E and it will be almost perfect, then go to C and the third is right on the money.

String clamp. Paul made this to help keep guitar in tune. *Photo courtesy of YFA*

Paul also prepped Chet's display guitars for the Country Music Hall of Fame.

These two pictures show him doing the final cleaning and setup on the legendary '59 that was Chet's main guitar for so many years when he was with Gretsch. The bench is at the Hall of Fame.

This only scratches the surface of the innovative tinkering and creativity Paul Yandell has done in his little workshop in Kentucky. He, like his friend and mentor, Chet, has never ceased looking for a way to make his guitars function better to get him closer to the ideal sound that he has in his mind.

Paul used his workshop for other things, too. Paul and Chet both had knife-oriented hobbies. Chet collected Case knives but Paul liked to get blade kits and make handles for Bowie knives.

Another shot of prepping the '59 for display. *Photo courtesy of Micah Yandell*

Prepping Chet's '59 for the last time. Getting it ready for its Hall of Fame display. *Photo courtesy of Micah Yandell*

One of Paul's hobbies was making Bowie knives. He did it all by hand and gave several of them away to his close friends. Micah has a couple of the knives that Paul made and I have two of them. He was also into collecting Case knives (Chet was, too) and many of his friends gave knives to him through the years.
— Marie Yandell

Here is an example of one of them.

"Cooper" Bowie. Paul was a craftsman and one of his hobbies was buying blade kits for Bowie knives and making pretty custom handles for them. *Photo courtesy of Derek Rhodes*

CHAPTER 21

ODDNOTES AND ADVICE

Interlude 10: A Little Style History

The Boys From Muhlenberg County

Some musical history essays repeatedly credit guitarist Arnold Schultz as being a thumb-style pioneer. Many sources give the impression that Arnold brought thumb style playing to Kennedy Jones and Mose Rager. In the essay "Arnold Schultz" by Kathy and Don Thomason the claim is made that Schultz was "a truly exceptional musician. Indeed, the consensus of those who heard him is that Arnold Shultz was one of the greatest blues guitarists who ever lived." But it is also fair to say that Kennedy Jones' son claimed his dad told him the Muhlenberg group had been playing the thumb style for years before they ever saw Schultz.

Schultz was a laborer, could have been an itinerant railroad worker and unfortunately, while no records were made of him, he was known in Kentucky. Because of this how well he played will always be speculative. It is really too bad that there are no known recordings of Schultz available so modern ears can form their own decision on Schultz's abilities. Paul felt Schultz was given too much credit for contribution to the Jones/Rager/Travis Kentucky thumb style that was part of his early roots.

Chet, Bill Monroe, and others were doing a show at the Station Inn one night when I asked Bill Monroe if he ever knew Arnold Schultz.

"Yes I played square dances with him in Rosine, Kentucky."

I then asked him if he played with a thumb pick. He answered "No, he used a straight pick and a Barlow pocket knife." He then said "He played a lot of runs."

Kennedy Jones Jr. told me that his daddy told him that he had been playing for about ten years before ever met Arnold Schultz. Kennedy learned his first guitar from his mother who played. So there are two people who knew and played with Arnold Schultz.

You can draw you own conclusions. Arnold Schultz may have been good guitar player but Kennedy Jones was the father of finger picking as we know it. To add a few more words, Kennedy Jones was the first guy to use a thumb pick in and around Kentucky. He told his son he was playing square dances when his thumb got sore. So when he saw a thumb pick

in a music store one time he bought one and tried it. (Thumb picks were offered to those who wanted to play Hawaiian steel guitar, which was popular in the twenties and thirties. Hawaiian guitar players used thumb picks and finger picks, sometimes called "thimbles" at the time.)

Mose Rager said Kennedy was the first to use a thumb pick and the first one to "choke the strings" in other words deaden the bass strings with his right hand. Mose's wife told me that Ike Everly played mostly rhythm.

Ike actually played very well, playing a lot like Mose Rager and Merle Travis. Ike made several TV appearances with his sons after they got famous. Ike tried, like Merle, to bring the style north and did some radio work in Chicago but he never caught on. Merle Travis expanded the style by incorporating more sophisticated chords, probably learned from piano players. His songwriting ability gave Merle a definite advantage over Ike Everly. Merle initially made his mark as a songwriter and singer.

Merle Travis put his own spin on the style taking it up another notch. When he started using that Super 400 he got a sound and tone that had never been gotten before out of a guitar. Chet took the style to the moon. Chet's love of all styles of music made his playing something to behold.

Bits of Advice

I'll tell you a few things that I've learned over the years which may or may not be correct but this is what I think.

To sound the best you can you need first a good sounding guitar, setup right, so you can play your best. Then have a good sounding amp ... not a lot of power. The powerful ones never have any tone. A 50 watt amp is just fine. Then have a good reverb. Most amps have terrible reverbs. A good outboard digital one is the best but even then, don't overuse it. For echo, a good digital delay, like the Boss DD-3 is good. I have one of those I used to use on the road. Another thing ... don't try to blow everybody's ears out playing loud. Playing loud isn't anything to brag about.

After he retired, Paul made this observation:

There's not many of us left that play thumb-style anymore. All I do is just play Chet's stuff. Just like Odell Martin did, and a lot of other guys.

Almost every lick I know I stole from Chet, so, as Chet used to say, "I steal from the biggies." I don't consider it a great feat to just play like someone else.

On a certain guitar forum the posters would go on for days about the difficulty of playing Chet's version of "Cascade." The sticking point being that the first chord form on the song requires a reach of the left hand little finger that is an awkward, and for some, impossible to reach.

Chet had large hands so "Cascade" didn't brother him very much. I don't know what it is about that tune but about every six months the forum goes through all this "nobody can play it as well as Chet did." I played it with Chet a few hundred times. Every time was an experience. You can either play it or you can't. I remember when Chet got the tape of it he then worked up all of those licks and later we recorded it. It is one of his greatest. Chet didn't like for people to argue over silly stuff like this. It's just a tune and many people can play it. It's not the second coming of Christ.

I like to hear a tune and be able to remember something of it. So much music today is just a mess of notes. What have you got left other than being impressed with the guy's technique? I'm not trying to prove anything or impress anybody. I just try to come up with something interesting and pretty. I don't mind anyone playing anything I record. There is not a whole lot of it that I've created. I do it because I love it and I do it to make a living. I've really never thought of myself as a trailblazer.

Paul's Guitars

The word "Currently" as used here is hard to accurately date with any certainty. However, when the 6120 CGP guitar came out in 2008 it became Paul's favorite guitar so this had to be written between 2003 and 2008.

Currently I have around twenty guitars but I haven't counted them in a while. My favorite guitar of course is the Nashville Classic. It sounds great, plays great and plays in tune better than any guitar I've owned. Other than the Nashville Classic I guess my favorites would be two of the archtops I have, a 1940s Gibson Super 400 and the D'Angelico New Yorker. I've used both on my CDs. I really enjoy playing rhythm on them.

Later on in life I owned one of the New Yorker D'Angelicos made by Heritage when someone bought the rights to the name. They were carved tops. I had a fellow at George Gruhn's to do inlays on the back of the peghead like the old ones and had a better pickguard made for it. It was a real good guitar and I recorded with it. I now have another old Super 400 so I didn't need two archtops. I also had one of the D'Angelicos made by Terada. It was pretty good but the first string didn't sound right so I sold it.

One of my more unusual guitars is one that is a copy of Merle Travis's and Lefty Frizzell's flat top that is in the Hall of Fame. It has a Bigsby style peghead on it. Mike Voltz did that for me and it can be seen on my Fingerstyle Legacy DVD. I made the pickguard and armrest. The guitar itself is a 1958 D-28. I shaved the braces in the top. I gave that guitar to my son Micah. I have another one that is a Gallagher and it, too, has a Bigsby neck also made by Mike Voltz.

Super 400. One of Gibson's legendary carved top models. For years this was their most expensive non-electric guitar. *Photo courtesy of Derek Rhodes*

Steve Wariner wanted to use some guitars that belong to Chet or were like Chet's old ones on a Chet tribute recording in 2009. He knew I had a guitar fixed up like Chet's D'Angelico. He kept it for a few months and used it on two or three tunes. It's an Epiphone Emperor Regent someone told me later on. I was at Gibson one day over in the Epiphone section and I saw it and I talked them out of it. I had just restored Chet's D'Angelico to its original electric form so it was easy to do mine. I had all the parts. I first put a Rickenbacker Vib-Rola like Chet's on it but those things work sideways and they are hard to get use to. I wired it out of phase and wired it regular. It sounds great but the neck is a little too narrow for my taste, about like the normal Gibson's. Steve liked it and got a great sound out of it for his sessions.

In my life I guess I have had sixty or more guitars and one thing I've learned is that each one had its own little problems you have to deal with. If you look hard enough you can find something wrong with any guitar.

"Re-necked" Martin. Martin D-28 with a Bigsby style neck installed similar to the one owned by Merle Travis. Gibson's Mike Voltz did this for Paul. *Photo courtesy of Derek Rhodes*

What is most important is how it plays and how it sounds. Some of the most beautiful guitars I've ever seen sounded terrible. I remember when Chet would get a new guitar he would look at it for a minute or two run the bridge up on it, plug it in and take a screwdriver and adjust the pickups and that was it.

I think what all of us (me included) should worry about is: "... Did I learn a new lick today? Am I a better player today than I was yesterday? Did I practice any?" If we are going to be guitar players these are the things we should think about.

On Buying "Chet Owned"

It seems every time you turn around there is a guitar owned by Chet, played by Chet, or looked at by Chet. Chet told me once that Gretsch sent him a lot of guitars for him to approve of, make suggestions and so forth. Unless there is some paper to prove that Chet had that guitar it would be silly to buy it just because someone makes claims about it. Besides, Chet must not have liked it if he didn't keep it.

Thumb Things

Do me a favor. Please don't call it "boom chick." It's Finger-Style. I don't care who says it, "boom chick" is incorrect.

I don't consider myself a finger-style guitarist. I consider myself a thumb-style player. Chet's a finger-style player. Lenny was a finger-style player. But I'm a thumb-style player. I think there's a big difference if you know what I mean.

Try to play in the groove! There are a few players around that play in the groove but it seems that playing fast is more important to some than playing with feeling. Pay attention to your thumb! Your thumb is the most important part of it.

I learned at an early age that what your thumb does is the most important. Odell and I always tried to play in the groove with our thumb. Chet and Merle had it down! When Chet would say something about a player he would say 'he has a good thumb.'

You should learn to control the amount of force (attack) that you strike the strings with your thumb. Your thumb volume should be lower than the treble strings. Chet could vary the sound of his thumb better than anyone. Chet always amazed me he could play soft or heavy with his thumb. Balancing thumb volume has always been a problem. If you listen to Chet's early records when he was using the D'Angelico he had a perfect balance between his thumb and his fingers. He also had that with the solid top 6120. Odell Martin had a great balance on his strings. I've tried to play like that all my life and it isn't easy. People don't play in the groove and make their thumb swing. Chet and Merle had it. Odell Martin had a great thumb. Eddie Pennington has a good feel. I've been working on doing that all my life.

One thing which has always bothered me about my playing is the D or 4th string is always louder than the 6th and 5th. I think it's because there is so much tension on them compared to the 6th and 5th strings. I have practiced for years to play with a lighter thumb.

A bigger thumb pick will give you a louder bass. When I play a nylon string I use a lighter pick. It's a problem that everyone has to deal with. Some players solve it, others never do. Some players really don't pay attention to their thumb.

The only person I ever saw who could do a decent job of using a flatpick to get thumb-style sound was Glen Campbell. It is nearly impossible to get the right feel with a straight pick. It's sort of like trying to paddle a boat with a broom: you can do it but not very well.

The Rager Thumb

As for using one's left thumb over the fingerboard Chet told me that chords sound different when you use your thumb. I think he meant that you can get a better grip on the chord.

The law of guitar playing, according to Segovia and the classical players, states the guitarist is to never, ever, use the left hand thumb for anything but a brace and support on the back of the guitar neck. Most popular guitar is played

D

The Rager Thumb. A diagram of an example of how the left thumb was used to hold down three strings for certain playing advantages. Not an easy technique to acquire. *Photo courtesy of the author*

T T 3 1 2 1

in a linear fashion, a series of single notes arranged in whatever melodic interpretation the guitarist has in mind. Use of the left thumb is similar to classical interpretation as a support appendage most often used on the back of the neck.

Classical, pop and jazz guitarists all use what is called the bar chord (*barre* when written on a score). The bar chord is pretty easy to spot when a guitarist uses it since their left index finger lays across three to six strings as the remaining fingers busily add notes. The neat thing about a bar chord is the guitarist can move the formation up and down the neck at will for different applications.

Thumb-style guitar is largely chord based. While your pop guitarist plays a series of single notes, the thumb-style guitarist is, to some degree, required to maintain the chord form on the guitar so they can maintain their alternating bass notes as they add melody notes with their remaining fingers.

To accomplish this they sometimes do what is called "thumb over" meaning the left thumb creeps over the neck on the low string side and is used to hold down the low E string. In some applications this is easier than the bar chord and can have practical applications.

Take a moment and consider the basic C chord. The first string is left open. The second string is fretted at the first fret with the index finger. The third string is open. The fourth string is fretted at second fret by the middle finger and the fifth string fretted at the third fret with the ring finger. The sixth string is generally not engaged unless the guitarist wants to move the ring finger as needed to fret the sixth string at the third fret.

The "Rager Thumb" is so called because Mose Rager was the first of the Muhlenberg County boys to change the application of the left thumb to the guitarist's advantage.

The diagram on page 253 is a D chord formed like a C chord and moved up two frets. This form lets you put it anywhere you want. The fourth finger is free to add melody or harmony notes. The two lowest strings, the sixth and fifth string are simultaneously covered by hooking the left thumb over the neck and firmly holding down those two strings at the third fret. This is not an easy thing to do. It takes a dedicated and very determined guitarist to learn how to make this work. The initial application is guaranteed to be very uncomfortable, even painful to some. But like a physical trainer would say, "No Pain, No Gain." As with so many other difficult techniques on guitar, time and determination, practice and more practice will make this little trick available.

It's an easy thing to miss when watching thumb-style guitarists. Chet used it a lot, particularly in his earlier years. Merle Travis who brought the technique out of Muhlenberg County and introduced it to the world, could hold down *three* strings, the sixth, fifth and fourth with his thumb when he wanted to. This is one of those things YouTube is good for: in just about every video of Merle Travis you can see him using the Rager Thumb. Quite a challenge.

Playing Rhythm

Not many guitar players can play good rhythm. Everybody wants to play the lead. I've seen a lot of players learn how to play a tune but don't know the chords to it. When you learn a piece you should also learn the chords.

Chet never wanted a heavy beat on 2 and 4 because he said it covered up his thumb, so he would have the drummer play kick drum and high hat cymbal on the off beat. As for one guitarist playing rhythm for another, I have played where there were three or four guys all playing at once. Everybody kept getting louder and louder and after a while it sounded like a train wreck! The trick is to soften up when you're playing with someone. Then when it's your turn, turn up and the other guy softens up.

I always took pride in playing good rhythm, I learned how to play in the groove and make it swing. It's very important to keep correct time. Most of the time, if some one has a problem with time, that person will rush. When I played with Chet I had to be careful to keep a steady beat and not get too loud. It takes a lot of practice to play rhythm.

No matter what you play there's always one part that gets you. Ever notice that? Every tune's got one part you think about all through the thing. "Boy I hope I get through that!" But I've learned if there's a hard lick somewhere there's another place to play it. There's always at least two places to play everything on a guitar. If you've got something hard to play work it out in a different position. It'll sound a little different but it might be easier to play.

I noticed some will talk about Clinics. Some clinics are just another concert at double the price. You can't learn much because there is so much played. If you remember one or two things you're lucky. A person would be much better off to spend $25 and buy one of Chet's tapes or DVDs and watch it. Someone asked Chet one time "How do you get to be a good guitar player?" Chet's answer was, "Get your guitar and go to your bedroom and practice 10 hours a day."

Nail care is an issue to many thumb style guitarists. Most of them use longer nails on their right hand for the tone the combination of fingertip and nail gives. Some, like Tommy Emmanuel, develop calluses so they don't need to deal with nails that can get inconveniently broken.

Paul, over the years, never said much about nail care except that he didn't do anything special beyond keeping them filed smoothly on the edges and once mentioned taking a little gelatin every few days. Unfortunately no one ever asked him what form it took. It could have been simple Jell-O. Still, nails do break and here he puts forth his view of emergency fix-it.

For many years when I would break a nail I glued a false one on and keep it on for about two weeks, but I never liked the tone I would get from it. Yesterday I tried something that I saw Chet do many times. That is, to cut a piece from a ping-pong ball and glue it underneath the edge of my fingernail. I tell you it's almost as good as the real thing and the tone is almost the same. I think I have solved another one of my problems!

CHAPTER 22

SOME GRUMBLES, SOME FUN, SOME LOVE

Paul was as human as the rest of us. When he posted his thoughts on the chatboards he was direct and to the point. Some of the chatboards could get quite contentious and more than once he would stop posting. It was always temporary because he had so much he wanted to share with people. He liked offering solutions to the problems, big and small as they applied to guitar maintenance. Here, he temporarily quits a forum over some now forgotten bit of pique.

If I'm right or if I'm wrong about it I've enjoyed as much of this as I can stand, I've enjoyed being on the Chetboard and the fellowship with everyone good luck to all. Maybe I'll see you on Life's Highway, good bye.

After about a week, Paul would be back and whatever it was that irritated him would be forgotten. Or at least not brought up again.

It seems since Chet died everybody has a quote that Chet made about how great they are and all that. It's funny to me that a lot of those quotes weren't around when Chet was still here.

Paul was always a little prickly about Les Paul. Les would occasionally exaggerate his role in creation and it got to Paul more than once.

Around 2004, at the NAMM show here in Nashville, Paul Rivera and I were standing, talking, when Ted McCarty came by being pushed in a wheelchair. I said to Paul, "Ask him about the Les Paul guitar." So Paul Rivera stopped him and asked him if Les designed that model.

Ted said, "No. I did." Gibson had to come out with a solid body model to compete with the Fender Telecaster so Gibson made the guitar. Les was hot at that time so Ted and another fellow went to upstate New York where Les and Mary were performing and showed it to Les. Les like it but wanted his tailpiece that he had designed put on it. They worked out a deal and it became the Les Paul guitar and everybody got rich. I doubt anything would have been invented if Les hadn't been around. Les is the Forrest Gump of the guitar business.

Marie and I have stayed for the Saturday night CAAS show the last two years. We stay until about 10:00 or half of it. The sound could be mixed a lot better. I think the first part of the show would be better if the first few performers were top Chet players. Those young kids don't have a clue as to what they're doing. Chet wasn't impressed about how many notes you could play in a bar. Speed is all about trying to impress other musicians. Most people couldn't care less.

Note: years referenced in the previous and next statements are unknown. Judging from his comments it may have been a year that had a lot of Django style players in attendance.

This year the highlight of the week was probably the Jerry Reed tribute. That was hard to top! As it turned out it probably would have been better to have done it in place of the Saturday night show. Mark Pritcher does a great job and it's tough to please everyone. I think some artists play too many tunes. Like Chet use to say "You have to know when to get off the stage."

In country music they won't play anything recorded before 1986 ... before Randy Travis. It's like nobody ever lived before them. The program directors don't worry about what the public wants. They're like the government. "They know what's best for you." Besides everybody wants to play like Albert Lee nowadays. Nothing against Albert Lee, but I don't play like Albert Lee. As far as the record business is concerned, thumb-style guitar playing is as about as popular as '61 Chevy's. You see one now and then but most of them are rusty.

People talk about "dings" you get on guitars as you own them or even how they come from factories. You should see the guitars Chet and I played on the road ... dings everywhere! It's really hard for even a guitar company to ship them without something happening to them. I don't know how many guitars I saw at Gibson that had come back from the dealers with the necks broken at the nut. It happens.

Buying a Nashville Classic or Country Gentleman with a little flaw for $1600 is a great deal. I think it would be a shame to cut up a great guitar because of a pinhead flaw in the finish. You have to ask yourself, are you buying a museum piece or a great sounding, great playing, guitar? When you play it does someone in the audience ask you if your guitar has any flaws or dings?

Can I Have Your Autograph?

Paul could succumb to being a fan in his own way. He had a normal "fan appreciation" for artists he saw on TV and in movies.

One night after the show with Jerry, the band had left the stage and I was turning off our amps. A voice behind me said "Is Jerry around?" I turned around and it was Roy Rogers! I almost wet in my pants! I said "He's up in his room. I can take you up there." We got on the elevator and went up to Jerry and Prissy's room. Roy was the nicest guy you could ever meet.

When I was with Jerry and lot of famous people came by his office. One day I was back in the studio and Jerry came back and said 'Look at this! It's Buford Pusser's gun!' It was a beautiful Browning Hi Standard 9 mm chromed and engraved with pearl grips. I held it for a few minutes and then went with Jerry up the hall where they were. Buford was a big dude! His face was scarred.

Once, when I was with Jerry, I was back in the studio control room. Jerry came back and said "Come up front." I got up and went to the front desk. There stood Audie Murphy as big as life! What a thrill to be in the presence of a great man such as him! He wanted to meet Jerry. I stood by and listened to everyone talk. A few months later Audie was killed in a small plane crash.

I was involved in a movie soundtrack once but there's really not much to tell. Myself and four or five other musicians got called to go to Memphis and record the sound track for the movie *Every Which Way But Loose*.

It took about two or three days. Clint Eastwood and Sandra Locke were there in the studio. Clint was nice to everyone and at one point in the middle of one of the tunes came over and sat down next to me. That didn't help my playing any. Actually it freaked me out a little. He said 'How you doing?'

I said, 'OK.'

On Saturday night after we had finished Clint bought our supper at a real nice place and we had a group picture made. That's about it.

We did the *Pat Sajak Show* once. They flew Chet and I out to Hollywood and we stayed in the Beverly Hilton hotel. They picked us up in a limo. It was a great trip. We did it at the large CBS studios. I went down the hall and went to the *All in the Family* set and sat in Archie's chair!

Sometimes Even Chet Could Be Impressed with an Autograph

Bettie Page, a famous pinup model of the 1950s, died in 2009. I remembered that Chet was a big fan of hers. Every now and then he would talk about her.

One year, on Chet's birthday at Cafe Milano, someone presented Chet with a letter from her wishing him a happy birthday. I don't think I ever saw Chet so surprised.

She was a good un'.

Computers

Chet didn't have a computer. He didn't want to waste his time fooling with one. His office computer for his secretary was a small Apple with a small screen. He didn't use a computer himself but he had some kind of word processor machine that he wrote letters on.

CHAPTER 23

PRESIDENTS AND PUNDITS

Chet, himself, played for presidents at White House functions from the Kennedy administration to, and including Bill Clinton. Here Paul describes meeting President Reagan.

We performed in Washington, DC with the National Symphony. I think Chet knew Larry Speakes, the White House spokesman during the Reagan administration. Chet and I were big Reagan fans so we were invited to lunch at the White House. Chet and I and Chet's manager, Fred Kewley, went.

They have a small dining room with five or six tables downstairs so we had lunch there. Then Larry Speakes said the President would like to meet us. We went upstairs to the floor where the Oval Office is. There was a Secret Service guy outside the door when we went in. President Reagan got up from his desk and greeted us. We all shook hands and Chet and he talked for a little while. President Reagan asked Chet how he slept the night before. He said when he couldn't go to sleep he would recite the poem "The Shooting of Dan McGrew" It has about forty verses to it. Then President Reagan gave each of us a set of cufflinks. Chet wore his for a while and I gave mine to my son Micah.

We stayed for about thirty minutes and then left. There is always a photo guy there taking pictures. In about three or four weeks we got the pics. It was a great thrill at the time. Another time Chet and I played for President Reagan and his wife. Chet played for President Clinton and his wife. We played so many great places. Carnegie Hall two or three times, the Plaza Hotel in New York City. We even did a tour with the Boston Pops Orchestra. It was a great twenty five years.

Paul sometimes came across as a person who regarded guitars as just tools of the trade and in many ways that's just what they were. But he recognized some guitars as being iconic and their sale moved him deeply.

In April 2007, Thom Bresh sold two of Merle's guitars. One was a Super 400 with P-90 pickups and a long handle on the Bigsby. It had a normally inlaid fingerboard. It was not the "Gibson Special" with the elaborately inlaid peghead that has Merle's name on the fingerboard.

The other was a real treasure, the Martin with the Bigsby neck on it. I have played that one a few times. The action, as I remember, was pretty low and the guitar had a deep tone to it. It gave you goose pimples to play it.

The neck is the same width as a Martin. It is shaped on the back sort of like one of the old Telecasters. That guitar has a deep tone but it's not real loud. It has a sweetness to it. We're lucky it survived Merle. I think it was Joe Maphis who said he went over to Merle's house when they all lived in California. Merle had that Martin on the wall with flowers growing out of it. Another time Merle was drinking and he couldn't get in tune so he threw it in the fireplace. Joe got it out.

You know, when I saw what they brought at auction (The Martin with the Bigsby neck sold for $264,000 and the Super 400 sold for $36,000) it brought tears to my eyes. It was almost like a good friend had died.

I don't play nylon guitar very much anymore. I'd rather play the electric steel string. One reason being everybody is playing a nylon and I'm sort of tired of the sound. Also I can play more different tunes on the electric and it has a vibrato.

Chet seldom played an acoustic guitar. I seldom play one and I have three great ones. I don't think the electric guitar will fade away.

I don't care much for acoustic guitars for one reason ... everyone sounds the same ... same tone etc. Take Paul Moseley; I don't know anyone who gets a better tone out of an electric guitar, but if Paul played an acoustic he would sound like everyone else. I love the sound of a good electric with a good player playing it.

Fun Stuff

Paul had a great sense of humor and loved good jokes.

Musicians and travelling salesmen always seem to have an inventory of good jokes at their beck and call. Being more of a salesman than a musician, I would hear a ton of jokes while on the road and I used to call Paul whenever I'd heard a really good one. He would listen and have a big grin on his face in anticipation of a great punch line. Then, when I would deliver the big finish, he would howl with laughter and I'd find myself laughing my tail off at how much he was enjoying it. And invariably, if he found it to be particularly funny, he'd turn to me while still chuckling and say "Man that was a good one. Chet would have loved that one, too!"
— John Lewis

One time when Paul was working with the Louvins, he was dating one of their sisters who lived in Chattanooga, TN. He would buy gas on credit to go see her when he wasn't on the road with them. One night, when he had taken her home and was on his way back to Nashville, it started coming a bad thunderstorm. Paul was driving a 1955 Pontiac convertible that he said was the sharpest thing you had ever seen. The body was white with a black convertible top and red interior. While driving through the thunderstorm a limb fell out of a tree and punctured a hole in the convertible top, the wind then caught it and ripped the top completely off the car. Paul had to keep driving in the pouring rain of the thunderstorm until he saw a house with a light on and it also had a barn beside it. The people there told him he could put his car in their barn. They also let him call Charlie Louvin in Nashville. Charlie came and picked him up and Paul went back a few days later and picked up the car and had a new top put on it.
— Robbie Jones

Sonny Thomas, a guitarist, had a guitar repair shop in his home in Nashville. Paul would bring Chet's guitars over to Sonny's for repair at times. I drove up to Sonny's one day for him to set up a new guitar for me. Sonny said that Paul had just left with one of Chet's guitars. Sonny was still laughing and he was showing me a guitar someone had made and left it there for him to look over. It had a metal plate on the head that said No.23. The guitar looked like a twelve-year-old kid had made it for a Scout project. Sonny said he was working on Chet's guitar and Paul was walking around looking at guitars in his shop. He picked the guitar up and was really looking at it. Sonny said he heard Paul talking out of the side of his mouth saying. "Number 23! Hell, I wonder what number 1 looked like?" That was 100% Paul Yandell.
— Gary Cochran

A Funny Dog Story

Here's an example of Chet's sense of humor.

Back in the late 1970s, after I had been working for him for a few years, I would go over to his office two or three times a week and have lunch at some place that he had run up on.

Anyway, one day I went over and Chet said "Let's just walk over to this new place." So we started walking. It was about four or five blocks and about half way there was a yard that had a chain link fence with heavy brush growing along the fence. I was walking on the inside as we were walking along the fence. All of a sudden, the biggest dog you ever saw jumped at me and hit the fence! He made the most blood-chilling roar you ever heard. I think it was a pit bull. It scared me to death but Chet almost died laughing. It was a practice of his to walk people along that fence and watch them when that dog came at them.

I remember when I had started with Chet we had to catch an early plane back to Nashville. I was driving us to the airport and I was feeling pretty good so I started whistling under my breath.

Chet said "I don't like to hear whistling early in the morning!" After that I didn't whistle very much.

A Les Paul Story

Here's a story Les told Chet and I when they were doing those albums. Chet said it wasn't true but it's funny anyway. Les said when Django was dying his son was at his side. Django looked at his son and said "Son don't ever play guitar because you'll never be as great as I am." Chet and I got a big laugh out of it.

One time Chet and I were sitting in first class flight going somewhere ... this was when I first started with him ... the stewardess came by and said to Chet, "Mr. Atkins, would you and your son like something to drink?"

Chet replied, "He's not my son! He's older than I am!" We had a good laugh about that. I always looked young until I got in my late fifties. Then, overnight I looked like I was eighty.

A few years back at a Chet Atkins Appreciation Society (CAAS.) I had changed the strings on my Sand guitar and didn't have anything to clip off the ends so I kind of wrapped them into loops at the headstock like a lot of people do. I stopped by Paul's table and he wanted to use my guitar to show someone a lick. Of course I was honored. By this time the strings had come out of the loops and were going in all directions. Paul looked up at me and said "You know people do cut those off." I can hear him saying that to this day.
— Eddie Estes

A Prank

Chet and Bill Carlisle were old friends. One day Chet told me to come over to his office. When I got there Chet said to me, "You know Bill hates Porter

Wagoner. I want you to write a letter from Porter to Bill giving him advice on his career."

I typed up a letter saying, "I think you have been doing great over the years, Bill, and I've been keeping an eye on you. If there is ever anything I can do for you to help you along please let me know." I signed it "Porter."

Chet mailed it to Bill in about three days Bill called Chet saying he knew he did it, raising all kind of hell about it.

We were having a sound check one time and he was singing that song about his dad. I was sitting behind him like I always do and I was playing fills behind him like I always do. I happened to play a fill I used to play behind the Louvin brothers. I'd heard Chet play it on an old Louvin Brother's record. He stopped playing and turned around and said, 'Don't ever play that lick again. I hate that song!'

Marie Yandell swears this happened:

Paul and Chet were booked for a small concert in summertime and Chet decided to wear white trousers for the show. Everything was fine until he and Paul were changing, getting ready for the show.

Chet looked in the dressing room mirror and saw that the colored underwear he was wearing was not a good idea since the trousers were, after all, white and made for summer. His boxers were of a dark material. (Rumors that they were Roy Rogers undies are total fabrications and not to be believed!)

A quick confab was held and Paul (who was wearing whities) and Chet exchanged underwear and the day was saved, the concert played and mutual passages through respective laundries made everything right in the world again.

A true bandleader among bandleaders to go the extra mile in his boss's underwear in time of need!

A Disneyland Story

Jerry Reed had performed at Disneyland, but had never toured the park. Paul drove all of us there in my car and we enjoyed an entire day walking all over Disneyland.

Jerry was worried about being recognized and drawing a crowd so he was wearing sunglasses with lenses that flipped up and down. He flipped those lenses so much that Paul finally told him that he was drawing more attention to himself by flipping the lenses than he would have without sunglasses at all.

They were playing at Knott's Berry Farm that night, so we finally headed to the parking lot only to find that not one of us remembered where Paul had parked the car. Bear in mind this was in the 1970s. There were no remote control clickers that would blink the lights or honk the horn. There were no cell phones to use to call a cab. So, we tromped all over the Disneyland parking lots until we found the car. Paul broke speed limits getting back to Knott's Berry Farm. Just in the nick of time, Jerry and Paul waltzed out on stage as though nothing unusual had happened and gave a dynamite performance.

— Jan Hite

Drummer Randy Hauser (played with Chet for twenty years) liked to engage Paul to the enjoyment of the other guys in the band. One day, Randy nudged Steve Wariner and said "Watch this."

"Paul! Isn't it a beautiful day, the sky is blue, the weather is great and we are right here at the ocean?"

Paul's reply was, "Ah, I guess, if you are into that kind of thing." We laughed about that for years.

— Pam Hauser

Playing in a minor key is just like driving on a damn muddy road. Hell, you think it will never end.

I was very fortunate to have been a close friend of Paul Yandell.

He was a great guitar player himself and he helped me a lot in my career as a musician and was one of my biggest cheerleaders and I miss him very much.

He was also a very funny person and I had many great times on the road with him and Chet driving to gigs sometimes just the three of us. Chet was always playing jokes on Paul and I. He loved to see us get flustered. My favorite time was when Chet took Paul and I to lunch to meet the founder and CEO of the Cracker Barrel restaurant.

We ate there pretty often because Chet did commercials for them we would all get lunch for free. Paul would complain about the crackers that they served and how stale they were and how they needed to improve on them by having a crisper, more crunchy, fresh cracker.

Chet invited us to lunch to meet the CEO at the Cracker barrel. We were all taken by the hostess to a table in the back. The four of us were seated and the CEO whose name was Dan introduced himself to us. We all sat down. There was a long silence while we looked at the menus.

Then Chet looked up, cleared his throat, and says to Paul: "Hey Paul, why don't you tell Dan what you think of the crackers they have here?"

Paul said, "Dammit Chet! Why did you have to tell him that?" He turned beet red. We all laughed about that for a long time.

Paul was a great guy and one of a kind.

— Pat Bergeson

A-1 Steak Sauce

Several years before my grandmother Yandell passed away she built a garage. She didn't have an automatic garage door opener, so my dad and mom thought it would be a great idea to install an automatic opener for her. So one Saturday my dad and I headed out to Kentucky to install the garage door opener. We worked all day long and accomplished our task of installing the garage door opener. It was getting late that day and we didn't want my grandmother to cook dinner that afternoon so we headed out back to Nashville.

We went through a little town by the name of Aurora, Kentucky and found ourselves very hungry and decided to stop at a family restaurant to eat. Once inside after looking at the menu the special was buffalo meat. Neither one of us had ever had buffalo meat so we decided we would try it. We ordered buffalo burgers with fries and coffee, we were ready for a treat. The waitress brought us our food and I think I took the first bite and then Daddy. We both looked at each other and I could read his expressions and he could read mine, the buffalo meat was horrible.

We decided the only way to solve this problem was to apply A-1 steak sauce, which was on every table in the restaurant. I got up and went to the first table and got a bottle and it was empty. I proceeded to the next table and next to realize that every bottle of A-1 was empty. We had a great big laugh off of this because we both realized that nobody else who had eaten previously liked the taste of the buffalo meat. We never passed the restaurant again that we didn't think of that Saturday and the experience of trying a buffalo hamburger. What a laugh we had!

— Micah Yandell

A Cat Story

Back in the 1980s, Chet and Leona had a large cat. It was more Leona's cat than Chet's. As time went by Chet started to dislike the cat for some reason. Finally he had Leona get rid of it.

The Christmas season was upcoming so Leona sent Chet a Christmas card from the cat saying how much he missed being there and how he felt Chet had been mean to him. We all thought that was so funny and clever of Leona.

Some years ago, Chet played Paul Masson's Winery out in California, about fifty miles from San Francisco. We were there for two or three days. One day Chet and I drove into San Francisco to Fisherman's Wharf to eat lunch.

After we ate we started walking around looking at the shops. Two women tourists walked toward us and one said to us 'Would one of you take our picture' She handed her camera to me. Chet said "Let me get in there with you!" and got in the middle as I took the picture. The women went on their way and as we continued walking down the street, Chet said "Someday they will look at that picture and they or someone they know will recognize me." We both had a good laugh.

Home Is Where the Heart Is

Recording was stressful and tiring to Paul. His energy level was usually drained when he got home. After recording, he didn't want to pick up a guitar until the next day.

Jet lag was another thing that bothered him after being on the road. When he got home He usually wanted to pull off his shoes, kick back and relax.

— Marie Yandell

Paul, Marie and Micah. *Photo courtesy of John Lewis*

In a *Talk of the Town* local TV clip there is a sweet bit of business of Chet talking of Leona.

The interviewer asked Chet if Leona still listened to him play after being married to him and his music for fifty years:

> Once in a while I'll play something and she'll turn and say "What is that, Daddy?"
> And I said, "That's a tune I wrote … 'Waiting for Suzy B.'"
> "Who wrote it?"
> "I did."
> "Well, that's great!"
> And then she goes back to reading the paper or watching TV.

Marie Yandell muses on being married to a guitar player:

> When we lived in East Nashville in a two bedroom house, which we did for forty one years. He kept guitars in his music room, some guitars and amps in the dining room. After we moved to Hendersonville in 2005, he had a room with a workbench in it and kept most of his guitars and amps in that room. His recording equipment was upstairs in the bonus room and he kept some guitars and a couple of amps in there too. So many guitars.
>
> He always kept a couple of guitars that he loved playing on a daily regular basis on guitar stands in the living room so that he could pick them up at any time when he was sitting around to play. He was very comfortable playing wherever and whenever he felt like it.
>
> When I was in the kitchen cooking, he'd sit in a kitchen chair and play his guitar. He always wanted to be around wherever I was in the house and he'd always have a guitar in his hands. If I was ironing in the bedroom he'd sit on the edge of the bed or the cedar chest or on a chair and play his guitar. If I was in the back yard gardening, he'd sit in a chair on the deck and play his guitar.
>
> When he was writing an instrumental, he always wanted me to hear what he was playing to get my opinion. His creative song and instrumental writing was always easier for him early in the morning.
>
> He always serenaded me in the mornings while I was cooking breakfast and/or washing dishes. Of course, during the day when I was at work, he mostly played in his music room or while sitting on the sofa watching TV. If he was watching something on TV he almost always had a guitar in his hands. Many times, if he heard music in a commercial, jingle or TV show that caught his ear, he'd take his guitar and figure out what they were doing. He liked to do his recording when I was not around to make noise though.

If he put his mind to it, he could pick up an instrument and master it, (as evidenced thru his playing of bass and banjo on some of Chet's recordings and fiddle, autoharp and mandolin on some of his own recordings.)

A Day on the Lake

As a boy I always enjoyed fishing. As years passed I found myself with a Ranger bass boat. My family, mother, daddy, Sheri and I starting going to Kentucky Lake each year for family vacation. One year before we left on our vacation daddy had visited with Jerry Reed and sometime during the conversation daddy mentioned how I was into fishing and he was going with me from time to time. When daddy started to leave that day, Jerry gave him a custom built rod with Jerry's name on it and a reel that someone had made for him. Daddy was all excited and was ready to do some serious fishing when we went to the lake.

As a child daddy always said he was not a good fishermen and always lost his dad's lures on Kentucky Lake. The following week in September we were in the cove near our condo on Kentucky Lake fishing. I was on the front operating the boat and daddy was in the back seat, the fishing was slow so we had great conversation throughout the afternoon. As I turned the boat and was heading back up the cove, I hear a commotion in the back of the boat. I turn around and see daddy sitting in his chair with no rod in his hand. I look further into the water and see Jerry's rod and reel sinking in the lake. I immediately turned

Micah's fishing/ pleasure boat. Many a fish story (and fishing pole story) started here. *Photo courtesy of Sheri Yandell*

the boat around and tried desperately to retrieve the rod and reel with no luck. Daddy seemed to be in shock and he said he made a cast and the rod and reel came out of his hand. We begin to laugh and as daddy and his humor would have it said "Someday someone will hook this rod and reel and discover it belonged to Jerry Reed." I went back several times and tried to hook the rod and reel, but I never had any luck. Daddy and I often laughed at this on our Saturday morning breakfast outings at the Cracker Barrel.

— Micah Yandell

Sunday Mornings

Sunday mornings will never be the same for me. Daddy would always come to our house where he and I would spend an hour or two playing while mother and Sheri went to church. This was a great time in my life for him to share and teach me the fundamentals of fingerstyle guitar playing. I still play on Sunday mornings, but it will never be the same without my daddy sitting here beside me at the kitchen counter showing me all the great tunes and licks.

— Micah Yandell

The Hazel Guitar

From a very early age I remember almost every one of my dad's guitars. I have fond memories of him working on them, improving the way they played and sounded. He was never afraid to try something new while searching for that perfect tone.

Mom and Sheri loved going antiquing so us guys we would let them go at their own pace while we piddled around looking at what we wanted to. On one of our many outings to Kentucky we headed to a little town called Hazel, Kentucky, known for its antiques shops. We were roaming around one antique store near the end of our day trip and over in the corner sat a Stratocaster body that was painted in yellow and pinstripe with black spider webs. The neck had been scalloped out on every fret. Daddy noticed the guitar and went straight for it. Much to my surprise he picked up the guitar held it in his hands and said 'I'm going to buy this!' They were asking six-dollars for the guitar. The guitar had no hardware and was in very bad shape. My thought at the time was this is a waste of six-dollars, but daddy saw beyond the ugly guitar and told me he could make the guitar into something special.

We went back to the home place that afternoon and upon arriving he headed to the garage and told me to find some paint stripper. We

The "Hazel" guitar. The Stratocaster Paul rescued and restored. *Photo courtesy of Derek Rhodes*

worked on the guitar until all the paint was gone down to the bare wood. Little did I know that daddy had every part at home to make this into a beautiful brown Fender Stratocaster. He worked at least two weeks on refinishing the body. He then assembled the guitar with the parts he had collected throughout the years. The picture below is a six-dollar Stratocaster that my dad brought back to life. To this day I will never take any amount of money for the six- dollar hazel strat.

— Micah Yandell

You Know What They Say About Paul …

He used to embarrass me when he introduced me on the show. He would say "This is Paul Yandell from Mayfield, Kentucky. He can play everything I can, only better." Or he would say, "He can play everything I can and play the harmony to it, too." He knew that wasn't true but he was being nice. He said that about a lot of players but nobody could play anything better than Chet could.

Even steel players respected him. Here are some of them … sidemen all.

Paul was never averse to helping a fellow picker make a living. Personally, he kept me eating in the winter and spring of 1985 with a weekend gig in Clarksville and some session work. He didn't have to hire me on the club gig as the band was already quite good sized. But we got along well and I busted my ass to do him a good job.
— Mike Cass
(Steel Guitar Forum)

Great player in his own right, and the ultimate sideman when that was called for—a rare combination, and getting more rare
— Dave Mudgett
(Steel Guitar Forum)

Paul and I played a club together for about two years after I got off the road in 1976. Knowing that I needed to acquire a lot of equipment to start a studio career he was always eager to loan or give me things I didn't have. The 1977 Les Paul Standard that I still play today is one that he found for me in a music store. He was very instrumental, (pun intended), in keeping me from having to go back on the road, and for that, I'll be eternally grateful!
— Gregg Galbraith
(Steel Guitar Forum)

I was a big fan of Chet and attended a concert featuring him and Paul in Orlando, Florida in about 1978. Chet was doing his usual good job with Paul doing his backup. In the middle of the concert, something happened to Chet's electric guitar that caused Chet to abruptly leave the stage for a while and go backstage to tend to it. He turned the show over to Paul and the rest of the band. They went wild with some great rock & roll classics featuring Paul playing some screaming string pulls and rock riffs. They really stole the show from Chet, but it was all in fun!
— Morgan Scoggins
(Steel Guitar Forum)

Paul was a good friend to me. Although we played many jobs together I think one of his closest friends was Sonny Thomas. Sonny never received the recognition he deserved as a player (and he is a great guitar player) he was also a gifted guitar repairman. Sonny was the guitar repair guy to Chet, Jerry Reed and Paul. Paul had Sonny refret a guitar for him just weeks before he died. Sonny told me that he thought Paul had him refret the guitar just so he would have an excuse to visit him in his last days. Sonny said "It was Paul's way of saying goodbye."
— Sid Hudson

(Steel Guitar Forum)

Jerry Reed joked: "Paul is so skinny, if he turns around sideways and sticks out his tongue, he looks just like a zipper!"
— Jan Hite

Paul was one of the most real people I ever knew, or will ever know. A rare trait.
— Randy Goodrum

Round or about the 2nd CAAS convention, Mark Pritcher had a table set up in front of the dining room for our banquet dinner. At that table he had name cards for Chet and Leona, himself and his wife Carole, Jim Farron and his wife and Paul and Marie (right in front of everybody!) Paul starts snatching up his and Marie's silverware and dinner plates and brought them to where Diane (my wife) and I were sitting. He didn't want to sit up there in the front beside Chet … too much attention … too much spotlight (anybody else would have killed to get to sit up there beside Chet and be seen with him) Paul said, "I want to sit here, with my friends!"
— Gayle Mosely

Once I told Paul he was one of my heroes. He said, "You ought to set your sights higher."
— Craig Dobbins

At CAAS in 2006, a youngster came over to Paul's table. I'm not sure how old he was, but I'd say that he was probably no older than twelve years old. He walked up and said, "Are you Paul Yandell?," and Paul responded with, "Well, I'm what's left of him," which drew laughter from those of us that were within earshot.

Paul asked him to play something for him, and the boy played a Jerry Reed song. Paul gave him a couple of picking tips on the song. After looking the guitar over, Paul saw something he thought would make the guitar play better and took the boy and the guitar to Kirk Sand's booth to get the guitar set up a little better.

A little bit later they went into the side room where some of the performers warm up. There, Paul sat down with the boy and gave him a guitar lesson.

Later on I told Paul how impressed I was with what he did to help the boy and he mentioned how Chet had helped him out back when he first auditioned at the Grand Ole Opry (the time that Chet let him use his guitar and amp). He also remarked at how when you ask the kids to play something for you, they don't get nervous. They just play, unlike many of us grown-ups who often get intimidated and nervous.

I wonder how the boy is doing now?
— Bill Bailey

At the CAAS convention a few years ago I was standing in the Belmont Room vestibule listening to a Travis style picker who had some very nice equipment. It was a Super 400 with P90s, just like the one Travis had and he was playing through one of the new reissue Standel 25L15 amps. He was a pretty good player but his tone had a little too much bite to it. While I was standing there with my arms folded, listening, Paul walked up beside me and stood there for a very few seconds listening. After just a few seconds, he elbowed me in the ribs and said, "Too many highs!" ... and turned around and walked off. Typical Paul. Direct and to the point.
— Richard Hudson

I used to open the case to my classical guitar and much too often I would find a broken D string. This used to frustrate the devil out of me and I couldn't figure out what was causing the problem. Well, one day I was over at Paul's house and we were just piddling around and telling stories. I looked up on the wall and saw this rather ordinary classical guitar hanging there. Somebody had cut away a section of the body to gain better access to the upper frets. I couldn't believe that somebody would have done that to a guitar.

As I sat there and started to play something on it, I noticed immediately that the D string was tuned way down. I offhandedly said to Paul "'Hey, the D string is turned down on this thing." He gave me that "Paul Look" that many of us came to recognize so well and then said "Well, of course it's turned down. That's what you do to keep it from breaking." I said, "Why do you turn down only the D string?" "Well, John," said Paul, "you turn down the D string because that is the one with the greatest tension on it."

Well, I looked it up on the Internet and sure enough. The D string carries the highest tension of all the strings. That gave me the explanation I had lacked all these years. Turns out that Paul was right as he always was, about all things guitar related.

Oh, I forgot to mention that the plain-looking guitar I was playing that day was the one Jerry Reed played on all of his hits! My God!
— John Lewis

I met Paul in the late 1980s. And over the years became very good friends. We would often talk about guitars, amplifiers and modifications to them. It was always a great honor to play with him. He was always a highlight for me each year at CAAS.

He told me once, " In order for a melody to be pretty, the notes need space."

He was one of my guitar heroes, mentor and very dear friend, a blessing in my life. He is truly missed.

— Paul Moseley

A Summation by Eddie Pennington

It is probably safe to say that there is no finer thumb picker in the Merle Travis style than Eddie Pennington.

From his website (used by permission):

Award winning Eddie Pennington is widely recognized among his peers as one of the greatest living thumbstyle guitarists. In venues throughout the United States and Europe, he has kept alive the sound popularized by Kentucky native Merle Travis in the 1940s. Because of his ability to adapt well-known tunes to the alternating bass rhythms that characterize "Travis pickin'," Eddie's performances have generated renewed interest in this challenging art form.

Eddie Pennington's love of the guitar—and his love of live performance—brings to life the rich musical traditions of western Kentucky, making him an entertainer appealing to all ages all over the world. His strong sense of place, combined with flawless performances of folk and contemporary guitar tunes, attracts and keeps a legion of loyal listeners.

Here, unedited, Eddie muses about his friend:

For a big ole guy that never quite followed the rules of learning to be a good guitar player I have been blessed to have been around some of the greatest players of all time, and one of the greatest I was ever around was Paul Yandell who I feel like is a big brother to me.

When I first started to get to be around the thumbpickers of Western, Kentucky one of the names they would mention in reverence was Yandell who came from Mayfield. Mose Rager spoke of him, and Gene Frances and Frank Hudson would often mention him when they spoke of Nashville picking. Odell Martin was the hero of the area I came from, and he deserved to be any guitar player's hero, but whenever his name was mentioned the name Yandell usually came up. I soon learned that Odell was a living breathing being, but I was not sure about guys like Merle Travis, Chet Atkins, and the Yandell guy. Those guys seemed more like immortal beings that appeared on TV and records, but were never reached by mere who pickers want to learn, like I was at that time. I would never have believed in 1975 that Paul Yandell would become one of the best friends I would ever have in this life simply because he was Yandell and had moved into the highest ranks of being a guitar player that folks like Mose Rager and the guys I knew granted to him.

After I met Odell Martin I just thought that I had reached the top of the guitar world, and at the time for me I pretty much had. But, it didn't take long being around him that you learned that he had someone that he loved very much and if advice was needed he would ask Paul. So my mind again put that guy way up on a cloud even more if someone like Odell Martin sought his advice.

I'm not real sure in my recall of the exact year that I first saw Paul Yandell in person, but I will never forget seeing him. He came to Gene Frances' picking day in Hopkinsville, Kentucky just to pick. It must have been in the very early 1980s maybe 1982 about the end of September. I was playing fiddle in Gene Frances' band by that time and was so sad that day because Odell was on the road and could not be there. It was sort of a cool and dampish day and everyone started talking about a special picker just arriving. I saw this real slim guy with glasses, and he seemed to frown as folks began to crowd around him. My friend Gayle Moseley said, "That's Paul Yandell" So we watched and soon Gene Frances had Paul headed toward the stage to pick. I got as close as I could without getting too close to bother him and was excited like a little kid gets before Santa appears in the parade. I think Paul was playing one of the new Gibson classical electric guitars that day, but I was not looking at his guitar. I was looking at Yandell the guy everyone that I knew spoke of in reverence. He lived and breathed, and then he played. I remember him playing "It Don't Mean a Thing If It Ain't Got That Swing" and I liked to have went wild because it was so good. Bobby Barber was there, and he was my Merle Travis hero, but I remember telling him how great that song was when Paul had finished. I didn't realize that he and Paul had been friends for years, and I just didn't realize that anyone could have been close with the mystical Yandell especially after hearing him play. After he played, he was cold, and although no one ever went into Gene's house on that day Paul went in for coffee. Gayle and I got up nerve and went in and we introduced ourselves to Paul. I know he was real impressed to meet us as he was trying to drink his coffee and get warm, but he was nice, sort of distant, but nice. Our friend Steve Rector had also slipped in and was telling Paul how he played solid backup guitar like Hawk Murphy. In all, we didn't bother him long, but I could brag that I had met the legend of Mayfield, Paul Yandell and he had even talked to me.

I saw Paul again I think in 1983 and 1984 at Gene's picking event. The next couple of years Odell was there, and Paul and Odell picked together. I remember a picture of the two of them picking and Gayle sitting in the back smiling like he had just eaten a big piece of watermelon.

Gayle started going to a club in Clarksville where Paul played on Sunday nights and got to know Paul. They soon became close friends and Gayle would tell me things that he and Paul talked about. Soon Paul would start visiting Gayle and every week at the square dance before we started, Gayle would show me a new tune that Paul had been helping him with. It was just great to be able to talk about somebody like Paul with his friend, and Paul was very good to Gayle. I developed great respect for him because of his friendship with Gayle.

The last time Odell Martin came to my house he had an old black face Fender Twin amp that Bobby Barber had bought from Thumbs Carlisle, and was trying to sell it for Bobby. The amp had some noise in it and I was afraid to buy an old amp like that as I was wanting something like the new Peavy's. That is another story about being too dumb to buy a great amp like that, but what I do remember was when I told Odell I was afraid to buy the amp because of the noise in it I remember him saying, "Ah, Paul Yandell could fix that in a New York minute." I didn't know at the time, but Odell was right, and if you knew Paul and your amp was not right he would fix it in a New York minute for you. I asked Odell one time why didn't Paul want to talk and be close with folks, and Odell said, "Paul Yandell is the greatest fellow in the world, but you just have to understand him."

Soon after that Odell died in a car wreck and left a big void in my picking life. A few months after Odell's death at the Saturday night square dance that I played for with Gene Frances I looked up as someone entered the back of the stage, and it was Paul Yandell. He actually came and played with us that night and I could brag and say that I had picked with Paul Yandell, even though it was on the fiddle I had been on stage with him.

In 1986–1987, I went to Mountain View, Arkansas, and was lucky enough to win a thumbpicking contest. After the 1986 contest, Gayle told me about going to Nashville to the Chet Atkins Appreciation Society's meeting. He told about Paul and Chet playing and that Chet had brought Thom Bresh to pick for the members. I sure wished I could become a member. In 1987, I heard about the CAAS meeting again and decided I'd just try and crash it. I did, and was received very great by the folks that put it on and was even invited to play. I got to see Chet play in person for the first time, and got to meet him. I saw Paul play with Chet, and the next day saw Paul do a show on stage by himself. Paul was ever so protective of Chet, and I remember someone asking why Chet didn't play and record more tunes like "Freight Train." Paul said, "Chet's on a major label and has to record new and fresh music.

If he only played the old tunes like he started with he'd have to be on the Red Robin label." I spoke to Paul at this event, and told him where I knew him from, but he didn't seem too impressed.

In 1988 a place called Libby's had a tribute to thumbpickers in honor of Merle Travis and Odell Martin. I knew many pickers by then, and I went over to play. Paul Yandell was the MC and as I started on the stage this pretty lady spoke to me and told me she was Paul's wife, Marie, and that the other ladies with her were Paul's mom and sister. She spoke to me like she knew who I was, but I didn't even know Paul was married. By then Paul was talking about me. He told the folks how I had won the contests in Arkansas, and one of the greatest things anyone ever said about me he said, "Eddie plays more like Merle Travis than anyone else in the world." I just couldn't believe that he even knew who I was much less tell all these things about me.

A short time after that he called me, and I was shocked, and he asked me if I would like an armrest on my Super 400 like Merle had on his. I had often looked at the pictures of Merle's guitar dreaming and wishing I could have something like that on my guitar. I told Paul that I wanted one so bad I didn't know what to do. He very quietly said, "I made you one and if you come down to the house I'll put it on for you." From that time on until his death he was always doing something to help me out. He'd fix any music instrument problem you had, and just looked for things to do for you.

As time passed I grew to know exactly what Odell Martin had meant when he said you just have to understand Paul. In understanding Paul I learned first, Paul was not a shy person, in fact he was the most direct speaking person I've ever met and I grew to love that more about him than anything else. He wasted no words. In a very short sentence, he could say more than most books hold. He was totally honest and when he told you something it was to help you to improve yourself.

Paul was a very private person, and he liked his space, but he opened up and came to you when he felt he needed to.

He seemed to have a hard shell, and although he spoke blunt, he did it in his way to be direct and usually to help who he was talking to. As I grew to know him better, I realized the hard shell was very thin, but he needed a hard shell because he was like a egg. He was hard on the outside, but the hard shell was very thin, and the inside was full of very soft tender emotions that were very delicate and sensitive.

I've not tried to talk of his wonderful music and the contributions he made there. They stand on their own, and always will, as only a handful of players in all time past and present will ever achieve what he did on the guitar. But, I wanted to speak about how wonderful the man Paul Yandell was and I wish that everyone could have known him

the way that I was fortunate enough to. He made one of the biggest impressions on me that I will ever have made on me in this life. I guess right next to my own Dad is where Paul Yandell stands in the impression he made on me. He nurtured me in my playing, he taught me things I needed to know when I started traveling. He kept my amps and instruments repaired and in top playing shape. He was just one of the most important people that will ever cross through my life and I do count my blessings that I was fortunate enough to say that he was one of my best friends. I do miss him a lot, but I find peace in knowing that he was truly a good person and I believe in all my heart that he is more alive now than he has ever been and that I will get to be with him again someday.
— Eddie Pennington
August 13, 2012

CHAPTER 24

THE BEST OF TIMES ... THE WORST OF TIMES ...

Chet had a good life. He got out of the pressure of being a producer and got back to being what he always wanted to be ... a guitar player. He understood that he was a Legend and a bronze statue was made in his honor, two biographies written. Not bad for a poor kid from Luttrel. Chet eventually went into forced retirement. Cancer, his old enemy, kept recurring. He had a bout of colon cancer described in his first biography *Country Gentleman*, published in 1974. It didn't stop him then, however. He continued being Chet Atkins, releasing records and playing guitar. He hired Paul Yandell, left RCA and went back to his first love, that of being a guitar player. He still got respectable sales of his releases, made the TV rounds now and again and played a road show when he wanted to. The Cochran brothers, Russ and Michael, did a wonderful limited edition, profusely illustrated, biography called *Me and My Guitars*. As that book neared completion the day Paul dreaded came to pass. Chet Atkins' ability to play his beloved guitar ended. Chet's physical condition had just deteriorated too much. Paul, by then, had been posting on the misterguitar.us chat board, sharing his pain as he watched his great friend and mentor decline.

The Cochran book was supposed to have a frontal page with a hand signed "Chet Atkins CGP" but Chet was too ill to even do this simple task. A brain tumor removal had a devastating effect on Chet and his ability to play guitar was suddenly gone. Paul was obviously suffering as he staunchly defended the Atkins family's right to privacy and at the same time kept the chat board members posted on Chet's condition. Death finally claimed Chester Atkins and he did not go easily.

Posted by Paul Yandell on June 30, 2001, at 14:09:34. Notice, he still signs himself in lower case. He was that way until he died. Humble to the end.

It's my sad duty to inform everyone that Chet died this morning at 10:00 am. As of this time I don't know any more details. I feel as though I have lost another Father, paul yandell.

After a time had passed, he posted this:

I've taken almost all of his guitars to the Hall of Fame for storage and display. The Hall of Fame is going to keep his guitar collection for a while,

then they will be transferred to a more secure place. It takes a lot of room to store all those guitars. Chet left all his guitars in a trust which means they can't be sold or something like that. Chet's wife and the estate asked me to take care of the guitars and handle the transfer of them. It was very moving to see Chet's guitars moved from his house never to return.

What follows is Paul's actual public posting on the Chetboard about moving the D'Angelico on what was a truly sad day in his life.

On April, 4, 2004, he wrote:

Hi everyone. This morning I had a sad chore. Chet's wife gave the Hall Of Fame Chet's D'Angelico and I took it to them this morning.

I don't mind saying that I cried when I left. It was the ending to the process of getting his guitars placed. It will be on display by the last of May in the case with his others. Leona didn't want anyone else to have it. She told me that she knew that Chet wouldn't want anyone else to play it so she decided to give it to the Hall Of Fame so everyone could enjoy seeing it.
Thx, paul

Shortly before he died, Paul sent an email to the author in November 2010:

You can put it in the archive but don't post it on the forums. After I'm gone people can read it in the archives,
Thanks, paul

The "it" he spoke of was this:

Now here is something that, until now, only my family knows about. After Chet passed away Leona tried to give me Chet's D'Angelico. I refused it and suggested she put it in the Country Music Hall of Fame. She agreed and had me take it down there. I know Chet would never want anyone to have that guitar or play it but it made me feel good that Leona cared that much for me.

It is also a measure of the man because he chose not to post about Leona wanting to pass the guitar to him while he was still alive.

A few years ago the Country Music Hall Of Fame changed personnel and it is difficult for me to get to them anymore. But as far as I know they take care of them. I don't think I will ever get over losing him. He was the best friend I ever had.

At the one year anniversary of Chet's passing Paul wrote:

One year ago today I posted a message that I never wanted to post that Chet had died. The past year for me has been one of sadness. I don't think the world of guitar playing will ever be the same. We, in this forum, all play his licks and tunes but there is always something missing. We are still going through his tapes he made in his basement studio. I don't know how long it will be before anything is done about them. I don't have anything to say about what happens to them.

Chet told me after he got sick that he would like the CAAS to keep going after he was gone so everyone could get together and play. People come to the CAAS because of Chet and what he has meant in their lives and no matter how good the players are that come "there is only one Chet." At CAAS it would seem to me that out of four days Chet should have his own night of his music. It just makes sense. Chet is the reason that convention started and it has his name in the title.

The CAAS is really tough for me each year but Chet wanted it to go on so everyone could come together and play. Some people have asked me to appear on the main stage at CAAS to talk about Chet. It's very difficult for me to talk about Chet. I don't like to perform on the big stage either because of the sound. In order to be heard to the back of the room you have to play loud and I don't do that. To me that will always be Chet's stage and there are too many memories there for me to deal with.

Chet didn't play any about a year or so before he died. I think when he got to the point where he couldn't play it took away the one thing he loved the most.

I wouldn't play in front of him because I knew how much he wanted to play. It broke my heart. He left an empty spot in my heart that will be there as long as I live. It was like losing my father. He was the best friend I ever had.

Chet was not totally out of Paul's life. Not by a long shot. Paul Yandell made sure Chet was not forgotten. He poured out his memories on the chat boards and successfully convinced Gretsch to launch two truly different guitars, the 6122-59 and the 6120 CGP. He happily saw the reuniting of Chet's name with the Gretsch guitar models that were so instrumental in the fortunes of Gretsch Manufacturing.

Paul made five CDs of his own, *Forever Chet, Dream Train, In the Groove, One More Again* and *Drive On.* He made a teaching DVD, *Finger-Style Legacy,* in which he shared some of what he had learned about guitar playing in his life.

Then, his own disaster struck. Paul was diagnosed with prostate cancer. Typically, he kept quiet about it on the chat boards, not wanting people to make a fuss about something they could do nothing about. Surgery was done and it did not go all that well. Repairs were attempted and aggressive medication and radiation was applied. All this took its toll on Paul. Even as he steadily grew weaker due to disease and the medical side effects, Paul devoted as much energy as he could playing guitar. Marie said he did some of his best playing during the last year of his life. He recorded himself when he was able and continued to post on chat boards. He and his family enjoyed going back to the old farm in Mayfield for the nostalgic, sweet peace that the familiar country landscapes bestowed on them. Paul was, in short, refusing to let the dreaded disease take him down without a fight.

On Monday, November 24, Craig Dobbins posted this sad news on the Chetboard at Marie Yandell's request, part of which is printed here:

Paul Yandell Obituary

by craigdobbins – Mon Nov 21, 2011 3:59 pm
Paul T. Yandell, CGP, who was born in Mayfield, Kentucky, on September 6, 1935, passed away quietly at his home in Hendersonville, TN with his family at his side after a long battle with cancer on November 21, 2011. He was a devoted husband and nurturing and loving father who lived his Christian life and treasured his family.

He was preceded in death by his parents, Theodore B. "Ted" and Imogene Ridings Yandell. He is survived by his wife of fifty years, Marie Jones Yandell; his son, Paul Micah Yandell and his wife, Sheri Yandell, of Hendersonville, TN; his sister, Yvone Lambert of Boaz, KY; his brother, Forrest Yandell of Kalasin, Thailand; nieces, Susan Butler of Boaz, KY; Betsy (Amos) Sanchez of Murfreesboro, TN, and a nephew, Greg (Christa) Yandell of Hendersonville, TN, as well as three great nephews and one great niece.

He was a member of New Life Baptist Church in Nashville, TN as well as the American Federation of Musicians Local 257, Nashville, TN.

Paul was an accomplished player by the time he left high school in Western Kentucky, arriving in Nashville in 1955. Little did he know he would end up playing for the most renowned guitar player in the world. He joined Chet Atkins in 1975 supporting Chet in his career that lasted for twenty-five years.

He started his career with The Louvin Brothers, which lasted until 1959, with Paul playing on many of their greatest hits. After serving in the army, Paul joined the Kitty Wells & Johnny Wright show where he stayed from 1961–1969 after which he worked for about a year with George Hamilton, IV. He then joined Jerry Reed in 1970 and as Paul says he "went to college" learning from Jerry Reed. Paul stayed with Jerry until sometime during 1975.

Making his place in Nashville's musical community as a session player, Paul played on many hit records with artists such as Chet, Jerry Reed, Dolly Parton, Steve Wariner, Hank Thompson, Perry Como, Roger Whitaker, Kitty Wells, Johnny Wright, The Louvin Bros., Les Paul, Woody Herman, The Everly Brothers, and Mary Chapin Carpenter. He appeared on TV shows such as The *Dinah Shore Show, The Tonight Show, The Today Show, The Pat Sajak Show, The Merv Griffin Show* and *Nashville Now.*

After Chet died in 2001, Paul released a solo CD entitled *Forever Chet* featuring many songs performed by Chet throughout his career. Other CDs released by Paul included *One More Again* released in 2003; *Dream Train,* released May of 2004 which featured many original tunes written by Paul and performed on the New Gretsch "Nashville Classic" that was co-designed by Paul and Fred Gretsch. The artwork for the cover of *Dream Train* was drawn by Steve Wariner, who is also featured on lap steel on one of the tunes. Following that was *In The Groove* released in 2005 and *Drive On* released in 2006. He was also instrumental in assisting with the reissue of Chet's Gretsch CGP guitar.

Merle Atkins Russell and Family presented Paul with the CGP (Certified Guitar Player) designation on August 11, 2011.

Steve Wariner, Eddie Stubbs & Fred Gretsch will deliver eulogies and Rev. Raymond Langlois will deliver the message. Friends and musicians in attendance will serve as honorary pallbearers.

Thus ends this particular chronicle of a sideman. It is of course incomplete. I doubt any work of this nature can be complete. But for me, the "work" has been a labor of love ... because I wrote about a friend.

THE LEGACY

Along with being involved in the creation of the 6122-59 and 6120 CGP guitars, Paul's legacy includes several CDs and DVDs released after his retirement. Some of the titles may be unavailable at this time. It is best to check with his estate for availability and pricing at:

Paul Yandell
1021 Kiser Ave.
Hendersonville, TN 37075
http://www.studio9kc.co.uk/paul/music_shop.html

CDs made by Paul Yandell

Forever Chet (*This CD is no longer available*)
Track Listing
Forever Chet
Down Home
Indian Love Call
Baby's Coming Home
Caravan
Yes Ma'am
Ready for The Times to Get Better
I'll Say She Does
Petite Waltz

One More Again
Track Listing
China Boy
Mystery Train
I've Been Lucky
Gallopin' Guitar
Clear Springs Rag
There Will Never Be Another You
Walk, Don't Run
City Slicker
Kentucky
Shadow Waltz

Dream Train
Track Listing
Dream Train
Lookin' Up
Mayfield
Say It Again
Clear Springs Blues #2
Kentucky Blue
Shanty Town
Shine
Arilyn Roe
My Pal
Nashville Boogie
SleepWalk

In The Groove
Track Listing
Mister Sandman
Avalon
Just One of Those Things
Bugle Call Rag
Stardust
In The Groove
Foggy Mountain Top
Cherokee
When I Stop Dreaming
Hawaiian Wedding Song

Drive On
Track Listing
Folsom Prison Blues
You Belong to Me
Rainbow
Blue Drag
C/J Ramble
Shavorana
Bells of St. Mary's
What Is This Thing Called Love
Sugarfoot Rag
(In Memory of Hank Garland and Odell Martin)
Georgia On My Mind

My Time
Track Listing
In Every Way
I'll See You in My Dreams
Time and Again
Looking Ahead
How about Now
Around the Corner
Just for Me
Twizzler
Windy and Warm
My Sweet Lord
Ms. Wanda

There is a National Thumbpickers Hall of Fame that maintains a facility at:

Merle Travis Music Center
750 Cleaton Road
Powderly, KY 42367

Paul was inducted 1999 in the Living Thumbpicker Category. They have a bronze memorial bench where there is a permanent memorial for Paul. A plaque says:

In Memory of Paul Yandell, CGP
A Great Friend and Picker
1935–2011

There is more to his legacy, of course, in the lives he touched. Some lives he touched only fleetingly but to some he was more than just a great friend and picker.
    Paul Yandell was Second to the Best.